Principles
and
Development
of
Jewish Law

by the same author

The Book of Temple Service (Yale Judaica Series, Vol. XII)

The Nature and History of Jewish Law (Yeshiva University Studies in Torah Judaism, No.9)

The Light of Redemption (Jerusalem, 5731)

Beyond the Moon and other Sermons (Jerusalem, 5734)

The Religious Foundations of The Jewish State (New York, 1977)

A Tale to Remember and other Sermons (Jerusalem/New York, 5743)

Tsemichat Ge'ulateinu (Hebrew, Jerusalem, 5744)

Principles
and
Development
of
Jewish Law

*The Concepts and History of Rabbinic Jurisprudence
from its Inception to Modern Times*

by
Mendell Lewittes

**Bloch Publishing Company
New York, N.Y.**

Published by Bloch Publishing Company, Inc.
Manufactured in the United States of America.

Library of Congress Cataloging-in-Publication Data

Lewittes, Mendell.
    Principles and development of Jewish law.

    Includes bibliographies and indexes.
    1. Jewish law--History.   I.   Title.
BM520.5.L44   1987   296.1'274   87-11778
ISBN 0-8197-0512-8
ISBN 0-8197-0506-3 (pbk.)

Dedicated to a True
Eshet Ḥayyil — A Woman of Valor
in honour of her eightieth birthday

MRS. EDITH RAJSKY

She is like the merchant ships; she bringeth her food from afar...
She stretcheth out her hand to the poor; yea, she reacheth forth her hands
*   to the needy...*
She maketh linen garments and selleth them...
Strength and dignity are her clothing...and the law of kindness is on her
*   tongue...*
Her children rise up and call her blessed...
Many daughters have done valiantly, but thou excellest them all

(Proverbs, chap. 31)

Contents

of the Talmud — Encyclopedias of the Halakhah —
Sephardi Ḥakhamim in the 18th and 19th Centuries —
Iraqi Ḥakhamim — North African Ḥakhamim — Ḥakh-
amim in the Ottoman Empire

Preface

In 1966 Yeshiva University published, as one of a series of Studies in Torah Judaism, my monograph on the Nature and History of Jewish Law, referring specifically to Rabbinic Jurisprudence, otherwise known as the *Halakhah*. The final chapter in the study was entitled, "Jewish Law and the Modern World," and dealt with the challenges to the authority and relevance of the Halakhah posed by the new religious movements in Jewish life and the rapid advances in modern technology. In the two decades since the appearance of that Study, some of the challenges mentioned therein have increased in intensity and scope, raising new questions concerning the viability today of traditional Jewish Law. The Halakhah, never static and indifferent to the changing circumstances in which we live, has responded to these recent developments with a corresponding increase in the current rabbinic literature addressed to these questions. The present volume is intended, in part, to bring us up-to-date in this aspect of the Halakhah.

One of the challenges to the Halakhah not dealt with to any extent in my previous monograph was posed by the establishment of the State of Israel. Can the Halakhah in its present codification serve to guide — let alone govern — a modern state, with all the complexities of modern life, in both its civil and criminal legislation, confronted as it is with plaguing social problems and precarious international relations? The present volume will review some of the answers to this thorny question, and record the measures already taken to enable halakhic principles and practices to play their proper role in the parliament of the Jewish state.

Another challenge to traditional Jewish Law today not dealt with in my monograph has been spawned by the feminist movement. Can the demands of modern women for greater participation in religious ritual be accommodated by the Halakhah as it stands today? We review the reaction to such demands by those who speak in the name of the Halakhah.

It is not only the response of the Halakhah to novel challenges that has moved me to write this expanded treatise on Jewish Law. Much of

1

the past record of its history has to be brought up-to-date, what with the ever-increasing publication of the results of recent scholarship in this field. Halakhic works hitherto hidden beneath the debris of centuries have been unearthed and brought to light, to take their rightful place in the history of rabbinic literature. New avenues have been explored to reveal both continuity and transition in custom and tradition. Though one volume cannot attempt to recapitulate all the results of this scholarship, an effort will be made here to cover its highlights and record its most significant conclusions.

Nor is this volume an academic or theological treatise, and therefore I have not engaged — except in the Epilogue — in any polemics with the opinions of others who have written on this complex subject. I express my own views, based upon years of study, with the hope that they will make some modest contribution to a true understanding of the Halakhah, both for the Jew who is interested in the religious tradition of his people, and for the non-Jew interested in the religious tradition of his Jewish neighbor. For the committed Jew, we hope this study will confirm his faith in the eternal validity of the Halakhah and its continued relevance in our modern society. Following the example of the saintly teacher Rabbi Nehuniah ben Hakaneh (*Berakhot* 4:2), I pray that "no wrong judgment will result from this effort, and that I have not erred in a matter of Halakhah."

I am dedicating this volume to a woman whom I have admired for many years for her exemplary courage and distinguished personality. Despite the loss of her husband at a rather early age, she carried on — together with her son and brother-in-law — the family business with unusual fortitude and acumen. I wish to acknowledge with deep gratitude her children's sharing in the cost of publishing this volume, as a loving tribute to their mother on the occasion of her eightieth birthday. May the Almighty grant her many more years of good health and active participation both in business and in *ma'asim tovim*.

Jerusalem 5747–1987

Introduction

The Halakhic Discipline

No one can gainsay that for centuries the Halakhah has determined the norms and practices of the Jewish people in all the countries of their dispersion, despite the vicissitudes of their history, so replete with expulsions and persecutions. Such a phenomenon can be grasped only if we understand the true nature of the Halakhah; namely, that it is not primarily a code of law. It has a religious connotation, a statement of faith, a commitment to one's Creator. Thus the Sages, the early codifiers of the Halakhah, in commenting upon the two chapters of the *Shema* — the Jewish declaration of faith — speak of two yokes, one following the other. "Why is the chapter of *Shema* (Deut. 6:4–8) recited (in the daily prayers) before the chapter of *Ve-Hayah Im Shamo'a* (*ibid*. 11:13–21)? So that one may first take upon himself the yoke of the Kingdom of Heaven, and then take upon himself the yoke of the commandments" (*Berakhot* 2:1). Hence, the most comprehensive code of Jewish Law, the *Mishneh Torah* of Maimonides, does not begin with the religious duties that a Jew is obliged to perform, but with what a Jew ought to believe in, the principles of his faith.

There are some who would remove this underpinning of faith from the Halakhah; they regard Jewish practice as the people's culture and folkways,[1] in part even as a result of the influences of their non-Jewish environment. Though it is not to be denied that certain practices sanctioned and enjoined by the Halakhah are cultural in origin, it is equally not to be denied that the foundation of Jewish Law — as we point out in the first chapter — lies in the faith that the Torah, the basis of Jewish Law, is the word of God.

Notwithstanding this premise, we do not read out of the community of Israel those secular Jews who reject Judaism as divinely ordained but cling to it as an expression of their belonging to the people who bear aloft its banner. Their observance of many of the customs of

---

1 E.g. Mordecai Kaplan's "Judaism as a Civilization."

Jewish tradition — their recognition, for example, of the Sabbath and the Festivals as special days even though they do not observe them as required by the Halakhah — is a recognition on their part of a unique tradition of the Jewish people. This is not too far removed from a recognition of the Divine Providence which has preserved Israel to this day, which ultimately may well lead to an acknowledgment of the giving of the Torah to Israel as the greatest manifestation of this Providence. This sanguine view is reflected in the Rabbinic homily on the verse in Jeremiah (16:11), *They deserted Me and did not keep My Torah.* "Would that they desert Me, yet keep my Torah; for the light of the Torah will bring them back to Me."[2]

The Sages refer to the Torah in general as a yoke.[3] It is, however, no ordinary yoke; it is a "magic" yoke that confines and restricts, but at the same time uplifts and inspires. It gives its adherents direction so that they should not flounder in the arbitrary ways of humanism, or fall into the morass of hedonism and moral obtuseness. It raises man from being a creature of animal instincts alone to a rational human being who reflects upon the consequences of his conduct. The Halakhah endows those who observe its precepts with a sense of purpose, giving their life both meaning and sanctity. It therefore embraces every aspect of human activity; both interpersonal relations — *beyn adam lehaveiro*, between man and his fellowman — as well as purely ritualistic duties and ceremonials — *beyn adam lemakom*, between man and God, both equally regarded as *mitzvot*, or religious imperatives. The Jew who accepts the burden of the Halakhah will turn to it for guidance in practically everything he undertakes.

Halakhah and The Ethical Life

Judaism, especially as it is reflected in the Halakhah, has been categorized as legalistic, concerned with the letter of the law and not its spirit. This derogation of Rabbinic Judaism, allegedly untouched by the

---

2   J.T. *Ḥagigah* 1:7 (76c), *Pesikta D'Rav Kahana* 15. Some editions read *ha'se'or*, the ferment, instead of *ha-ma'or*, the light.

3   *Pirkei Avot* (Ethics of the Fathers) 3:5. Cf. Rashi, *Rosh Hashanah* 28a: "The mitzvot were not given to Israel so that their observance be a pleasure, but were given to be a yoke on their necks," Rashi, *Megillah* 25a "Decrees of the King, to impose upon us His yoke, to make known that we are His servants and keepers of His commandments."

social passion of the Prophets of Israel, was first propagated by the founders of Christianity in order to justify their breakaway from Judaism.[4] A truly objective view, attested to by such Christian writers as George Foote Moore[5] and R. Travers Herford,[6] will demonstrate that Rabbinic Judaism, far from being a soulless regimen of perfunctory acts, is rooted in the ethical principles of justice and mercy. Illustrative of the ethical character of Rabbinic justice is the following incident related in the Talmud:[7] Some porters working for Rabbah bar Hana broke a cask of wine,[8] so he seized their cloaks in compensation. They complained before Rav,[9] who ordered Rabbah to return the cloaks. "Is this the Law?" he asked. "Yes," relied Rav, "for it is written *That you follow the way of the good* (Prov. 2:20)." Rabbah returned the cloaks. The porters continued to complain, "We are poor; we worked all day; we are hungry and possess nothing." Whereupon Rav said to Rabbah, "Pay them their wages." "Is this the Law?" he asked. "Yes," Rav replied, "for it is written *And keep the paths of the just (ibid.)*"

A commentator on Rabbinic Judaism made the following perceptive statement: "If the ethics of the Rabbis strike us now and then as a little sober and mundane and unexciting, it is partly due to this very feature that their teaching was so thorough, that it sought so earnestly to cover with a network of morality all the circumstances and details of life."[10] A corroboration of this thesis can be found in the recently published survey of the Halakhah and Morality by Shubert Spero.[11]

Halakhah and Aggadah

The wellsprings of Jewish morality flow not so much from the Halakhah as from that other branch of Rabbinic literature, the Aggadah.

---

4 Cf. S.W. Baron, *Social and Religious History*, Vol. II, p. 67, "The recurrent fulminations against the Scribes and the Pharisees found throughout the Gospels." See *ibid.* pp. 343–344.
5 *History of Religion*, N.Y. 1928.
6 *The Pharisees*.
7 *Bava Metzia*, 83a.
8 Rashi, "through negligence."
9 Abba Arikha, 3rd century Babylonian Amora, founder of the Yeshiva in Sura.
10 C.G. Montefiore, *Rabbinic Anthology*, Phila. 1960, p. xliii.
11 *Morality, Halakhah and the Jewish Tradition*, N.Y. 1983 (Vol. IX, Library of Jewish Law and Ethics).

While the Halakhah is rooted mainly in the Talmud, Aggadah is found both in the Talmud and in the homiletical discourses of the Sages collected in the various Midrashim. It is comprised of homiletic exposition of Scripture, moral exhortation, parable and proverb, folklore and legend. Its declarations are more hortatory than mandatory, expressive of the essence and spirit of Judaism. Two statements typical of the Aggadah are the following: "It matters not whether one offers much or little (referring to sacrificial offerings brought to the Altar), as long as his heart is directed to Heaven."[12] "What matters it to God if one slaughters (to prepare meat for human consumption) from the neck or the nape; the commandments were given to Israel only in order to purify mankind through them."[13]

Halakhah and Aggadah are not sealed off hermetically one from the other. On occasion, an halakhic ruling will find its source in legend. Thus, when Maimonides rules that the site of the Altar to be erected in the Holy Temple was delimited very specifically and is never to be changed, he adds, "It was on the site of the Temple that the patriarch Isaac was bound...This too was the place where Noah built an altar when he came out of the Ark. It is also the place of the altar upon which Cain and Abel offered sacrifice. There it was that Adam offered a sacrifice after he was created. Indeed, Adam was created from that very earth; as the Sages taught, 'Adam was created from the place where he made atonement'.[14] (According to some religious authorities, this site is located where the Dome of the Rock now stands).

And needless to say, homiletic preachment will invariably include one or more mandates of the Halakhah. Typical of such is the homily for *Parashat Ha'azinu* (Deut. chap. 32).[15] "Halakhah: If a Jew senses an affliction in his ear, may he heal it on the Shabbath?[16] Thus have our Sages taught, Even if there is a doubt whether life is in danger, the (restrictions of the) Shabbath are set aside, and this affliction of the ear may be healed on the Sabbath if danger to life is involved. The Rabbis have said, 'If you seek to be free of affliction in your ear or in any other

---

12   Mishnah *Menaḥot* 13:11.
13   *Gen. Rabbah* 44:1. See, however, Maimonides' *Guide etc.*, trans. M. Friedlander, Part III, p. 126, esp. n. 4.
14   *Hilkhot Bet ha-Beḥirah* 2:1.
15   *Deut. Rabbah, ad loc.*
16   The Sages prohibited the use of medicine on the sabbath lest one compound it, except where the ailment may endanger life. See, however, below p. 00.

limb, incline your ear to the Torah and you will enjoy life.'" Thus are linked together the two branches of Rabbinic literature, combining the prescriptions of the Halakhah with the preachments of the Aggadah to shape the moral and ethical character of the observant Jew.[17]

Halakhah: The Leap To Action

Isaiah (29:13) decried the perfunctory performance of the command-ments devoid of an awareness of their inner meaning in the following words: *Because that people has approached Me with its mouth and honored Me with its lips; but it has kept its heart far from Me, and its worship of Me has been a commandment of men learned by rote.* In keeping with the spirit of this chastisement, the Sages insisted that ritual performance is meaningful only if accompanied by an awareness — called *kavanah* — that it is God Who has commanded the ritual and to Him we must direct our thoughts. Thus, referring to the verse (Exodus 17:11) *And it was that when Moses would lift his hand Israel prevailed*, they explained,[18] "Do, then, the hands of Moses determine victory or defeat in battle? Rather, this teaches that as long as (the children of) Israel were looking heavenwards and subjecting them-selves to their Father in heaven they would prevail; otherwise, the enemy would prevail." They also taught, "The Holy One, blessed be He, requires the heart (i.e. the proper intention), as is written *But the Lord sees to the heart* (I Sam. 16:7)."[19]

Nevertheless, the Rabbis did not discount completely a *mitzvah* performed without the required *kavanah.*[20] Better to act imperfectly

---

17 As a general rule, however, we do not accept an aggadic statement as normative and binding; the two realms remain separate as far as required practice is con-cerned; cf. J.T. *Pe'ah* 2:6. See, however, M. Elon, *Hamishpat Haivri* (Jer. 5733), pp. 144ff. The late Chief Rabbi Kook advised that the Halakhah and the Aggadah be combined in study so that they become united (*Orot ha-Kodesh* 1:25).

18 Mishnah, *Rosh Hashanah* 3:8.

19 *Sanhedrin* 106b.

20 Cf. *Berakhot* 13a–b. In the mitzvah of *tekiat Shofar*, the accepted ruling is that the intention to fulfill a mitzvah (*kavanah la'tzet*) when performing it is an absolute requirement; see *Rosh Hashanah* 29a. Prayer, characterized by the Sages "worship of the heart" (*Ta'anit* 2a), requires also intention of the heart (*kavanat ha-lev*). Maimonides describes this *kavanah* as follows: "One should dismiss from his mind all (alien) thoughts, and see himself as standing in the presence of the *Shekhinah*" (*Hilkhot Tefillah* 4:16; see also Mishnah *Berakhot* 5:1 and *Tosafot Pesaḥim* 115a *s.v.*

than not to act at all; for there is always the hope that some day the act will be performed as it should. The greatest mitzvah is the study of the Torah, yet the Sages advised, "At all times a person should engage in Torah and mitzvot even if not for their own sake (i.e. with some ulterior motive); for from acting not for their own sake he will ultimately arrive at performing them for their own sake."[21]

This seemingly ambivalent attitude towards performance without proper intention can serve to clarify a fundamental difference between Judaism and Christianity. Christian theologians speak of "the leap of faith," that one must believe even though what he is called upon to believe is patently absurd (*credo quia absurdum est*).[22] And the moment one takes this leap of faith and says "I believe" he achieves salvation. Thus the essential message of Christianity ends at the leap of faith.[23] Judaism, however, though it begins with a leap of faith — an affirmation that God's commandments are not arbitrary or absurd, but were given for the good of mankind — goes on to a leap of action. Our religious commitment tells us to act, to perform the mitzvot, endowing performance with a significance of its own. This explains the centrality of the Halakhah in Jewish life.

The tendency to perform the mitzvot as "a commandment of men learned by rote" has been fairly common through the ages, but was restrained by both word and the example of Judaism's spiritual leaders. They constantly reminded their flock of the moral values of Judaism and the importance of *middot tovot*, desirable character traits. Many of the maxims of *Pirkei Avot* (Ethics of the Fathers) were recorded for that purpose, and hence it became a popular tract, included in the prayer-book and the text for Sabbath afternoon discourses during the summer. Maimonides, beginning his *Mishneh Torah*

matkif). R. Ḥayyim Soloveitchick of Brisk (1853–1918) added another *kavanah* to prayer; to understand what one is praying, though this is not an absolute requirement. Countless Jews pray in Hebrew though they do not understand the language. Similarly, the Sages have ruled that one fulfills the mitzvah of reading the Megillah on Purim by listening to the reading even though he does not understand the meaning of the words; see *Megillah* 18a.

21 *Pesaḥim* 50b; cf. J.T. *Ḥaagigah* 1:7 (76c). Cf. Rashi *Ta'anit* 7a, "He studies because the Lord his God commanded him and not in order to be called 'Rabbi'." See also *Tosafot ad loc. s.v. vekhol.*

22 Attributed to St. Augustine; see Bartlett's *Familiar Quotations*, p. 69a, n. 1.

23 A view no doubt stemming from Christianity's premise that man is innately and incorrigibly evil ever since the fall of Adam.

with the fundamental principles of the Torah, follows immediately with *Hilkhot De'ot*, which may be rendered "the laws concerning man's virtues and vices," before he proceeds to codify the actual manner in which the mitzvot are to be observed. The Biblical basis for the requirement of good character, beyond the above fulfilment of ritual requirements, is the injunction *Do what is right and good in the eyes of the Lord* (Deut. 6:8).[24] What is "right and good" signifies the moral values of Judaism, especially as they relate to interpersonal relationships.

Reminders of these values are particularly appropriate nowadays in the light of recent developments in Jewish life. There is a marked movement to the colloquial "right" in religious matters, a tendency on the part of many observant Jews — their spiritual leaders included — to introduce into the Halakhah more stringent and rigid rulings which emphasize form more than substance. Thus we find an insistence upon a particular type of hat and cloak as a token of one's religiosity, or the wearing of a *sheitel* (a wig, worn so that a woman's natural hair not be exposed)[25] albeit the most fashionable and alluring one. The more serious consequence of such accretions to the Halakhah is the attitude on the part of those who accept them towards those who do not accept them, the former branding the latter as non-observant and deviationist. A rigid concept of the Halakhah has also led to a denial of a "history" to the Halakhah, which in turn has led to a denial of the significance of our most recent history, especially the establishment of the State of Israel. When an ultra-Orthodox publisher of a *lu'aḥ* (Jewish calendar) was asked why he made no note of *Yom ha-Atzma'ut*, Israel's Independence Day, he replied, "It is not included in the Shulḥan Arukh," ignoring the fact that the Shulḥan Arukh preceded the State by several centuries.

Religious Jews have welcomed the recent phenomenon of *ba'alei teshuvah*, the return of many who had led a life completely devoid of Jewish observance and identification back to the traditional observance of Torah and mitzvot. It is only to be regretted that most of the institutions which guide them on their way back present only that interpretation of Judaism described above. Neophytes are the most likely to adopt this narrow, one-sided view of traditional Judaism,

---

24 See N. Leibovitch, *Studies in Devarim*, Jer. 5743, *ad loc.*
25 For differing opinions, see *Rema* to Sh. A. *Oraḥ Ḥayyim* 75:2 and *Mishnah B'rurah ad loc.*

unaware of its many enriching facets both in theory and practice. Judaism of "the right" denigrates all non-Jewish secular culture, and excludes from the curricula of its educational institutions all subjects not directly related to Talmudic studies and non-essential for the limited careers open to its followers. Such "closed" minds become closed even to innovative thinking in the exposition of Jewish Law, unable to adapt the law to new circumstances, let alone to new perceptions. The inevitable consequences of such attitudes are the growing intolerance manifested in the Jewish community, increasing polarization, lack of mutual respect, and the absence of any serious dialogue among the proponents of divergent views that are legitimately within the parameters of authentic Judaism. That such attitudes are not part of the Talmudic heritage can be seen from its history as it is — we hope — authentically portrayed in this volume.

1

Creation and Commandment

ויצו ה׳ אלהים על האדם לאמר
— *And the Lord God commanded the man, saying* (Gen. 2:16)

Rationale for Divine Commandment

The cornerstone of traditional Judaism, more particularly Rabbinic or Halakhic Judaism, is its faith in the revelation of God's word to Israel at Sinai as recorded in the Pentateuch (Exod. chaps. 19–20; Deut. chap. 5). Revelation of God's word, however, did not begin with the giving of the Torah at Sinai; it began with the creation of man.[1] Just as Creation was the result of God's will,[2] so was it His will that man — the crowning glory of His work — live in accord with His will. For man to do so, he must perforce know God's design for human conduct. In the words of the prophet, *He has told you, O man, what is good and what the Lord requires of you; Only to do justice and to love kindness, and to walk modestly with your God* (Micah 6:18).

Thus, revelation of God's directives for humanity is construed as a logical necessity, following from our concept of the purpose of Creation and the existence of man upon earth. Saadia Gaon, the first of the medieval Jewish philosophers (d. 942), explained such revelation as the greatest boon to mankind. He says,[3]

---

1 Cf. M. Buber, *The Prophetic Faith*, p. 195, "The Creation itself already means communication between Creator and creature."
2 Cf. Saadia Gaon's translation of *vayomer* in Genesis, "And He willed."
3 *Emunot ve-De'ot*, trans. S. Rosenblatt, New Haven, Yale Univ. Press, 1948, pp. 137–138.

"Now His first act of kindness towards his creatures consisted in His bringing them into being...In addition to that, however, He also endowed them with the means whereby they might attain complete happiness and perfect bliss. This means the commandments and the prohibitions prescribed for them by God.
Now this remark may immediately arouse the attention of the reflecting mind, prompting it to ask, 'Could not God have bestowed upon His creatures complete bliss and perfect happiness without giving them commandments and prohibitions? Nay, it would seem in such case that His kindness would have contributed even more to their well-being, because they would be relieved of all exertion for the attainment of their bliss.'
"Let me then say in explanation of this matter that on the contrary the better course is God's making His creatures' diligent compliance with His commandments the means of attaining permanent bliss. For according to the judgement of reason, the person who achieves some good by means of the effort that he has expended for its attainment obtains double the advantage gained by him who achieves this good without any effort, but merely as a result of the kindness shown him by God."[4]

According to Maimonides, "the general object of the commandments is two-fold: the well-being of the soul and the well-being of the body ... The well-being of the body is established by a proper management of the relations in which we live one person to another. This we can attain in two ways: first by removing all violence from our midst ... Secondly, by teaching everyone of us such good morals as must produce a good social state."[5] Though Maimonides was here referring specifically to the laws of the Torah, there is no doubt that the foregoing two-fold object applies equally to mankind in general. That this is so can be seen from the first communication of divine law to man. From the verse *And the Lord God commanded the man* etc. (Gen. 2:16) the Sages inferred that man was commanded seven injunctions, known in halakhic literature as "the seven commandments for the children of Noah."[6] These form the basic code for all humanity, regardless of race or creed. They include a directive to set up a regime

---

4   Cf. *Avot*, end of chap. 5, "The reward is commensurate with the painstaking."
5   *Guide of the Perplexed*, trans. M. Friedlander, part III, p. 129.
6   *Sanhedrin* 56b.

of law and order (*dinim*)[7] and the prohibition of idolatry, murder, and sexual immorality. Indeed, archeological discoveries have now unearthed several codes of law of the ancient Middle East, most prominent of which is the Code of Hammurabi, who lived approximately at the time of the Patriarch Abraham.[8] These codes include several of the seven Noahide laws, though missing is the most fundamental one prohibiting idolatry.

In a profound essay analysing the first chapters in Genesis,[9] Rabbi Joseph B. Soloveitchik delineates two stages in the creation of Adam, a pre-commandment one and a post-commandment one, corresponding to the two levels of man's nature. At the lower level is the creature who is an integral and undivided part of creation in general. Here man is like the beast of the field, a creature of instincts, unreflective and unchanging, unchallenged and unmystified by the vastness and complexity of Creation. Such a being is non-normative, not singled out from the rest of Nature by any specific commandment from God.[10] At such a level, what is left for man is to enjoy the satisfaction of his instincts in an abundantly blessed Nature, an existence that is purely hedonistic.

But subsequently man was raised to another level, separating and elevating him from the rest of Creation. Here man develops a human consciousness, facing a world that challenges his curiosity and intellect. This places man, according to Rabbi Soloveitchik, in an existential framework that is tragic, filled with conflict and confusion. At this stage, man was the recipient of the first divine command, *And the Lord God commanded Adam etc.* (Gen. 2:16). This second stage did not eliminate from man's nature the first non-normative stage, a creature of instincts, and thus gave rise to man's dialectical nature. Only if man

---

7   Naḥmanides, in his commentary to Gen. 34:13, says that the *dinnim* given to the sons of Noah are the civil laws similar to those given to the Israelites.

8   For a listing and description of these codes, see U. Cassuto, *Commentary to Exodus*, Jer. 1953, pp. 179 ff.

9   *Confrontation*, Tradition, N.Y. 1963. See also *The Lonely Man of Faith*, Tradition, 1965.

10 All nature, plants and animals and humans alike, were given one injunction, to reproduce themselves so that the cycle of Nature would be unbroken, and the results of God's creative efforts would endure as long as He willed it; see Gen. 1:12, *Fruit tree making fruit according to its kind*, and *ibid.* 1:22, *And God blessed them saying, "Be fruitful and multiply...and the fowl will multiply in the land."*

13

is ready to submit to God's commands can he reach some sort of balance, and realize to some extent the purpose of his existence.

Another aspect of man's dialectical nature pointed out by Rabbi Soloveitchik resides in the tension between man's freedom and his submission to God's commands. On the one hand, man's freedom is axiomatic: this is the meaning of the phrase *He created him in the image of God* (*ibid.* 1:7). On the other hand, once man was commanded by God, he was in effect asked to surrender his freedom. "With the birth of the norm, man becomes aware of his singular human existence of being unfree, restricted, imperfect and unredeemed, and at the same time being potentially powerful, great and exalted, uniquely endowed, capable of rising far above his environment in response to the divine moral challenge. Man attains his unique identity when, after having been enlightened by God that he is not only a committed but also a free person, endowed with power to implement his commitment, he grasps the incommensurability of what he is destined to be."[11]

Divine or Human

Now we may well ask ourselves, Were these primordial laws made known to man by means of Divine revelation: or perhaps man, through his innate rational faculty, came to realize that he can construct a happy and peaceful society only if such laws are observed and enforced? The Rabbis of the Talmud concede that certain moral precepts could have been learned from Nature even if they had not been communicated by direct revelation.[12] The Rabbis also distinguish between those laws called in the Bible *ḥukim* (statutes) and those called *mishpatim* (judgments); of the latter they say, "Even if they had not been written in the Torah, they would have been written down anyway."[13] Nevertheless, there is sufficient reason for their having been divinely commanded and not left to man's reasoning alone.

11 In the light of this description, we can understand the statement of the Sages, "Only he is free who occupies himself with the Torah" (Avot 6:2). The universality of this idea I found in a statement by a non-Jewish writer "...for the first time in my life (writes a man who has been searching for God and the meaning of life's existence) I felt what true liberty is: to place oneself beneath God's yoke." (*Report to Greco*, Nikos Kazantzakis, Bantam ed. p. 452.

12 *Eruvin* 100b.

13 *Yoma* 67b.

Maimonides, in discussing the seven Noahide laws, makes the following distinction:[14]

"Everyone who accepts the seven commandments and observes them scrupulously is one of the righteous gentiles and has a portion in the world-to-come. However, this is only if he accepts them and observes them because the Holy One blessed be He commanded them in the Torah; and there it was made known to us by our teacher Moses that the sons of Noah had been commanded them before (the giving of the Torah). But if he observes them because of a conclusion based on reason, he is not deemed a resident alien (*ger toshav*)[15] or a righteous gentile, but one of their wise men."

This assertion is in line with the rabbinic statement, "Greater is one who is commanded and performs than the one who is not commanded and performs."[16] For there is a psychological difference between laws which are handed down by secular authorities and those decreed by divine legislation. The former, lacking divine authority, are more easily abandoned when their performance is challenged, either by difficult circumstances or by intellectual argument; whereas the latter, bearing the stamp of a heavenly command, are more readily honored despite such challenges.

U. Cassuto, in discussing the codes of the ancient Middle East, makes the following observation:[17]

"The legal tradition of the ancient East in all its branches was secular and not religious. The sources of the law were, on the one hand, custom, and on the other hand, the will of the king. In all the collections of the aforementioned codes, we see that the law does not issue from the will of the gods. This is in contradistinction to the laws of the Torah, which are religious and moral instructions handed over in the name of the God of Israel." Perhaps this is what the Psalmist was referring to when he said, *He issued His commands to Jacob, His statutes and judgments to Israel. He did not*

---

14 *Hilkhot Melakhim* 8:11. See however *Encyclopedia Talmudit*, Vol. VI, p. 290, n. 11 for a variant reading of the final phrase.
15 Cf. Rambam *ibid.* 8:10 for a description of *ger toshav*.
16 *Kiddushin* 31a.
17 *Op. cit.* above, n. 11.

do so for any other nation; He did not make known to them any judgments (Psalms 147:10–19).[18]

It is only because the social, as well as the ritual, laws have been included in the Torah and thus incorporated into the framework of *mitzvot*, that they subsequently became the burden of the prophetic passion for social justice.

In this pre-Sinaitic period of history, God did not proclaim commandments to any nation; He did, however, speak to individuals. He let them know that though He is commanding them, He is not depriving them of their innate freedom, the choice to obey or disobey. At the same time, He warned them of the dire consequences of disobeying. Thus He said to Cain, *If you do right, there is uplift; but if you do not do right sin crouches at the door. Its desire is towards you, but you can be its master* (Gen. 4:7). Unfortunately, Cain yielded to his passion and aggressive instincts, killed his brother, and set a pattern of bloodshed for his descendants. For ten generations God was patient with disobedient mankind,[19] until corruption and violence became so widespread that it could no longer be tolerated, and humanity was almost swept away by the Deluge.

One individual remained with his family to rebuild human society on the basis of the seven Noahide laws. One law in particular, with dire punishment for its violation, was spoken by God to Noah, the law against murder. *Whoever sheds the blood of man, by man shall his blood be shed; for in the image of God was man created* (*ibid.* 9:6). Another injunction given to Noah was *You must not eat flesh with its life-blood in it* (*ibid.* v.4); namely, before human consumption of animal flesh is permissible, the animal first has to be killed.[20] This is the law known as *ever min ha-ḥai* (a limb torn from a living creature); no doubt to teach man that even sub-human living creatures are not to be abused or caused unnecessary pain (in Rabbinic parlance, *tza'ar ba'alei ḥayyim*).

Though the Deluge was designed to give humanity a fresh opportunity to reconstitute itself on the basis of law and order, it did not change human nature. Right after the flood God acknowledged that *the devisings of man's heart are evil from his youth* (*ibid.* 8:20). Several

---

18 See Targum and commentators *ad loc.* to *yeda'um*.
19 *Avot* 5:2.
20 Adam had not been permitted to eat the flesh of animals; his food was restricted to vegetables and fruit (Gen. 1:20; *Sanhedrin* 59b).

generations after Noah man again demonstrated his evil inclination; he dared defy God, substituting rule by man in place of rule by Divine decree. *Come let us build us a city, and a tower with its top in the sky, to make a name for ourselves (ibid.* 11:14). It was not long before the world lapsed into the idolatrous and corrupt ways of their forebears.

Selection of Abraham

At this critical juncture in the history of early man, there appeared an individual who not only lived in accord with God's word, but resolved to teach it to all who came within the scope of his influence. Here was a new hope for mankind that out of this individual's family would emerge a people that would commit itself unreservedly and at all costs to hearken to God's commandments and walk in His ways. This individual was Abraham, of whom God said, *For I have known him*[21] *so that he may instruct his children and his household after him to keep the way of the Lord by doing what is just and right (ibid.* 18:19). The Lord sealed this hope by making a covenant (*b'rit*) with Abraham. He appeared to Abraham and said to him, *I am God Almighty; walk in My ways and be whole-hearted. I will make My covenant between Me and you, and I will make you exceedingly numerous.... I will establish My covenant.... as an everlasting covenant throught the ages to be God to you and to your offspring after you.* The Lord also included in the covenant the promise that *I will give to you and to your offspring after you the land you sojourn in, all the land of Canaan, as an everlasting possession, and I will be their God (ibid.* 17:1–8). God then requested Abraham to seal the covenant on his part and on the part of his offspring by the rite of circumcision (*ibid.* 10–13).

Four generations later the family of Abraham had multiplied into a people of twelve tribes, the people of Israel. Forged by the travail of bondage in Egypt,[22] sensitized by its own suffering to the suffering of all victims of man's inhumanity to man, [23] the people were led by Moses to the foot of Mt. Sinai to hear from the Almighty Himself the divine charge for all peoples. For the time had now arrived once again

---

21 Cf. J.P.S. translation, "For I have singled him out."

22 Cf. Deut. 4:20 *You the Lord took and brought you out from the iron furnace.*

23 Cf. Exod. 23:9, *You shall not oppress a stranger, for you know the feelings of the stranger, having yourselves been strangers in the land of Egypt.*

for God to communicate with mankind, through a people chosen and choosing to receive His word.

The commandments which the children of Israel were destined to hear at Sinai were not designed for one people alone, even a chosen people; they were designed for all peoples. The Talmud, commenting on the verse *The Lord came from Sinai, He shone upon them from Seir, He appeared from Mount Paran* (Deut. 33:1), asks, "What was God doing in Seir, what was He doing in Paran? This teaches us that the Holy One blessed be He offered the Torah to every nation, but they refused to accept it; only Israel accepted it."[24] The Midrash elaborates on this scenario and portrays it as follows: God appeared to the children of Esau and asked if they would accept the Torah. They queried, What is written in it? God answered, *Thou shalt not kill*. This, they retorted, we cannot accept, for we live by the sword. Then God appeared to the children of Ammon and Moab, offering them the Torah. They also asked, What is written in it? When God told them *Thou shalt not commit adultery* they said they could not accept that, for it is against their life-style. Then God appeared to the children of Ishmael with the same offer, and again the question was asked, What is written in it? Again the Torah was rejected, on the grounds that *Thou shalt not steal* contradicted their life-style. Only the children of Israel responded positively and said, *We shall do and we shall hear* (Exod. 24:7).[25]

We now arrive at that cataclysmic event which is the basis of the principle of faith we began with, *Torah min ha-Shamayim*, the Torah is a heavenly document bearing the message of the Divine for all humankind.

---

24 *Avodah Zarah* 2b.
25 *Yalkut Shimoni* to *parashat Yitro*, sec. 286.

2

Revelation at Sinai

וכל העם רואים את הקולות
And all the people perceived the voices (Exod. 20:15)

Degrees of Revelation

Maimonides, in postulating thirteen principles of faith as the basis of
Judaism, places the principle of *Torah min ha-Shamayim* as number
eight. Preceding it are two antecedent principles: number six, that of
prophecy in general, and number seven, the unique prophecy of
Moses. For the revelation of God's word at Sinai was a manifestation
of prophecy, albeit unique both in its essential character and in its
being a one-time happening, *a mighty voice, not to be repeated* (Deut.
5:18)[1]

To fully understand the uniqueness of Sinai, we should distinguish
three categories or degrees of Revelation. First is the one in which
there is a sensation of an overwhelming Presence, so effulgent that the
person experiencing it is completely absorbed by it to the extent that he
loses his individual identity. The children of Israel went through such
an experience at Sinai. The Talmud relates, "At every word that issued
forth from the mouth of the Holy One, blessed be He, the soul of the
Israelites departed."[2] This type of revelation is mystical, where the

---

1   Cf. Rashi *ad loc.*, "He (God) did not reveal Himself publicly ever again."
2   *Shabbat* 88b.

essence of the revelation is not a verbal or even symbolic message — and certainly not the revelation of God Himself, for he is unrevealable[3] — but a revealing of the heavenly spheres (*sefirot*) emanating from Him. Such revelational experiences are described in the literature of the *kabbalah* and later we shall try to define their influence upon the Halakhah.[4]

The second category of Revelation is that of Prophecy. It is the revelation of a message which the Almighty wishes to transmit to mankind through selected human beings.[5] *I spoke to you persistently... I persistently sent you all My servants the prophets, to say "Turn back, every one of you from your wicked ways and mend your deeds"* (Jer. 35:14–15). We usually identify prophecy with foretelling the future, for very often the message consists of foretelling the dire consequences of evil conduct. God speaks to the prophets in order to inform them what He is planning to do, and why: *My Lord God does nothing without having revealed His purpose to His servants the prophets* (Amos 3:7). Thus God revealed to Abraham what He was planning to do to the evil community of Sodom: *Shall I hide from Abraham what I am about to do?* (Gen. 18:18)

Uniqueness of Revelation at Sinai

The third and highest degree of Revelation is the one which took place at Sinai. It was unique in several of its aspects. First of all, this was not a revelation to an individual but to an entire assemblage, a people. Secondly, the revelation of God's Presence was somehow clearer than in other revelational experiences: *Then Moses and Aaron, Nadab and Abihu, and seventy elders of Israel ascended; and they saw the God of Israel, under His feet there was the likeness of a pavement of sapphire like the very sky for purity* (Exod. 24:9–10). Thirdly, in contradistinction to other prophetic messages, which were invariably communicated when the recipient was in some sort of ecstatic trance, the recipients at Sinai were fully conscious and aware that God was

---

3   Cf. Exod. 33:20, *And He said, "You cannot see My presence, for no man can see Me and live."*

4   For a description of non-Jewish revelational experiences, see William James, *Varieties of Religious Experience.*

5   For the views of medieval Jewish philosophers on the phenomenon of prophecy, see I. Husik, *History of Medieval Jewish Philosophy* (Phila. 1947).

speaking to them directly. Finally, the message was verbal, clear and forthright, consisting of specific commandments, and not a general moral exhortation or symbolic figure typical of almost all other prophetic communications.

True, we are told by the Rabbis that the children of Israel heard only the first two commandments — *I am the Lord your God* etc. and *Thou shalt not have any other gods* etc. — directly from the voice of the Almighty.[6] *"You speak to us,"* they said to Moses, *"and we will obey; but let not God speak to us lest we die"* (Exod. 20:19). Beyond that, it was only Moses who continued to receive direct communication from God; and he in turn transmitted the divine messages to the people. Thus Moses became the prophet *par excellence*, enjoying a degree of prophecy higher than anyone before or after him.[7]

For the people of Israel the experience at Sinai was more than the revelation of God's word couched in universal commandments. It was a *b'rit*, a covenant between the universal God and a particular people, as is written, *And the Lord said to Moses, "Write down these commandments, for in accordance with these commandments I make a covenant with you and with Israel"...And he wrote down on the tablets the terms of the covenant, the Ten Commandments* (Exod. 34:27–28). Covenant implies reciprocity, God's promise and Israel's promise. God's promise was essentially the statement *You shall be for Me a treasured possession (segulah) from among all the peoples* (*ibid.* 19:5); namely, special providential care to secure the blessings which had already been promised to the Patriarchs for their descendants. Israel's promise was expressed very tersely, *We shall do and we shall hearken* (*ibid.* 24:7); namely, to keep the commandments proclaimed at Sinai.[8] This was the response given to Moses when he read to the people the *sefer ha-b'rit*, the Book of the Covenant.[9]

The Sages characterize the ceremony of the Sinai covenant as one of conversion, such as a proselyte must undergo when he accepts the

---

6   *Makkot* 24a.
7   Cf. Deut. 34:10, *There did not arise in Israel another prophet like Moses."*
8   See *Shabbat* 88a for the rabbinic comment on this declaration.
9   The *sefer* most probably included the message given to the Israelites in the days prior to the actual proclamation of the Decalogue (Exod. chap. 19).

Jewish faith.[10] The Halakhah sees the Sinai covenant as the conversion of the Israelites from the status of *b'nai Noah*, obliged to observe only the seven Noahide laws, to the status of *b'nai Yisrael*, committed to the observance of *taryag mitzvot*, 613 commandments, 365 of these negative and 248 positive.[11] These commandments are the basis of Jewish Law, the matrix out of which the Sages of the Talmud developed the Halakhah, which in turn fashioned the character and culture of the Jewish people.

The proliferation of the commandments from 10 to 613 came about as God communicated again and again to Moses, adding precept to precept and injunction to injunction. These revelations of God's prescriptions for His chosen people took place in the *Mishkan*, the Tabernacle erected in the wilderness, also called *Ohel Mo'ed*, the Tent of Meeting. It became, in effect, a portable Sinai, as is written, *There I will meet with you, and I will impart to you — from above the Ark's cover, from between the two cherubim that are on top of the Ark of the Testimony — all that I will command you concerning the children of Israel (ibid.* 25:22). The Sages differ as to the scope of the divine communication to Moses at Sinai before the setting up of the Tabernacle.[12] However, it is reasonable to assume that more than the Ten Commandments were revealed on Mt. Sinai. For it is written, *The Lord said to Moses, "Come up to Me on the mountain and wait there, and I will give you the stone tablets, and the Torah and the commandment*

---

10 *Keritot* 9a. See, however, *Nedarim* 31a, "Israel, as soon as Abraham was sanctified, no longer are considered *b'nai Noah*, but sons of Abraham." Conversion of non-Jews to Judaism and their inclusion in the peoplehood of Israel is indicated in several places in Scripture. In Deut. 23: 4–9, the Torah excludes certain tribes from being *admitted into the congregation of the Lord*; implying that members of other non-Jewish tribes may be admitted. In Exod. 12:48, Scripture states *If a stranger who dwells with you would offer the Passover-offering to the Lord, all his males must be circumcised; then he shall approach to offer it; he shall then be as a citizen of the land.* From this verse we see that circumcision is a requirement for the conversion of a male. In addition, the Sages ruled that immersion in a ritually proper pool of water (*mikveh*) is also required, both for the male and the female convert. For other requirements and procedures of conversion, see *Yevamot* 46a–47b and *Yoreh De'ah* 268.

11 *Ḥullin* 101b. *Makkot* 24a. Commentators differ as to which mitzvot are counted to comprise this number; see especially Ramban's comments to Rambam's *Sefer ha-Mitzvot* and *Sefer ha-Ḥinukh*.

12 *Zevaḥim* 115b.

which I have inscribed to instruct them" (ibid. 24:12).[13] Later we shall have occasion to refer to the divine communications recorded in the Book of Deuteronomy, spoken when the children of Israel were encamped in the plains of Moab, posed for their entry into the Promised Land.

The Basis of our Belief

Is there any historical evidence for the theophany at Sinai? Upon what do we base our belief that it was the Creator's voice that proclaimed the Decalogue; and that — as popular saying would have it — "The *Shekhinah* (God's Presence) was talking through the throat of Moses?"[14] The contention of nineteenth century Biblical criticism that it was impossible, because of the primitive nature of Israel's culture at the time, for the Decalogue to have been promulgated in the days of Moses has long been discredited by both textual and archaeological findings which substantiate the historicity of the Bible in general, including the Pentateuch.[15] Faith in *ma'amad har Sinai* is based upon the unbroken tradition which preserved the testimony of the actual eye-witnesses of the theophany, the Israelites who had heard with their own ears the proclamation *I am the Lord your God.* Thus did Moses exhort the people, *But take utmost care and watch yourselves exceedingly so that you do not forget the things that you saw with your own eyes... and make them known to your children's children, the day you stood before the Lord your God at Horeb* (Deut. 4:9–10). It is a perverse argument to maintain that such a living tradition as described in the

13 Some have interpreted the phrase *and the Torah and the mitzvah* to be in apposition to the *the stone tablets*; see Cassuto, *Commentary to Exodus* and JPS. On the other hand, the Sages would include practically all of Jewish Law from beginning to end; see *Berakhot* 5a. Rashi follows Saadia's interpretation that all 613 commandments are implied in the general injunctions of the Decalogue. I am inclined to accept the opinion that *the Torah and the mitzvot* refer to the laws recorded in Exod. chaps. 21–22, i.e. the *mishpatim* which were given at Sinai; see Rashi to Exod. 21:1.

14 Cf. *Zohar, parashat Pinḥas,* 232. For a full discussion of the origin of this phrase see Z. Gotthold in *Sefer ha-Yovel* of Rabbinical Council of America, Jer. 5745, p. 39, n. 35.

15 See Cassuto, *op. cit.* p. 163, and his *Torat ha-Te'udot,* Jer. 5713; also M.H. Segal, *Masoret Ubikoret,* Jer. 5715; W.F. Albright, *From the Stone Age to Christianity,* the Introduction; John Bright, "Modern Study of Old Testament Literature" in *The Bible and the Ancient Near East,* N.Y. 1965.

theophany is merely the product of the imagination of later generations.

Our faith is further buttressed by our historical experience. God did not announce his presence at Sinai as the Lord Who created heaven and earth; rather *I am the Lord your God Who took you out of the land of Egypt, the house of bondage* (Exod. 20:2).[16] Indeed, we are called upon to recognize our special relationship to God by the command *Remember the days of old and reflect upon a history of generations; ask your father and he will tell you, your elders and they will inform you* (Deut. 32:6–7). We of the twentieth century, who look upon a history of well nigh 3500 years since Sinai — a history replete with successive crises and salvations — can only find therein confirmation of the truth of the Torah and its divine provenance. The return of the Jews to the land of their Fathers after so many centuries of exile and dispersion, and the establishment therein of the sovereign State of Israel, are but the latest witnesses to the truth of Biblical assurance that the Torah is *your life and the length of your days* (*ibid.* 30:20).

Furthermore, our faith in Moses as the true spokesman of the Almighty is rooted in the historical experiences of our forefathers. Maimonides affirms this as follows:[17]

16   Yehudah Halevy, *Kuzari* 1:25.
17   *Hilkhot Yesodei ha-Torah* 8:1. No doubt Maimonides here was alluding to Christianity, based as it is upon faith in the miracles performed by Jesus. Another veiled attack against Christianity can be seen in the following statement: "If a person, either Gentile or Jew, will rise and perform a miracle, and then say that the Lord sent him to add or subtract a mitzvah (of the Torah), or to interpret a mitzvah differently from what we received from Moses, or said that the mitzvot Israel was commanded to observe were not for all generations but were temporary; he is a false prophet, since he came to contradict the prophecy of Moses" (*ibid.* 9:1).

In a passage missing from most printed editions of the Code because of the censor, Maimonides refers specifically to Jesus, condemning him as one who "caused Israel to be destroyed by the sword, their remnant to be dispersed and humiliated. He was instrumental in changing the Torah and causing the world to err and serve another beside God." For the full text, see A.M. Hershman, *The Book of Judges*, Yale Univ. Press, New Haven, 1949, p. xxiii.

Not all medieval rabbis shared Maimonides' view of Christianity. The Tosafists (*Sanhedrin* 63b. *s.v. assur*) maintained that a non-Jew is not considered idolatrous if he ascribes to God a partner *(shituf)*. Menahem ha-Meiri (see below, p. 137) maintained that the discriminatory legislation in the Talmud against non-Jews pertained only to the ancient heathen, but not to those nations (i.e. Christians) "who are defined by religious and moral paths."

"Israel did not believe in Moses because of the miracles he demonstrated; for one who believes because of miracles still doubts; perhaps the miracle was effected through magic. All the miracles that Moses performed were done according to the need of the moment, and not in order to substantiate his prophecy... The Israelites believed in him because of their experience in Sinai. They it was who saw and heard — and not some stranger — the fire and the sounds and the torches. Moses approached the thick cloud and a voice spoke to him and they heard, "Moses, Moses, go tell them thus," as is written, *And the Lord said to Moses, 'Behold I come to you in a thick cloud in order that the people may hear when I speak with you and so have faith in you forever"* (Exod. 19:9).

The Humaneness of Biblical Law

A further confirmation of our faith in *Torah min ha-Shamayim* may be found in its very contents: *What great nation has statutes and laws as righteous as all this Torah which I have set before you this day* (Deut. 4:8). What other society proclaimed millenia ago principles so universally acknowledged today! In what other ancient peoples do we find a day of rest for manservant and maidservant (Exod. 20:10), or a ruling that a slave is to be freed if his master knocked out his eye or tooth (*ibid.* 21:26–27). Those laws which are cited by Christians to this day to prove the cruelty of the Old Testament, such as *an eye for an eye and a tooth for a tooth*, might seem primitive if interpreted literally. However, they were never so interpreted by Judaism's oral tradition.[18] How did the Sages arrive at such a perception, if not from the general thrust and tone of Biblical legislation.

The economic and social legislation laid down by the Torah in the 25th chapter of Leviticus, though placed within the framework of an agricultural society, can serve as the basis for the most progressive legislation in modern industrial society, as they reflect the Torah's unmatched concern for man's dignity and equality of opportunity.[19]

18   *Bava Kamma* 83b–84a. See N. Leibovitch, *Iyunim Ḥadashim b'Sefer Vayikra*, Jer. 5743, pp. 390 ff.

It is true that much has been discovered in recent years of the laws of other ancient peoples of the Near East which bears a marked resemblance to the laws of the Torah, a fact which has led some to discount the originality and the uniqueness of the Revelation at Sinai.[20] This resemblance, however, can in no way diminish our faith in the divine origin and unique character of the Torah. For the Torah's divine character does not rest upon its terms of reference, but upon its unique moral attributes; a fact which can be ascertained by a comparative study of the various ancient codes of law. Among all the ancient codes, that of Sinai alone endured as a living testament and preserved for all humanity the universal and eternal principles of freedom and justice. And eternal principles of necessity proceed, not from ephemeral man, but from a Supreme Lawgiver, the Eternal Himself.

The revelation of the laws of the Torah took place as the Israelites were on their way to the Promised Land. There it was that these laws would enable them to organize a society unsullied by the barbarism and moral degradation of their neighbors. *Do not follow the practices of the land of Egypt or of the land of Canaan, and do not follow their statutes* the Torah admonished them (Lev. 18:3). The revelation was not designed to create a completely strange and unknown society by abolishing all customs and institutions prevalent at the time. "Scripture speaks of the commonplace," say our Sages[21] and its laws deal with life as it was lived in ancient times. Indeed, many laws of the Torah confirm or modify the practices of the Patriarchs. *The ways of the Lord to do justice and righteousness* (Gen. 18:19) were known to Abraham, and Scripture testifies that *he listened to the voice of the Lord, keeping His mandate, His commandments, His laws, and His teachings (ibid.* 26:5).[22] The practice of the Israelites not to eat the thigh

---

19 Cf. the statement of Henry George, a famous economist in the late 19th century, in his book *Progress and Poverty* (N.Y. 1879). "It is not the protection of property, but the protection of humanity, which is the aim of the Mosaic code. At every point it interposes barriers to the selfish greed which, if left unchecked, will surely divide men into landlord and serf, millionaire and tramp, ruler and ruled."

20 U. Cassuto, *op. cit.* pp. 178 ff., and Y. Kaufman, *The Religion of Israel*, Chicago 1960, pp. 166 ff.

21 *Bava Kamma* 5:7.

22 On the basis of this verse, the Sages imputed to Abraham the keeping of the entire Torah, even laws found only in the Talmud (*Yoma* 28b). See also Ramban to Gen. 38:8, "The early wise men before the period of the Torah knew that there is a great advantage in levirate marriage, and it included not only the deceased's brother but

muscle that is on the socket of the hip (*gid ha-nasheh*) began before Sinai.[23] Commands concerning the Sabbath (Exod. chap. 16) and other statutes (*ibid.*)[24] were already handed down before the Decalogue.

Maimonides goes further than other classical commentators in underscoring the contemporaneity of the Laws of the Torah. Many of them, he claims, can be understood only in relation to the prevailing customs of the then pagan world. Since a primary object of the Torah was to abolish idolatry and utterly uproot it, it forbade rounding the corners of the head (Lev. 19:27) and the wearing of garments made of linen and wool (Deut. 22:11) because these were the customs of heathen priests. In explaining the laws of sacrificial worship — a mode of worship which Maimonides deemed much inferior to that of prayer and supplication — he begins his argument as follows: "It is impossible, according to the nature of man, to suddenly discontinue everything to which he has been accustomed... The general mode of worship among all men, and to which the Israelites were also accustomed, consisted in sacrificing animals. It was in accordance with the wisdom and plan of God that He did not command us to give up all these rituals of service; for to obey such a commandment would have been contrary to the nature of man, who generally adheres to that to which he is accustomed."[25]

The Rationality of Biblical Law

We must not assume that out of this approach Maimonides would argue for the obsolescence of even a single law of the Torah and a justification for its abandonment. While the rationalists among Jewish philosophers insist that all the commandments of the Torah are explicable in terms of human reason, they acknowledge the limits of the

other relatives as well; but the Torah restricted such marriage to the brother only."

23 See, however, discussion in *Ḥullin* 101b. See also J.T. *Mo'ed Kattan* 3:5(82c), "Do we learn from what occurred before the giving of the Torah?" See also Rambam, *Commentary to Mishnah, Ḥullin* 7:6, "Pay attention to this important principle... What we refrain from doing or what we do is so only because we were so commanded by God through Moses, and not because God so commanded to the prophets who preceded Moses." A fuller discussion of this principle can be found in Zvi H. Chajes, *Kol Sifrei Maharitz*, (Jer. 5718), Vol. 1, chap. 11.

24 See *Sanhedrin* 56b and Rashi *ad loc.*

25 *Guide for the Perplexed*, ed. M. Friedlander, Part III, p. 151. This view was severely

human intellect and the obligation to observe the commandments even though their logic may escape us. No one has stated this more forcibly than Maimonides himself. In summing up the laws of sacrifices, he concludes,

"It is fitting for man to meditate upon the laws of the Holy Torah and to comprehend their full meaning to the extent of his ability. Nevertheless, a law for which he finds no reason and understands no cause should not be trivial in his eyes... Come and consider how strict the Torah was in the law of trespass.[26] Now if sticks and stones and earth and ashes become hallowed by words alone as soon as the name of the Master of the Universe was invoked upon them, and anyone who comported with them as with a profane thing committed trespass and required atonement even if he acted unwittingly, how much more should man be on guard not to rebel against a commandment decreed for us by the Holy One, blessed be He, only because he does not understand its reason... or to regard the commandments in the manner he regards ordinary affairs."[27]

Thus Maimonides did not spare himself the effort to include in his compendium of Jewish Law all the laws, down to their smallest detail, of the building of the Holy Temple and the sacrificial worhip therein, though he found no reason for all of them.[28]

Nevertheless, the rationalist insists that we are obliged to search out the reasons which prompted the Lawgiver to enjoin the Law. By understanding the rationale of the *mitzvot* we are supplied with an added motivation for ready compliance with them. Furthermore, in expounding the purpose of a mitzvah we are better able to achieve the ultimate goal of all the mitzvot; namely the refinement of character, something which a perfunctory observance for the sake of compliance alone cannot achieve. Of this we are certain, the Torah does no

criticised by Naḥmanides; see his commentary to Lev. 1:9.
26   I.e., the profane use of an object dedicated to use in the Temple; Lev. 5:15.
27   *Hilkhot Me'ilah* 8:8.
28   See Guide, III: chap. 26.

violence to human reason and logic; and we are not called upon — as others are — to believe that which is absurd.[29]

Further internal evidence of the super-human wisdom of Mosaic law can be found in its comprehension of Nature. All the species of birds mentioned in Leviticus (11:13–19) as forbidden food could not have been known to Moses through personal experience alone. Hygienic values which only modern medical research have been able to disclose inhere in such specific regulations as circumcision on the eighth day, or ritual impurity of a woman during her menstrual period.[30] It is by no means strange that the Sages have interpreted the verse *Be most careful for yourselves* (Deut. 4:15) to imply an injunction that one must take all measures to conserve not only one's life, but one's health as well. A physician pursues his profession with the sanction of the Torah:[31] and indeed one is cautioned not to dwell in a city that has no physician.[32] Even those who may not recognize the undoubted soundness of mind and body which a Torah regime confers upon its adherents can point to no single law of the Torah as being injurious to man's mental or physical health.

The Torah Against Asceticism

The divine origin of Mosaic legislation must not lead us into the false assumption that it was designed for super-human creatures; or at best for extraordinary individuals who have somehow exorcised from their natures the temptations of the flesh to which ordinary individuals are subject. The Sages state categorically: "The Torah was not given to the

29   Cf. *Pesaḥim* 119a, "What is the meaning of the phrase *and cover themselves elegantly* (Isaiah 23:18)? It refers to one who discloses things which the "ancient of days" covered; namely, the reasons of (the laws of) the Torah."

30   The Israelites were not the only ancient people which observed the rite of circumcision, or regarded the menstruating woman as unclean. But the Torah transferred local custom into divine fiat, and prescribed the details of performance in complete harmony with man's nature. Studies have appeared in various medical journals to substantiate this fact. For references see Leo Jung, *The Jewish Library* (N.Y. 1934), Vol. 3, pp. 359 ff.

31   *Bava Kamma* 85a. See also J.D. Bleich, *The Obligation to Heal in Jewish Tradition*, in *Jewish Bioethics* (N.Y. 1979).

32   *Sanhedrin* 17a.

ministering angels."[33] The laws of the Torah are within the capabilities and comprehension of unexceptional human beings; the only qualification being that they have a sense of commitment to the covenant of Sinai.

The Torah does not call for ascetic practices or a denial of the satisfaction of man's instinctual drives.[34] Priests are not enjoined to be celibate; on the contrary, a husband is enjoined not to deny his wife her conjugal rights (Exod. 21:10).[35] Only one day in the year does the Torah command that it be a day of *afflicting one's self* (Lev. 16:29).[36] This phrase could easily have been interpreted to imply some sort of flagellation; but the Sages, fully aware of the Torah's non-ascetic character, expounded, "Does this mean that one should sit in the hot sun to make himself suffer? No, for we learn that it is a command only to refrain from food and drink."[37] Indeed, the Torah forbids self-inflicted wounding of the flesh or other excessive manifestations of mourning (Deut. 14:1). For many occasions the Torah prescribes rejoicing; and one Sage goes so far as to aver that a person will be called to account for the things he could have enjoyed but denied himself.[38] Thus the nazirite is called a sinner because he denied himself the mere pleasure of wine.[39] And we recite a benediction when we see the fresh blossoming of the trees in Spring, thanking God for having created beautiful things in this world for people to enjoy.[40]

Despite the "humaneness" of the Torah's commandments, it must be acknowledged that human beings in general have fallen far short of its prescriptions for a healthy and peaceful society.[41] Man's greed and arrogant lust for power have too often led him astray from the path of justice and righteousness. The history of human affairs is indeed depressing, a sad tale of "man's inhumanity to man"; replete with conflict and strife. The irony of such history lies in the fact that so

---

33 *Berakhot* 25b.
34 Cf. Rambam, *Hilkhot De'ot* 3:1.
35 Moses was an exception; see Rashi to Num. 12:1.
36 JPS translation: "self-denial".
37 *Yoma* 74b.
38 End of J.T. *Kiddushin*.
39 *Nedarim* 10a.
40 *Berakhot* 43b.
41 Cf. *Avodah Zarah* 2b, "Have you observed the seven commandments?" Also *Bava Kamma* 38a, "He saw that the sons of Noah, who had accepted upon themselves the seven commandments, did not fulfill them."

much of man's injustice and cruelty has been committed in the name of God and religious principle. Nevertheless, it is the firm conviction of Judaism that a time will come when mankind will elevate itself from the morass of bloodshed and tyranny to the heights of universal brotherhood and peace. This is the unique message of the the Prophets of Israel.

The Prophets and the Halakha[42]

Moses was not the only person who received a message from God to be transmitted to Israel for the edification of all mankind. The Biblical prophets also conveyed the word of God. But God's manner of communication with the prophets was not the same as with Moses. The former received their messages by means of a vision, in an ecstatic trance, whereas Moses received the Torah directly, *as a man talks to his neighbor* (Exod. 33:11). This difference in the method of communication is a result of the difference in the content and purpose of the respective revelations. Moses was asked to charge the people with specific and detailed injunctions regulating every phase of life, the letter of the Law; the prophets were summoned to exhort the people to proper compliance with the Law by clarifying its spirit and basic purpose; namely, social justice and the brotherhood of man under the fatherhood of the One God.

This distinction between the two methods of divine revelation is significant for Jewish Law. The Sages, basing themselves upon the verse *These are the commandments which the Lord God commanded Moses for the children of Israel on Mount Sinai* (Lev. 27:34), posited the principle that "From now on a prophet may not introduce anything new," i.e. no new legislation in the corpus of Jewish Law.[43] The Talmud makes a distinction between *divrei Torah*, statements found in the Pentateuch, and *divrei kabbalah*, statements found in the books of the Prophets, and stipulates that one may not infer from the latter an interpretation of the former.[44] Maimonides bases this principle upon

---

42 A full discussion of this subject can be found in *Kol Sifrei Maharitz*, (op. cit.) chap. *Torat ha-Neviim*.
43 *Shabbat* 104a.
44 *Ḥagigah* 10b; *Niddah* 23a.

two other verses: *You shall not add anything to what I command you, or take anything away from it* (Deut. 4:2; 13:1), and *This mitzvah which I enjoin you this day...is not in heaven* (*ibid.* 30:11–12). "Why then," asks Maimonides, "did the Torah say *The Lord your God will raise up for you a prophet from among your own people like myself; him you shall heed* (*ibid.* 18:15)? Not for the sake of making law, but to enjoin the people to observe the Torah and warn them against transgressing it."[45]

The distinction between the Torah of Moses and the Prophets is also reflected in halakhic rulings assigning different degrees of sanctity to the Torah (i.e. the Pentateuch) and to the Prophets and the Writings (*Ketuvim*, or Hagiographa): "Scrolls of the Torah and of the *Humashim* (individual books of the Pentateuch) may be wrapped in mantles used for scrolls of the Prophets and the Writings; but scrolls of the Prophets and the Writings may not be wrapped in mantles used for scrolls of the Torah and the *Humashim*. One may place a scroll of the Torah or *Humashim* on top of a scroll of the Prophets or Writings; but one may not place a scroll of the Prophets or Writings on top of a scroll of the Torah or *Humashim*.[46]

This line of demarcation between Mosic law and prophetic preachment is not a solid line. The Sages were hard pressed to explain certain laws which ostensibly are based upon prophetic passages. For example, there is a dispute among Tannaim concerning the prohibition of a *kohen* marrying a proselyte, each Tanna supporting his opinion by inference from a verse in Ezekiel.[47] Another dispute, whether or not one is permitted to carry an object in the public domain on a Festival, is based upon a passage in Jeremiah.[48] One explanation offered by the Sages for such seemingly prophetic provenance is the assertion that such laws first mentioned by the Prophets were actually an oral

---

45　*Hilkhot Yesodei ha-Torah* 9:1–2.

46　J.T. *Megillah* 3:1 (73d). This follows the principle, "We may raise something to a higher degree of sanctity; but we may not lower it to a lower degree" (*Menahot* 99a).

47　*Kiddushin* 78a. Ezekiel presented a special problem because "his words contradict words of the Torah, and only Elijah will be able to explain them" (*ibid.* 45a). Fortunately, the Sages were able to interpret those difficult passages and decided not to exlude his book from the *Kitvei Kodesh* (Holy Writings). See also *Mo'ed Kattan* 27b, where many laws of mourning are derived from Ezekiel; and *Sanhedrin* 81a.

48　*Betzah* 12a.

tradition handed down by Moses.[49] Another reconciliation between theoretical principle and the actual practice is the assertion that the prophets were bringing to the attention of the people practices originally sanctioned by Moses but which in the course of time had been forgotten.[50]

We shall see in a later chapter that the Rabbis were anxious to preserve the distinction between laws which have the force of a Biblical injunction (*d'oraita*) and those which have the force of a Rabbinic injunction (*d'rabbanan*). Those practices which the Sages deemed to have the force of Mosaic law they attributed to an oral tradition (*halakhah l'Moshe mi-Sinai*); just as they decided which laws derived from Rabbinic exegesis have the force of Biblical law, and which they deemed to be Rabbinic in origin even though based upon an inference from Scripture (*asmakhta*).[51]

The תורה was given for the purpose of being written. But the נביאים's prophecies weren't written, unless ה said. Usually נבא is for that generation, & may not correspond to other generations. Prophecies couldn't be written outside של נבא'ה.

---

49   *Mo'ed Kattan* 5a.

50   *Megillah* 3a.

51   See *Rosh Hashanah* 19a, "*Divrei kabbalah* are like *divrei Torah.*" For other discussions of this problem, see *inter alia*, Zvi H. Chajes (*op. cit.*) chap. *Torah ha-Neviim*, chap. 1; I.H. Weiss, *Dor Dor ve-Dorshav*, Vol. 1, pp. 71 ff.; Eliezer Levi, *Yesodot ha-Halakhah* (Tel Aviv 5720), pp. 83–89: B. Epstein, *Torah Temimah* to Lev. 27:34; C.G. Montefiore and H. Loewe, *Rabbinic Anthology* (Phila. 5720), p. CIV.

What is essential for us to understand is the complementary relationship between *divrei Torah* and *divrei Kabbalah*, the former being normative and the latter inspirational. Together they represent the unique character of Jewish Law, where spirit is embodied in specific legislation. Thus in determining the letter of the law, the Sages were mindful of the verse in Proverbs, *Its ways are ways of pleasantness.*[52] At the same time, they realized that the lofty purpose of Mosaic law would easily vaporize into vague sentimentality if not held fast by adherence to its manifold prescriptions.

52   See *Gittin* 59b; *Sukkah* 32a; *Yevamot* 15a and 87b.

'ה dictated the תורה to משה, the exact words were
written by משה. One סברא says משה wrote from בראשית to בראשית
on כתיב then it was written as it happened. The rest were
dictated to משה in the מדבר של, The תורה was given
משה by משה. Another opinion says that nothing was written
until the 40th yr. (נויזת עשיית) (נוזת תורה)
[נאר-זרו the תורה was given ~~פרשה~~ by 'ה word by word, Why
doesn't it start w/ "וזאת ה לפני"

3

This Is The Torah

וזאת התורה אשר שם משה לפני בני ישראל
And this is the Torah which Moses set before the children of Israel
(Deut. 4:44)

Maimonides explains his eighth principle, *Torah min ha-Shamayim*, as follows:

"That we believe that the entire Torah which we possess today is the Torah given to Moses, and that it was given in its entirety by the Almighty. In other words, we have received it as one receives a spoken communication, though exactly by what method is known only to the recipient, Moses. He was like a scribe who writes down everything dictated to him, including the historical events and the commandments...Every letter in the Torah contains wise and wonderful statements perceived by those granted wisdom by God.[1] Moreover, the accepted interpretation of Scripture is also from the mouth of the Almighty, so that the manner in which we perform today the mitzvot of Sukkah and Lulav and Shofar and Tzitzit and Tefillin etc. is the same manner in which God communicated it to Moses, who in turn communicated it to us."[2]

1   A reference to the Sages who expounded the Torah; cf. *Sifre* Num. 134 (verse 27:11) "The Torah gave wisdom to the Sages to expound."

2   *Commentary to the Mishnah, San.* chap. 10. See *Gittin* 60a for discussion whether sections (*parshiyot*) of the Torah were committed to writing at the time of their being communicated to Moses, and before he passed away he joined the scrolls together into one whole scroll; or perhaps Moses retained in his memory the various communications and did not commit anything to writing until he had received the final communication.

35

The Book of Deuteronomy

This sweeping assertion of Maimonides, undoubtedly including the Book of Deuteronomy, raises problems even for the believing Jew.[3] From the Torah itself and from certain rabbinic comments it would appear that the Book of Deuteronomy (*Mishneh Torah*)[4] is largely a review by Moses himself in his own language of the events and commandments already recorded in the earlier books. The introductory verse to Deuteronomy reads *These are the words which Moses spoke to all Israel*, instead of the usual verse *And the Lord spoke unto Moses saying*, which introduces other sections of the Torah. In Deuteronomy, when Moses transmits a message from the Almighty, he does not seem to be quoting Him directly, word for word, but seems to phrase it in his own words. Thus there are linguistic variations between what is recorded in the earlier books as God's command, and what is recorded as such in Deuteronomy. This is seen most strikingly when we compare "the blessings and the curses"[5] recorded in chapter 26 of Leviticus with those recorded in chapter 28 of Deuteronomy. The Sages acknowledged that the former were dictated to Moses by the Almighty, whereas the latter were the words of Moses himself, and they base upon this difference a halakhic ruling. In the public reading of the Torah in the synagogue, the chapter in Leviticus must be recited by one person without interruption, whereas in reading the chapter in Deuteronomy we may interrupt to call up another person in the middle of the section.[6] Furthermore, the Sages derived an important

---

3   We are not concerned with the views of the Bible critics who assert that Deuteronomy was not composed before the reign of King Josiah (see II Kings, chap. 22), if not later. We are trying to understand the traditional point of view as set down by the Sages of the Talmud.

4   This phrase appears in Deut. 17:18, where it means "a copy of the Torah", and not — as the name Deuteronomy suggests — a repetition of the Torah. It is remarkable that Maimonides called his great compendium of Jewish Law *Mishneh Torah*; see Introduction to the code for his explanation of the name and the stricture of the Ravd. Feeling that this name is too pretentious, especially since it is the usual appellation given by the Rabbis to Deuteronomy, Maimonides' code is usually referred to as the *Yad ha-Ḥazakah* (see the last verse in Deut.), since the numerical value of the word *Yad* is 14, the number of books into which the code is divided.

5   Generally referred to as the *Tokhaḥah*, chastisement.

6   *Megillah* 31a.

lesson from this difference. Rabbi Levi said, "Come and see that the attribute of a person of flesh and blood is not the same as that of the Holy One blessed be He; the Holy One blessed Israel with 22 letters and cursed them with 8 letters, whereas Moses our teacher blessed them with 8 letters and cursed them with 22 letters."[7]

Another problem with the text of Deuteronomy is the version of the Decalogue recited by Moses, which varies in several of the commandments from the version recorded in Exodus. Moses seems to be quoting the Sinaitic revelation verbatim, and yet introduces several changes both in language and in substance. The Sages resolve this problem by stating categorically that both versions were pronounced by the Almighty simultaneously. "Both *Zakhor* (*Remember the Sabbath day* in Exodus) and *Shamor* (*Keep the Sabbath day* in Deuteronomy) were spoken in a single utterance; something which the mouth cannot speak and the ear cannot hear."[8] In his commentary to the Torah, Nahmanides explains that it was not the variation in the language which prompted the Rabbis to make that assertion — after all, there are other variations in language besides *Zakhor* and *Shamor* — but the difference in the nature of the respective commandments, *Zakhor* being a positive commandment and *Shamor* a negative one.[9] What Moses did here when he repeated the Decalogue was to tell the children of Israel that when God said *Zakhor* He meant *Shamor* as well. This perhaps would explain the phrase *As the Lord your God commanded you* which Moses added to both the fourth and fifth

---

7　*Bava Batra* 88b. We have here a play upon the numerical values of the letters which open and close the section in respective versions. For a contrary point of view see Rashi to Deut. 28:23, where Moses is said to be more considerate in his chastisement than the Almighty. Nahmanides, in his commentary to Lev. 26:16, explains that the *tokhaḥah* in Lev. refers to the first (Babylonian) exile; whereas the *tokhaḥah* in Deut. refers to the second exile, i.e. the present Diaspora after the destruction of the Second Temple.

8　*Shevuot* 20b. The *Mekhilta* to Exod. 20:8 resolves apparently contradictory legislation in the Torah with the same assertion that God spoke both rulings at once. In that context, the assertion signifies that God Himself excepted a particular instance from a general rule. Thus, despite the general rule that a man may not marry his brother's widow, an exception is made if the widow is childless (the law of *Yibbum*).

9　The command to "Remember" is fulfilled by the positive act of reciting the verses in Gen. 2:1–3 which speak of the Sabbath of Creation, and the benediction blessing God Who sanctifies the Sabbath (the *Kiddush*). The command to "Keep" calls upon us to desist from labor on the Sabbath.

commandments. The Sages, however, explained this additional phrase to mean that God commanded these injunctions prior to Sinai, at Marah.[10]

The problem with Deuteronomy is not only with what Moses did say, but also with what he did not say. The Sages aver that the mitzvot which were given to Moses at Sinai and in *Ohel Mo'ed*[11] were repeated at the plains of Moab, the locale of Moses' address recorded in Deuteronomy.[12] Nevertheless, many mitzvot included in the address are not mentioned in the previous books.[13] Nahmanides explains that in his farewell address Moses stressed those laws which were most relevant for the people about to enter the Promised Land, particularly the warnings against idolatry. It was not necessary, for example, for Moses to repeat the special laws pertaining to the priesthood, since priests are diligent in their performance and do not require reiteration of their duties. Nahmanides insists that the laws recorded only in Deuteronomy were given to Moses at Sinai, but were not transmitted by him to the Israelites until they were in the plains of Moab since they were of little relevance for the Israelites who were to perish in the wilderness.

Another problem dealt with by the Sages concerns the final eight verses of Deuteronomy, which begin *And there Moses the servant of the Lord died.* "Is it possible that Moses died and then wrote his obituary?" Two opinions are advanced to resolve this problem. One asserts that these verses were written by Joshua and added to the text of the Pentateuch. The contrary opinion rejects such a premise, asking "How is it possible that the command given by Moses to the Levites to take the *Sefer Torah* (Deut. 31:26) was a scroll with verses missing?" Rather, we must assume that until these final verses God spoke and Moses wrote; when it came to these final verses God continued to speak and Moses continued to write, but with tears in his eyes.[14] The special character of these verses is reflected in an halakhic ruling: "These eight verses in the Torah are read in the synagogue by one

10 *Sanhedrin* 56b.
11 See above p. 22.
12 *Zevaḥim* 115b.
13 For a listing of these mitzvot, see J. Reider, *Deuteronomy*, (Phila. 5697), p. xxviii, n. 29.
14 *Bava Batra* 15a.

38

individual only;" that is, we do not interrupt the reading of these verses in order to call up another person to the reading.[15]

To resolve these problems I suggest that we examine the concept of "tradition" in Rabbinic literature; namely, the transmission from master to disciple of the teachings of the Torah. There are two terms to designate this process, one from the point of view of the teacher, and the other from the point of view of the disciple. The clearest example of this we find in the opening statement of *Tractate Avot* (Ethics of the Fathers). To describe Moses' receiving the Torah from Sinai (i.e. from the Almighty), it employs the verb *kibbel*, from which we derive the term *kabbalah*, which signifies our tradition.[16] However, to describe the handing over of the Torah by Moses to Joshua it employs the verb *masar*, from which we derive the term *masorah* or *masoret*, which also means tradition.[17] *Kibbel*, received, implies that the disciple received an exact and specifically worded teaching; whereas *masar*, handed over, implies the handing over of a more general idea of the subject involved, thus allowing the disciple to formulate the teaching as he best understands it. Traditional teaching transmitted by either method enjoys equal validity and sanctity.[18]

In these two methods lies the difference between the earlier books of the Pentateuch and Deuteronomy. In the former there was *kabbalah*, Moses receiving an instruction that was to be transmitted to Israel verbatim; whereas in the latter there was *mesirah*, Moses being given the freedom — more to the point, the responsibility — to transmit the instruction in the manner best suited to the circumstances of the moment. Of course, in such case the disciple is one who can be trusted

---

15 *Menaḥot* 30a. Maimonides (*Hilkhot Tefillah* 13:6) has a rather strange interpretation of this ruling. Here again he mentions that Moses heard the verses from the mouth of the Almighty. See also *Tosafot Rosh Hashanah* 27a, *s.v. aval.*

16 Only in post-Talmudic literature does *kabbalah* also designate the mystical teachings of Judaism. The Sages also designated the Prophets as *kabbalah*, see above p. 31. For Rabbinic use of the terms as oral tradition, see Ḥullin 137a and Rashi *ad loc.*, "The Torah of Moses is called *Torah* because it was given for all generations; whereas (the teaching of) the Prophets is called *kabbalah* because they received each prophecy from the Holy Spirit according to the need of the hour and the generation and the occasion."

17 For the Rabbinic use of the term *masoret* as tradition, see *inter alia Yoma* 21a, *Megillah* 10b, *Bava Batra* 99a. See also below, p. 46, for its use in a technical sense.

18 Cf. *Eduyot* 1:3, "One is obliged to transmit (a ruling) in the very language of his master."

to phrase the instruction he received in such a manner that it conveys the subject properly, in accord with the intent of the master. Such a disciple of the Almighty was Moses, as the Torah testifies, *Throughout My household he is trusted* (Num. 12:7). To such an extent was Moses trustworthy that he did certain things without first asking God's permission, and yet God conceded that what he did was proper. "Three things Moses did on his own and the Holy One blessed be He agreed with him; he added one day (to the days of preparation for receiving the Decalogue at Sinai; Exod. 19:10); he separated himself from his wife; and he broke the tablets."[19] Though the method of instruction differed, the resultant recordings of the Almighty's teachings in the Pentateuch possess equal sanctity; and therefore a scroll of the Torah which does not contain all these recordings is invalid.

Incidentally, we have here an indication of that basic principle of the Halakhah that we possess two Torahs, the Written Torah and the Oral Torah,[20] a concept we shall explain in greater detail in the next chapter. And this is why Maimonides included in the same principle of *Torah min ha-Shamayim* both the Written and the Oral instruction received by Moses.

Safeguarding the Text

Before passing away, Moses enjoined the people that as soon as they cross the Jordan into Canaan they should *set up large stones, coat them with plaster, and inscribe upon them all the words of the Torah...most clearly* (Deut. 27:2–8).[21] In the Book of Joshua (8:3) we are told that

19   *Shabbat* 87a. Maharal of Prague makes a somewhat similar distinction between Deuteronomy and the earlier books. He says, "The difference between Mishneh Torah and the rest of the Torah lies in the two categories of the Torah; one from the point of view of the Holy One, blessed be He, Who is "the giver" (*noten*) of the Torah, and the other from the point of view of Israel, the receivers of the Torah... In the Mishneh Torah it was necessary for Moses to add explanations for the benefit of the recipients" (*Tiferet Yisrael* 43). See also Ibn Ezra's commentary to Exod. 20:1.

20   *Shabbat* 31a.

21   This last phrase in the Hebrew text, *ba-er heitev*, which can also mean "well expounded," cf. Deut. 1:3, was interpreted by the Sages to imply that the words of the Torah were to be inscribed in seventy languages (*Sotah* 32a), corresponding to the seventy nations that branched out from the sons of Noah (Gen. chap. 10). This is a token of the universal character of the Torah.

Joshua fulfilled this charge *and inscribed on the stones the copy of the Torah of Moses which he had written for the children of Israel.*[22] This was a reference to the scroll of the Torah which Moses had written on longlasting parchment and entrusted to *the kohanim, bearers of the Ark of the Covenant, and to all the elders of Israel* (Deut.31:9). When Solomon built the Temple we are told that *the kohanim brought the Ark of the Lord's Covenant to its rightful place, to the shrine of the Temple, to the Holy of Holies, underneath the wings of the cherubim* (I Kings 8:6). And even though it says there that *there was nought in the Ark save the two stone tablets which Moses had placed therein in Horeb* (v. 9), the Sages aver that the scroll of Moses was also brought into the Temple together with the Ark.[23]

As soon as Joshua had taken over the leadership of the Israelites after the death of Moses, he was commanded by God *Let not this Book of the Torah cease from your lips, but recite it day and night,*[24] *so that you may observe faithfully all that is written in it* (Josh. 1:8). However, it was the responsibility of the *kohanim* who ministered in the Temple to safeguard the Torah, for they were charged with the duty to teach its precepts to the people,[25] and to act as judges on the basis of the Torah's legislation.[26] Unfortunately, the priests neglected their responsibility, as we read in Jeremiah (2:8), *The priests never asked "Where is the Lord?" and the guardians of the Torah did not know Me.*

As a result, ignorance of the Torah — especially its forthright condemnation of all forms of idolatry — was widespread. Indeed, for a long time the Torah lay hidden and forgotten until discovered in a recess in the Temple by the priest Hilkiah, who had been supervising repairs to the building. When its contents were read by the scribe Shaphan before the king Josiah, the latter assembled all the people *and*

---

22 Opinions are divided as to how much of the Torah was inscribed on the stones; see Radak *ad loc.* and *Torah Temimah* to Deut. 27:8.

23 *Bava Batra* 14a–b. See the discussion there whether the scroll was placed inside the Ark, or on a shelf extending from the side of the Ark.

24 This phrase, *but recite it day and night,* was adopted by Rabbinic tradition as an admonition to all Israel to study Torah constantly; cf. the benediction before the Shema in the evening service. The Sages, however, did concede that one fulfills this injunction by reciting the Shema morning and evening (*Menaḥot* 99b). See also *Yalkut Shimoni* to Joshua, sec. 6.

25 Lev. 10:11; Malachi 2:7.

26 Deut. 17:9. See also M. Lewittes, *Religious Foundations of the Jewish State* (N.Y. 1977) pp. 9–10.

read to them all the words of the Book of the Covenant found in the House of the Lord (II Kings 23:2). He then had them pledge *to keep all the mitzvot... with all their heart and soul* (*ibid.* v.3). Josiah immediately instituted compliance with the Torah's commandments and destroyed all vestiges of the idolatry that had been practiced in the days of his grandfather Manasseh. He also ordered the Levites, who taught all Israel, to put back the Ark, which apparently had been removed by Manasseh, into the Temple (II Chron. 35:3).[27] No doubt, the scroll of the Torah of Moses was also restored to its place near the Ark.

Incidentally, reading of the Torah before an assembly of the people is a provision of the Torah itself, which prescribed that the people assemble once in seven years so that *they may hear and that they may learn to fear the Lord and observe all the words of the this Torah* (Deut. 31:12).[28] We shall soon see how such public reading of the Torah once again served to keep alive the words of the Torah in the hearts and minds of the people of Israel.

Ezra the Scribe

It was only after the destruction of Solomon's Temple by Nebuchadnezer, and after the return of a fraction of the exiled Judeans to Zion, that there appeared an individual who "restored the Torah to Israel" and made its provisions known to the people at large. *The entire people assembled as one man..: and they asked Ezra the scribe to bring the scroll of the Torah of Moses which the Lord had commanded Israel. And Ezra the priest brought the Torah before the congregation, men and women, and all who could listen with understanding. He read from it... from the first light until midday... the ears of all the people were given to the scroll of the Torah* (Nehemiah 8:1–3). Subsequently Ezra instituted the public reading of sections of the Torah in the synagogue on Monday and Thursday mornings, and Saturday mornings and afternoons.[29]

---

27 The Rabbis interpret the verse in II Chron. to mean that Josiah, seeing that the Temple would be destroyed, ordered the Ark to be hidden in underground tunnels which had already been prepared for this purpose by King Solomon (*Yoma* 52b).

28 For the details of this mitzvah of Assembly (*hak'hel*) see Mishnah *Sotah* 7:8.

29 *Bava Kamma* 82a. see *Tosafot ad loc. s.v. kedei* why Mondays and Thursdays were chosen. *Soferim* 16:10 speaks of 175 sections, or *sidrahs*, into which the Pentateuch was divided, which indicates that the reading cycle was completed

Ezra's work was so important that he is compared by the Sages to Moses as a giver of the Torah.[30] This man was no prophet; by his time the period of prophecy had come to an end. The rebuilding of Jewish life after the catastrophe of the *Ḥurban* required no new revelation; needed was a *sofer*, a scribe who would not only spread the words of the Torah among the people, but would make them the standard of daily practice. This man of the hour was Ezra Hasofer, *a ready scribe in the Torah of Moses* (Ezra 7:6).[31]

Ezra was bold indeed. In order to make sure that all the people would be able to read the Torah, he had copies written in the Assyrian script then in vogue in place of the ancient Canaanite script of the days of Moses.[32] In addition to the regular readings of the Torah in the synagogue, Ezra also instituted that these readings be translated, verse by verse, into the vernacular, which for a thousand years was Aramaic.[33] Scrupulous care was exercised by Ezra and his associates, the *Soferim* or Scribes, to copy the text of the Torah exactly, for any change in the wording might signify a change in the law.[34] "Why were they called *Soferim*?" asks the Talmud. "Because they would count all

once in three and a half years, or twice in a *Shemittah* cycle of seven years. In Talmudic times, this was the practice in Eretz Yisrael, but in Babylonia the rabbis instituted a yearly cycle; see *Megillah* 29b; Rambam, *Hilkhot Tefillah* 13:1, and *Jewish Encyclopedia s.v.* "Triennial Cycle." The *Sidrahs* are also known as *Parshiyot*, though technically speaking the latter are the divisions of the text into paragraphs. See Rambam, *Hilkhot Sefer Torah*, chap. 8, for a listing of these *parshiyot*.

30   *Sanhedrin* 21b.

31   See *Religious Foundations of the Jewish State, op.cit.* pp. 54 ff.

32   *Sanhedrin* 21b. Cf. discussion in J.T. *Megillah* 1:11.

33   *Nedarim* 37b; J.T. *Megillah* 4:1. For rules concerning procedure, see Mishnah *Megillah* 4:4 (*Megillah* 23b–24a). See also *Tosafot Megillah* 23b *s.v. lo* and *ibid.* 24a *s.v. ve'im* re practice in Middle Ages; and Y. Kapaḥ *Halikhot Teiman* (Jer. 5728) p. 68 that Yemenite Jews continued the practice till recent times. The official translation (*Targum*) was the one attributed to Onkelos; see *Shaarei Teshuvah* (ed. Z. Leiter, Pittsburgh 5706, sec. 330), "The Targum referred to by the Sages is the one presently used (i.e. Onkelos); other translations do not possess the sanctity of this translation." For translations of Bible in general see M.L. Margolis *The Story of Bible Translations* (Phila 1917).

34   Cf. R. Yishmael's warning to R. Meir, who was a scribe , "My son, be very careful in your vocation for it is a heavenly one; if you were to omit or add even one letter the entire world would be destroyed." (*Eruvin* 13a).

the letters of the Torah."[35] Thus to indicate the exact middle of the Pentateuch as far as the number of letters is concerned, they instituted that the letter *vav* in the word *gaḥon* (Lev. 11:42) be written extra large; and to indicate the middle as far as the number of verses is concerned, the letter *gimmel* in the word *vehitgalaḥ* (*ibid.* 13:33) be written large.[36]

The Talmud speaks of *Mikra Soferim* and *Ittur Soferim*, indicating that the *Soferim* did make some slight editorial or stylistic emendations in the text.[37] Most important was their fixing of the text where they found two or more versions of the same passage; at times retaining the written text (*ketib*) but inserting an instruction that it be read differently (*keri*). To Ezra is attributed the ruling that certain words are to be written with dots over them to indicate that their inclusion in the text is doubtful. In *Avot D'Rabbi Natan* (34:5) we read as follows: "Thus said Ezra, 'If Elijah will come and ask me why I have written these words (that do not belong), I will reply that I have placed dots over them (to indicate their doubtful inclusion). And if he tells me that these words do belong, I will remove the dots from them.'"[38] Subsequent generations exercised scrupulous care that the exact wording of Scripture be preserved free from error, and even if one letter in a scroll of the Torah is found to be incorrect or missing it is invalid for public reading until corrected.[39] And a person who permits a scroll to remain uncorrected for more than thirty days is said to ignore the admonition in Job (11:14) *Let not unrighteousness dwell in your tents*.[40] The anxiety to preserve the text in its original form is also demonstrated in the fact that scrolls of the Torah to this very day do not contain any vowel or

---

35   *Kiddushin* 30a. In the Talmud, *Soferim* also refers to the early exegetical scholars, as in the phrase *divrei soferim*. In J.T. the term was applied to teachers, in the Aramaic *safra, safraya*. See also Mishnah *Kiddushin*, end of chap. 4.

36   In our *sifrei Torah* today, the middle verse is Lev. 8:7. See *Tosafot Shabbat* 55b *s.v. ma'aviram* that our *masoret* varies in many instances from that of the Talmud. Even some rabbis of the Talmud were not certain of the correct *masoret* (*Kiddushin* 30a). For a listing of the variations between our scrolls and what is recorded in the Talmud, see R. Akiva Eger, *Gilyon Hashas*, to *Shabbat* 55b.

37   *Nedarim* 37b. See commentaries *ad loc.* for the meaning of those terms.

38   For a listing of these dots, see *Soferim* 6:3.

39   *Sh. A. Oraḥ Ḥayyim* 143:4 and *Mishnah Brurah ad loc.* n. 25.

40   *Ketubot* 19b.

cantillation signs even though this makes reading from the scroll so much more difficult.[41]

The Soferim

How authentic was the text in the hands of the *Soferim*? Was it composed at the time of the events described therein, as tradition claims; or did it originate at a time far removed from those events, as Bible critics of the school of Wellhausen claim? Biblical scholars of recent days, both Jewish and non-Jewish, examining the results of archeological discoveries — particularly literary remains of the Biblical era — have exposed the theories of the 19th century Bible critics to be a string of fantasies without any basis in actual fact.[42]

Yehezkel Kaufman, in his monumental work on the History of the Israelite Faith, offers a cogent argument against those who would question the authenticity of the Pentateuch. There are many stories in the Book of Genesis concerning the Patriarchs which are in contradiction to the laws laid down in the subsequent books of the Pentateuch; such as Abraham marrying his sister and Jacob marrying two sisters. Had Ezra and his colleagues felt free to tamper with the text in order to make it more consistent with the religious norms of his time, they undoubtedly would have eliminated those parts of the text which might prove embarrassing or contradictory. It was the sense of the sacredness and inviolability of the Biblical text which had come down to them from ancient times that insured that copies of the Torah were free of updating corrections, with the exception of the slight emendations mentioned above.

In the period following Ezra, standard copies of the Torah were kept in the Temple to serve as models for the copyists, and in fact "correc-

---

41 *Sh. A. Yoreh De'ah* 274:7, based upon a responsum of Ramban that "we only (may make a copy) as it was given from Sinai." See also *Soferim* 3:6.

42 See, *inter alia*, S. Schechter, *Seminary Addresses* (Cincinnati, 1915), pp. 35–39; M.D. Cassuto, *Torat ha-Te'udot*; M.L. Margolis, *The Hebrew Scriptures in the Making* (J.P.S. Phila., 1922); J. Bright, *Modern Study of Old Testament Literature* (in the Bible and the Ancient Near East, N.Y., 1961).

tors" of scrolls of the Torah were paid from Temple funds.[43] Nevertheless, copyists are human, and undoubtely some errors might have been made in transcribing the text. In fact, it is reported that three scrolls found in the Temple had variant readings, and it was decided to accept as valid the reading common to two out of the three scrolls.[44] Since this was before vowels were introduced into Hebrew writing,[45] the proper vocalization was standardized by the oral tradition kept alive by the public readings in the synagogue, known as *mikra*, literally "reading". In the period of the *Tannaim*, who flourished in the century after the destruction of the Second Temple in the year 70 of the Common Era, there was a difference of opinion among them as to whether the written text, called *masoret*, or the vocalization took precedence in determining the law.[46] However, we do not find any controversies based upon variant versions of the text, for this was fixed and uniform.

There were discussions among the Sages — it seems that some of them were quite heated and lengthy — as to the inclusion of certain books in the canon of the *kitve kodesh*, the Hagiography or Holy Writings. The first controversy of this sort surrounded the Scroll of Esther. The sages were reluctant to include it in the canon of Scripture "lest it arouse the envy of the Gentiles." They finally yielded, however, to the persuasive arguments of Queen Esther herself, and found support for doing so in a verse in Exodus (17:14).[47] The inclusion of *Kohelet*, the Book of Ecclesiastes, was also questioned, until a reexamination of its major conclusion convinced the Sages that it should be sanctioned.[48] It was the opinion of Rabbi Akiva that "all the Writings are holy, but *Shir ha-Shirim*, the Song of Songs, is most holy," which led the Sages to decide in favor of its inclusion.[49] Books which were

---

43   *Ketubot* 106a. See also *Mo'ed Kattan* 3:4 and *Kelim* 15:6, reference to *Sefer ha-Azarah*, the Scroll of the Temple Court. Some read *Sefer Ezra*, the Scroll of Ezra. The ruling was that a scroll could not be written from memory, only from a standard copy (*Megillah* 18b; *Sh. A. Yoreh De'ah* 274:2). For further discussion, see Gerhardsson, B., *Memory and Manuscript, Oral Tradition etc.* Uppsala, 1961.

44   *Soferim* 6:4.

45   *E. Levita (1469–1549)* marshalled all the arguments indicating the post-Talmudic origin of vowelization in his *masoret ha-masoret*.

46   *Sanhedrin* 4a.

47   *Megillah* 7a. An expanded version is found in J.T. *Megillah* 1:7 (70d).

48   *Shabbat* 30b and *Yadayim* 3:5. See above, p. 33, n. 45, with referece to the Book of Ezekiel.

49   *Yadayim ibid.* For further discussion, see S.Z. Leiman, *The Canonization of Hebrew Scripture*, Hamden, Conn., 1976.

composed before the period of the Talmud but after the days of Ezra were not included in the canon, and therefore were designated as *Seforim Ḥitzonim*, Excluded Books; namely Apocrypha.[50]

The Masoretes

Shortly after the period of the Talmud critical editions of Scripture were produced by the so-called masoretes, from whom we derive the present-day Masoretic text. They decided which version of the several existing ones should become standard, especially where to retain a "full" spelling — that is, to include certain letters which serve as vowels — and where to retain a "deficient" spelling. This will account for the few differences in our present-day text from that in the Dead Sea Scrolls.[51] Maimonides, who flourished in the second half of the twelfth century, writes that he still found many mistakes in the scrolls of the Torah as far as the *parshiyot*, or paragraphs, are concerned, and therefore he included a proper listing in his *Mishneh Torah*. He then continues, "And the scroll upon which I relied in this matter is the one well-known in Egypt, and which was in Jerusalem for many years serving as the model for the copyists. Everyone relied on this copy because it was corrected by Ben Asher, who examined it for many years and reviewed it many times; and I relied upon it for the scroll of the Torah which I wrote in accord with the *halakhah*."[52]

None of the variations mentioned above is of a substantial nature to change the meaning of the text as far as Jewish Law based upon Scripture is concerned. Thus, we may truly assert today, as the Sages did in their day and Maimonides in his day, that "the Torah which is now in our hands is the same given to Moses our teacher."[53]

---

50   The Talmud occasionally quotes the Proverbs of Ben Sira (Ecclesiasticus) as if it were Holy Scripture, but this does not imply its erstwhile canonization. R. Akiba condemned those who read *Seforim Hitzonim* (*Sanhedrin* 10:1). He probably was referring to those Jews — like the early Christian sectarians — who read them publicly in the synagogue, thus regarding them as sacred Scripture.

51   See A. Dupont-Sommer, *The Dead Sea Scrolls*, N.Y., 1956, pp. 20 ff., and M. Burrows, *The Dead Sea Scrolls*, N.Y., 1955, pp. 301 ff.

52   *Hilkhot Yesodei ha-Torah* 8:4. Maimonides was here referring to the copy of Aharon ben Asher, known as *keter Aram Tzova*; see M. Breuer, *Keter etc.* Jer., 1976, p. 3. For many years this copy was in a synagogue in Aleppo, Syria, but since 1948 it is in the National Library in Jerusalem.

53   Maimonides, *Commentary to Mishnah, Sanhedrin* chap. 10 (p. 143 in Kapaḥ, ed.).

From the faith in the divine origin of the Torah, affirmed in his eighth principle, flows Maimonides' ninth principle, that the Torah is immutable. "This Torah of Moses will not be abrogated; nor will another Torah be given in its place. Nothing will be added to it or subtracted from it; neither in the text nor in commentary."[54] Maimonides codifies this principle in his *Mishneh Torah* in more forthright language: "It is clear and explicit in the Torah that it is an obligation that endures forever and ever. There is neither change, nor subtraction, nor addition, in it, as is said, *Everything which I command you that you shall observe to do; you shall not add to it, nor take away from it* (Deut. 13:1). And it is said, *That which is revealed, it is for us and for our children forever, to do all the words of this Torah* (ibid. 29:28).

There is no doubt that Maimonides found it necessary to emphasize this principle in order to deny the allegation of both Christianity and Islam that the New Testament or Koran have replaced the Torah of Moses as God's final word.[55] It must, however, be understood that the eternity of Biblical law does not mean that every law of the Torah is eternally in effect. Laws in general are dependent upon certain conditions of time and place, and fall into desuetude when those conditions are absent. Thus all the laws concerning sacrificial offerings are not in effect today in the absence of the *Bet ha-Mikdash*.[56] The laws of the Jubilee Year and those concerning a Hebrew servant (*eved ivri*) have not been in effect ever since the exiling of the Ten Tribes.[57] However, these laws have not been annulled, they are temporarily suspended. When the original conditions laid down for them are restored, the laws will once again come into effect. For this reason Maimonides included

---

54 How this principle can be reconciled with rabbinic exegesis and legislation will be clarified in the following chapters.

55 Cf. comment of Y. Kapaḥ in his ed. of *Commentary to the Mishnah* (Jer., 5725, p. 144, n. 77).

56 The Sages found a substitute for the offering of sacrifices in the *Bet ha-Mikdash* in the study of the laws concerning the sacrifices; see *Menaḥot* 110a. See also *Avot D'Rabbi Natan* 4:5. Once as Rabban Yoḥanan b. Zakkai was going out of Jerusalem, R. Yehoshua followed after him and beheld the Temple in ruins. "Woe unto us," cried R. Yehoshua "that the place where the iniquities of Israel were atoned for is laid waste!" "My son," Rabban Yoḥanan said to him, "be not grieved; we have another atonement as effective as this. It is acts of loving-kindness, as it is said, *For I desire mercy and not sacrifice* (Hosea 6:6)."

57 *Arakhin* 32b.

in his Code laws which are not currently observed, such as the laws concerning sacrificial offerings. It is the hope of traditional Jewry that they will once again be observed, with the coming of the Messiah and the rebuilding of the Holy Temple in Jerusalem.[58]

---

58 See, however, *Vayikra Rabbah* 27:12: "R. Pinḥas and R. Levi and R. Yoḥanan in the name of R. Menaḥem Diglaya: In the future, all sacrifices will cease, but the sacrifice of thanksgiving (*korban todah*) will never cease.

4

Halakhah — Law and Life Together

הליכות עולם לו: אל תקרי הליכות אלא הלכות
The eternal ways are His (Habakuk 3:6)
"Do not read "ways;" read "laws""*

The Oral Law

The Talmud relates:[1] It once happened that a certain gentile
approached Shammai and asked him, "How many Torahs do you
(Jews) have?" Shammai replied, "Two; a written Torah and an oral
Torah, the gentile retorted, "I believe that you have a written
Torah, but I do not believe that you have an oral Torah. However,
convert me on condition that you teach me the written Torah."
Whereupon Shammai rebuked him and showed him out with a
reprimand. The gentile then approached Hillel (with the same
request) and Hillel accepted him for conversion. The first day Hillel
taught him *aleph, bet, gimmel, daled*, but on the morrow he taught
him the reverse. Whereupon the gentile said, "Didn't you teach me
the opposite yesterday?" Hillel replied, "You have to rely upon me
(to teach you the written Torah); then rely upon me for the oral
Torah."

That the Written Law has to be accompanied by an Oral Law is a
logical necessity. No written text is simply handed over to a pupil
without the teacher adding some clarification; nor can a code of law
encompass in detail all the possible circumstances to which a
particular law may apply. For a society to be based upon law and

---

*   *Megillah* 28b
1   *Shabbat* 31a.

50

order it cannot be governed by kings alone; it must have philosophers as well. An philosophers, as the ancient Greeks understood, are both teachers and judges; teachers so that the citizenry should not be ignorant of the law, and judges to interpret the law. In the Torah, such men of wisdom and learning are called *zekenim*, "elders;" in the Talmud they are called *hakhamim*, "sages." Thus the Talmud explains the designation *zaken* as "the person who has acquired wisdom."[2] More often, the scholars are called *talmidei hakhamim*, "disciples of the wise;" for only that one can achieve the status of a *hakham* if he is first a disciple of the wise and makes the study of the Torah his major interest in life.[3] Invariably, we shall refer to the rabbis of the Talmud as "the Sages."

Moses our Teacher

We have said in a previous chapter that Moses was the prophet *par excellence*; or as Maimonides refers to him, "the father of all the prophets." But Moses was distinguished not only as the *navi*, the prophet who conveyed the divine code of law; in Jewish tradition he is more familiarly known as *Moshe Rabbenu*, "Moses our teacher." For Moses was also the teacher *par excellence*, the prototype of the *zaken* or *hakham* mentioned above.[4] He was the forerunner of the scholar and sage who studies and analyzes the Torah in order to fully comprehend its meaning and determine when and where it applies.

This is how the Talmud describes Moses' role as a teacher:[5] Our Sages taught, How was the order of *Mishnah*? (*Rashi*: How did the Israelites learn the Oral Law?). Moses learned Torah from the mouth of the Almighty. Then Aaron entered (*Rashi*: and sat before Moses), and Moses taught him a chapter. Aaron then moved and sat at the left of Moses; Aaron's sons entered and Moses taught them a chapter. The sons then moved, Elazar sitting to the right of Moses and Ittamar to the left of Aaron. Then the elders entered and

2   *Kiddushin* 32b.
3   Similarly, the wise men in ancient Greece were not called *sophos* "wise men," but *philosophos*, "lovers of wisdom;" cf. *Tosafot Shabbat* 116a, *s.v. philosopha*.
4   Cf. *Sanhedrin* 13b; also H.A. Wolfson, *Philo* (Cambridge, Mass. 1947), Vol. II, p. 18.
5   *Eruvin* 54b.

Moses taught them the chapter. Consequently, Aaron heard the lesson four times, his sons three times, the elders twice and the rest of the people once. After Moses left, Aaron reviewed the lesson with all being present. After Aaron left, his sons reviewed the lesson. After the sons left, the elders reviewed the lesson. Consequently, everyone heard the lesson four times.

In teaching the Torah, Moses not only repeated to his pupils the exact words which God commanded him to "speak to the children of Israel." He also added to the words of the Law explanatory remarks, clarifying passages which required clarification and explaining in detail how the laws were actually to be carried out. Many of these explanations of the text were part of divine revelation, as Maimonides avers in his eighth principle of faith:[6] "Moreover, the accepted interpretation of Scripture is also from the mouth of the Almighty, so that the manner in which we perform today the mitzvot of Sukkah and Lulav and Shofar and Tzitzit and Tefillin etc. is the same manner in which God communicated it to Moses, who in turn communicated it to us."

There were even circumstances for which the law had not been revealed to Moses orginally, and he was compelled to say to those who questioned him in a matter of law, *Stand by and let me hear what instruction the Lord commands concerning you* (Num. 9:8). Thus, the law of *Pesah Sheni* (*ibid.* 9–14) and the laws of inheritance (*ibid.* 27: 1–11) became part of the Written Law only because of petitioners who were demanding their just rights.[7]

Moses was the one who had to decide the most difficult cases (Exod. 18:26). Undoubtedly, in many such cases it was not necessary for him to turn to God for further instruction; he was able to render a decision on the basis of a logical inference from the text itself, or even on the basis of what the Talmud calls *s'vara*, a reasonable assumption.[8] Such decisions, or other instructions given by Moses which were not explicit in the text, were transmitted orally

6   Quoted above, p. 35. Undoubtedly this is too comprehensive a generalization; otherwise the innumerable discussions in the Talmud regarding the detailed observance of these mitzvot would largely be superfluous. Even those details which the Talmud declares to be *halakhah l'moshe mi-Sinai* (e.g. *Menahot* 35a) are not literally so; see below, p. 58.

7   Other instances where Moses had to turn to the Almighty for further instruction are those of "the blasphemer" (Lev. 24; 10–16) and "the gatherer of wood" (Num. 15:32–36); cf. *Sanhedrin* 78b.

8   See E. Berkowitz, *Hahalakhah kohah vetafkidah* (Jer. 1981, chap. 1).

from master to pupil over the generations, constituting an essential and indisputable part of the Oral Law.

Indeed, there are certain areas where the Torah itself did not prescribe any specific legislation, but left the matter for the *hakhamim* to lay down the rules in the Oral Law. Thus, concerning work on the intermediate days of the Festivals (*Ḥol ha-Mo'ed*) we are told[9] "Scripture gave it over to the *hakhamim* to tell us on which day work is forbidden and on which day it is permitted; which type of work is forbidden and which type is permitted." Even for the types of work prohibited on the Sabbath the Mishnah asserts, "Scripture is scanty but the Rabbinic rulings (*halakhot*) are many."[10]

If not for the Oral Law, which defines that which is vague and specifies that which is written down only in general terms, Jewish life could not have been organized into a community of distinctive practice and creed.

The Midrash offers the following explanation why the Oral Law was not written down: When God told Moses *Write down these words* (Exod. 34:27) Moses requested that the Mishnah be written down. However, God foresaw that the Gentiles will translate the Torah and read it in the Greek, and they will then claim that they are the Israelites (to whom God gave the Torah). But God will say to the Gentiles, "You say that you are My children; only they who possess My secret lore (*mistorin*), which is the Mishnah, are My children."[11] Indeed, it is only the children of Israel, possessing the Oral Law, who have been able to maintain the Written Law, the Torah of Moses, as the enduring basis of the "law of life." The nations who do not possess the Oral Law have found it necessary to substitute man-given testaments for the divine Testament of Sinai.

The Torah is not in Heaven

With the passing away of Moses, divine revelation of Torah law ceased. The Torah, once having been revealed by God to Moses,

---

9   *Ḥagigah* 18a. See Rashi *ad loc.* that it is through the procedure of *Kiddush ha-Hodesh* by which the Rabbinic court determines which day is the first of the month that the Rabbis determine which days are to be celebrated as Festival days.

10   *Ḥagigah* 10a.

11   *Pesikta Rabbati*, beginning of chap. 5. Cf. *Tanḥuma Ki Tisa* 17.

was given over fully to man to understand and interpret from the written text. Questions could no longer be asked directly of the Almighty. Thus the Talmud relates that three thousand laws were forgotten during the days of mourning over the death of Moses. The people then asked Joshua to turn to Heaven for instruction but he refused, citing the passage *It* (the Torah) *is not in heaven* (Deut. 30:12).[12] The same verse was cited a millenia and a half later by another Joshua, the *Tanna* Rabbi Yehoshua, in a dispute between Rabbi Eliezer ben Hyrcanus and Rabban Gamaliel concerning the uncleanness of an oven constructed of sections and held together by sand. Rabbi Eliezer called upon supernatural manifestations, such as a carob tree transplanting itself and a river flowing upstream and the walls of the house of study bending down, but Rabbi Yehoshua rebuked all of them for interfering in a Rabbinic dispute. Finally, Rabbi Eliezer called upon Heaven for witness that the law is according to his opinion, and a voice from Heaven proclaimed, "Why do you rabbis dispute Rabbi Eliezer; in every matter the law is according to his opinion." Whereupon Rabbi Yehoshua stood up and said, *It is not in heaven*. The Talmud then concludes, "For the Torah has already been given over from Sinai, and in the Torah it is written, *Bend the law after the majority* (Exod. 23:2)."[13]

"The Torah was given over to the man;" that is, to men qualified by virtue of their position and learning. These men, the *ḥakhamim* mentioned above, are also known as *rabbanan*, "our Rabbis." Their expositions of Scripture and their discussions in matters of Jewish Law comprise the *Torah-she-b'al-Peh*, the Oral Law. The decisions based upon these discussions are known as *Halakhah*, the norm and practice in traditional Jewish life.

The term *Halakhah* is derived from the Hebrew root *halokh*, "to walk;" for Halakhah is the law which points out the *way* of life for the Jewish people, as it is written, *Enjoin upon them the laws and the teachings* (the *torot*); *and make known to them the way they are to go and the practices they are to follow* (Exod. 18:20). In a more restricted sense, as first employed by the *Tannaim*, *Halakhah* (plural, *halakhot*) referred to an oral ruling handed down by the authorities

12 *Temurah* 17a.
13 *Baba Metzia* 59b. The simple meaning of the verse from Exodus is that one should not follow a multitude if they pervert justice; but the Sages have employed this phrase as confirmation of the principle that majority rules; see *Rashi ad loc.*.

as distinguished from a specific teaching of Scripture, known as *mikra*.[14] To distinguish rulings transmitted without direct reference to Scripture from those attached to the verse from which the ruling is derived, the former are called *halakhot* and the latter *midrash* or *midrash halakhah*.[15] Later, *Halakhah* came to mean the accepted or authorized opinion when a ruling was in dispute. In the course of time, certain principles were established in order to determine which opinion to follow in a matter under dispute.[16] The term is also used generically to denote the legal parts of Jewish tradition in contradistinction to *aggadah*, the homilies of the Sages.[17]

The Sages were anxious that the distinction between the *Torah she-bikhtav* (the Written Law) and the *Torah she-b'al-Peh* (the Oral Law) be scrupulously maintained; and therefore they ruled, "Teachings which were given orally may not be transmitted in writing, and teachings given in writing (i.e. Scripture) may not be transmitted orally."[18] In fact, Rabbi Yoḥanan, an *Amora* of the third century, went so far as to say, "They who write down *halakhot* are committing the Torah to burning."[19] The reason for such a stringent ruling appears to me to be twofold: First of all, it is essential that no commentary to Scripture, exegetical or otherwise, ever be added to and included in the sacred text;[20] the original text is divine, any commentary is human. Secondly, it is essential to preserve both the fixity of the original text and the fluidity of all commentary.

The text of the Torah itself is not subject to any emendation, addition or subtraction; but its interpretation and the application of its teachings may vary according to the authority of the day and the particular needs arising from the circumstances of the day. This can best be illustrated by the case of Rabbi Yoḥanan mentioned

14 *Ḥagigah* 1:8 and 10a.
15 *Kiddushin* 49a.
16 *Eruvin* 46b.
17 See above, Introduction, p. 5. For a detailed discussion of all aspects of Halakhah, see *Encyclopedia Talmudit*, Vol. IX, under rubric *halakhah*.
18 *Temurah* 14b.
19 *Ibid*. This ban applied only to the writing of texts for public reading or teaching. Teachers themselves did have private notes for personal reference called *megilat setorim* or "hidden scrolls;" see *Shabbat* 6b; Rashi *ad loc*. and Rambam, *Introduction to Mishneh Torah*.
20 As happened to some passages in the Talmud.

above. Despite his condemnation of the writing down of *halakhot*, he himself, together with his colleague Resh Lakish, would consult a book of Aggadah; justifying their practice on the grounds of the overriding necessity of preserving the midrashic teachings. "It is better," they said, "that (one rule of) the Torah be cancelled, so that the Torah itself (i.e. in its broader sense of the corpus of traditional teaching) not be forgotten.[21] As we shall see later, this same consideration led to the compilation of the *Mishnah*. and ultimately to the committing to writing of practically every halakhic and aggadic thought.

The Judge in Charge at the Time

By the very nature of divine revelation Torah in its broader sense possesses a twofold character, the fixity of the Written Law and the flexibility of the Unwritten Law; for Revelation is the dialogue between God and man, God Who is Eternal and man who is subject to the accidents of time. Thus from the very beginning there is imbedded in the words of the Law an "eternal contemporaneity," a contemporaneity of relevance to life in every vicissitude and circumstance. Thus we can understand the Rabbinic comment to the verse *Then you shall go to...the judge who will be in charge at the time* (Deut. 17:9). "Would it enter your mind that you should go to the judge who is not in charge at the time. Scripture is teaching us here that one should go to (i.e. accept the jurisdiction of) the judge of his day."[22] Only the judge of the day appreciates and understands the requirements of his day.

While the judge of the day did not operate in a social vacuum, he also did not operate in a legal or halakhic vacuum. His judgment could not be the result of hasty or capricious decision; nor could his interpretation of the Mosaic code be shifting and arbitrary. The Oral Law did not resemble the quicksilver that changes shape at the slightest pressure. First of all, it was based upon and circumscribed by the text given at Sinai, which served as the seed which bore the

21   *Temurah ibid.* Cf. *Gittin* 60a.
22   *Rosh Hashanah* 25b.

fruit of most Rabbinic interpretation. Even where the ruling was not derived directly by an inference from the Biblical text, the Sages would seek confirmation in the text by a method called *asmakhta*,[23] thus investing the Oral Law with the binding authority of divine revelation. To confirm this authority the Sages asserted, "Even that which an advanced disciple would instruct in the presence of his master was already revealed to Moses at Sinai."[24]

That such a categorical statement is not to be taken literally can be seen from a piquant story told in the Talmud:[25] When Moses ascended heavenward (to receive the Torah) he found the Holy One, blessed be He, sitting and binding coronets (in the shape of small strokes) to the letters of the Torah. Whereupon Moses asked, "Master of the Universe, who is restraining You?" (that You have to add coronets). God replied, "There is a certain person who will be born many generations hence — his name is Akiva ben Yosef — who will expound heaps and heaps of *halakhot* from each and every stroke." Moses then requested that God show him this scholar. "Turn backwards," said God, and Moses found himself sitting in the eighth row of Rabbi Akiva's academy. Moses was unable to follow the discussion and he became downhearted. At one point, Akiva's disciples asked "Master, whence did you derive this teaching?" Rabbi Akiva answered, "This is a ruling handed down by Moses from Sinai." Hearing this, Moses became comforted. (No doubt because he was recognized as the first link in a chain of tradition to which new links would be added in every generation). Every judge in charge was bound to respect these precedents

---

23 No doubt, many halakhic rulings were handed down orally without any specific reference to a Biblical verse. Other rulings were taught from decisions rendered by Sages in a particular case and not based on inference from Scripture or from questions raised in the academies, and only later did the Sages find confirmation of the law in an expounding of the text. Thus, *halakhah* preceded *midrash*; cf. statement in J.T. *Berakhot* 2:3 (4c), "Whenever a proposition is not clear, the Rabbis support it by reference to many Biblical passages;" and J.T. *Pe-ah* 2:6(17a), "Rulings derived from expounding Scripture are more numerous than those derived from oral interpretation." See also Y.N. Epstein, *Mavo'ot le-Sifrut ha-Tannaim*, Jer. 5717, p. 511. For further details of *asmakhta*, see *Encyclopedia Talmudit*, Vol. II, pp. 105 ff.

24 J.T. *Pe'ah ibid.*

25 *Menahot* 29b.

handed down in the name of Moses; they were designated *halakhah l'Moshe mi'Sinai*.[26]

The Vesting of Judicial Authority: Semikhah

Moses was also the orginal source of the authority vested in "the judge of the day." When he gathered, at the behest of the Almighty, seventy elders to share with him the overtaxing task of leading the children of Israel (Num. 11:16), he laid the foundation for the vesting of authority to administer justice and decide questions of Jewish Law. This official granting of authority, endowing the recipient with the power to apply the laws of the Torah to any case at hand, is called *Semikhah*, literally the laying on hands, an act first recorded when God commanded Moses, *Take Joshua son of Nun, a man of spirit, and lay your hand upon him* (*ibid.* 27:18). Semikhah not only conferred the authority to judge; it also conveyed the power to transfer this authority to another, thus enabling the creation of an unbroken chain of traditional authority passed on from master to disciple and from generation to generation.[27] In the course of time, Semikhah was not effected by the laying on of hands, but by conferring the title "Rabbi."[28]

26 Many post-Talmudic authorities discussed this halakhic category, especially Maimonides in his *Commentary to the Mishnah (Introduction)*. For modern discussions of this term, see *inter alia,* M. Kasher, *Harambam Vehamekhilta* etc., New York 5703; H. Revel, *Hamasoret B'Sifrei HaRambam*, New York 5702; *Encyclopedia Talmudit*, Vol. IX, pp. 365 ff.

27 Cf. *Avot* 1:1: "Moses received the Torah from Sinai and committed it to Joshua, and Joshua to the elders, and the elders to the Prophets (in *Avot D'R. Natan*, "the elders to the Judges and the Judges to the Prophets"), and the Prophets committed it to the Men of the Great Assembly." Cf. Rambam, *Hilkhot Sanhedrin* 4:1.

28 *Sanhedrin* 13b. Certain scholars, though their scholarship and teachings were recognized, were not given Semikhah for one reason or another, and thus are quoted without the title "rabbi;" see *Kiddushin* 49b re Ben Zoma and Ben Azzai, and *Bava Metzia* 85b–86a re the Amora Shmuel. It is interesting to note that the early Sages, e.g. Hillel and Shammai, are cited by their names alone without any title. Beginning with Gamaliel the Elder (1st Century C.E.) the title *Rabban* was given to the Nasi of the Sanhedrin (see *Arukh ha-Shalem* under *Rabban* for reason); the title *Rabbi* to the Sages in Eretz Yisrael, and the title *Rav* to the Babylonian Sages. This led to a popular saying, "*Rabbi* is greater than *Rav; Rabban* is greater than *Rabbi;* his name alone is greater than *Rabban*."

The Sages found it necessary to limit the conferring of Semikhah by individual Rabbis; one had to first obtain the consent of the *Nasi*, the chief authority in Jewish life in Talmudic times.[29] Candidates for Semikhah had to possess certain qualities, besides knowledge of the Law, as specified by Jethro when he advised Moses to appoint judges and said to him, *Seek out from among all the people capable men who fear God, trustworthy men who spurn ill-gotten gain* (Exod. 18:21).[30] Semikhah was deemed so essential for the continued vitality of Jewish life that one Sage sacrificed his life in order to perpetuate this chain of Jewish jurisprudence. The Talmud relates: "Once the wicked kingdom (Roman Empire, in the days of Hadrian) decreed that both the giver and the receiver of Semikhah will be killed and the city in which it is given will be destroyed....Wherupon R. Yehudah b. Bava went to a place situated between two big mountains, between two cities, between Usha and Shefar'am, and conferred Semikhah upon five Sages: R. Meir, R. Yehudah, R. Shimon, R. Yose, and R. Eleazar b. Shamua...He said to them, "My children, flee." "And what will happen to you?" they asked. "I will remain before them as a stone that cannot be upturned." It was told that they (the Romans) did not leave the place until they pierced the body with 300 iron spears until it became like a sieve."[31]

The Supreme Authority: the Sanhedrin

With the exception of Moses, no individual, regardless of his erudition, could make decisions binding upon all Israel. For such comprehensive authority a duly constituted body, comprised of individuals duly authorized by virtue of the Semikhah conferred upon them, was necessary. Such a body was first constituted when Moses

---

(*Teshuvat Rav Sherira Gaon*, addendum to *Iggeret Rabbenu Sherira Gaon*, A. Heiman ed. (Jer. 5727), pp. 106 ff.; also cited in *Arukh s.v. Abbayye*).

29   J.T.*Sanhedrin* 1:2 (19a).

30   Cf. Deut. 1:13, *Pick from each of your tribes men who are wise, discerning, and experienced.* See also Rambam, *Hilkhot Sanhedrin* 2:7, "Each judge must possess seven qualities; wisdom, humility, awe, spurning wealth, love of truth, beloved by the people, and a good reputation; all these are specified in the Torah."

31   *Sanhedrin* 14a.

gathered the seventy elders mentioned above.[32] In the days of Ezra, when autonomous Jewish life had to be reestablished in Eretz Yisrael after the return from Babylonian exile, the supreme governing body is said to have been comprised of one hundred and twenty members who are referred to as *Anshei Knesset ha' Gedolah*, "Men of the Great Assembly."[33] Subsequently, as the body was reconstituted in the days of the Hasmoneans, it consisted of seventy-one members and was known as "the Great Sanhedrin," a term of Greek origin meaning "Council". It is also referred to in Rabbinic literature as *Bet ha-Din ha-Gadol*, the Great Court of Law.[34]

Fixing the Calendar

One of the chief prerogatives of the Great Court, crucial for all Israel, was the fixing of the Jewish calendar, which determined the days on which the Festivals were to be celebrated. Maimonides states unequivocally that proclaiming the beginning of a new month (*Rosh Ḥodesh*) and deciding whether or not a thirteenth month should be added to the year in order to reconcile the lunar and solar years (*Ibbur ha-Shanah* intercalation) "can be performed only by the *Bet Din ha-Gadol*, and that is why today we do not proclaim the new month by sighting the new moon[35] since we do not have a Great Court, just as we no longer offer sacrifices in the absence of the Holy Temple....And here we have a great principle of

---

32 Mishnah *Sanhedrin* 1:1.
33 Based on this tradition, the parliament of the modern State of Israel is designated "the Knesset," and consists of 120 members. Some sources speak of 85 elders; see *Religious Foundations etc.*, *op. cit.* pp. 226–227, notes 11 and 15. For their activities, see *ibid.* pp. 57 ff.
34 For a description and history of this body, see S.B. Hoenig, *The Great Sanhedrin* (Phila. 1953 and H. Mantel, *Studies in the History of the Sanhedrin* (Harvard Univ. Press, 1961). For the exact number of the Sanhedrin's members, see Hoenig, *op.cit.* pp. 62 ff.
35 A procedure still followed by the Karaites and the Moslems. Many commentators, especially Saadia Gaon (see *Otzar ha-Geonim l'Sanhedrin*, Mossad Harav Kook, Jer. 5727, p. 95), maintain that this procedure was more or less *pro forma*; the day of Rosh Hodesh was determined beforehand by astronomical calculation. Cf. Rambam, *Hilkhot Kiddush ha-Hodesh* 1:6, "If members of the

our faith that when we say today, 'Today is Rosh Ḥodesh and today is Yom Tov' it is not because of our calculation, but because the Great Court that was in Eretz Yisrael already fixed that today is Yom Tov or Rosh Ḥodesh."[36] The authority of the Court in this regard was so exclusive that even if it had erred in its calculation and declared the "wrong" day to be Rosh Ḥodesh, their declaration became law. Thus when R. Yehoshua contended that the testimony accepted by the Nasi of the Sanhedrin Rabban Gamaliel was false, he nevertheless traveled on the day which according to his calculation was Yom Kippur.[37] Hence the Court could deliberately postpone the proclamation of the New Moon of Tishri so that Yom Kippur should not fall on a Friday or a Sunday.[38]

The Sanhedrin and the Torah she-b'al-Peh

The Sanhedrin was much more than a Court of Law. Its chief function, in fact, was to expound and interpret the Torah's legislation for all Israel. Thus Maimonides states, "The Great Sanhedrin of Jerusalem is the root of Torah she-be'al-Peh. Its members are the pillars of instruction; out of them go forth statutes and judgments for all Israel."[39] Once it proclaimed a decision it dared not be questioned; any scholar who defied its ruling and acted, or caused another to act, contrary to its decision was liable to punishment by death, as is written *The man who would act deliberately and not*

court found by calculation that the new moon could not possibly be seen... if witnesses nevertheless did appear and testify that they saw the new crescent it was certain that they were false witnesses." The laws and procedures of *Kiddush ha-Hodesh* are dealt with in Tractate *Rosh Hashanah*; of *Ibbur ha-Shanah* in *Sanhedrin*, chap. 1.

36   *Sefer ha-Mitzvot*, Positive Mitzvah 153. Cf. *Hilkhot Kiddush ha-Hodesh*1:5. Maimonides stressed this point because many disagreed and maintained that *Kiddush ha-Hodesh* could be performed by an ordinary Bet Din; see strictures of Ramban to *Sefer ha-Mitzvot*. Re the fixing of the calendar, see M. Kasher, *Torah Shelemah*, Vol. 13.

37   Mishnah *Rosh ha-Shanah* 2:8–9; *Sifra* to Lev. 23:2. For different versions, see H. Heller ed. of *Sefer ha-Mitzvot* (Mossad Harav Kook, Jer. 5706), p. 73, n. 15.

38   *Rosh Hashanah* 20a.

39   *Hilkhot Mamrim* 1:1.

hearken....to the judge, that man shall die (Deut. 7:12).[40] A token of its supreme authority was its seat of judgment; as long as the *Bet ha-Mikdash* stood, it convened in the Chamber of Hewn Stones, part of which was in the hallowed precincts of the Holy Temple.[41]

The Sanhedrin's powers of interpretation of Jewish Law were practically unlimited. At times, it would base its ruling upon a deviation from the simple meaning of the Scriptural text.[42] Nor did they hesitate to abrogate a law of the Torah or administer a punishment not prescribed by the Torah, if they deemed it necessary for the general upholding of the Law.[43] They ruled that one should forego the fulfilment of a Biblical command if in doing so he would violate a law of the Sages, who in the period after the destruction of the Temple assumed the prerogatives of the Great Sanhedrin.[44]

The Sages assumed these powers because of their conviction that their interpretation of the Scripture was part of the Divine revelation. It was this conviction which prompted them to postulate absolute and total acceptance of their teachings. Thus they applied the verse *Because he has despised the word of the Lord* (Num. 15:31) to the person who says, "The entire Torah is from Heaven except this inference or this *kal vahomer* or this *Gezerah shavah.*"[45] Even when opinions were divided, where one Sage would declare something prohibited and another equally emphatically assert that it is permitted, the consensus was, "Both opinions are words of the

---

40   Tractate *Horayot* deals with this law. The offending scholar is called *zaken mamre*, "a rebellious elder." The Sages went so far as to expound the verse *You must not deviate from the verdict they announce to you to the right or to the left* (Deut. 17:11) to imply "Even if they tell you that the right is left or the left is right" (*Sifre ad loc.*). However, J.T. *Horayot* (1:1, 45d) disagrees and asserts that if they tell you that right is left you are not obliged to obey. See Ramban and *Torah Temimah ad loc.*

41   Mishnah *Middot* 5:4, *Yona* 25a. Cf. *Rosh Hashanah* 31a–b, the seats of the Sanhedrin after the destruction of the Temple.

42   *Yevamot* 24a; *Sotah* 16a; J.T. *Kiddushin* 1:2 (59d).

43   *Yevamot* 89b, 90b.

44   Mishnah *Betzah* 5:2. Cf. J.T. *Sanhedrin* 11:3(30a) and *Sifre ad loc.*, "*You shall come* etc. (Deut. 17:9), this includes the Bet Din in Yavneh."

45   *Sanhedrin* 99a. For explanation of *kal va-homer* and *gezerah shavah*, see below, p. 66.

living God."[46] However, after a decision was taken and a certain opinion was declared to be the Halakhah, every member of the Sanhedrin was bound to accept it. This does not mean that a decision taken at one time became the decision for all times. A Sanhedrin was "the judge in charge *at the time*," implying that it was competent to reverse the decision of an earlier Sanhedrin, within certain limitations. Maimonides puts it this way, "A Great Court that interpreted Scripture by means of the rules of interpretation[47] according to their sights and rendered judgment, and another Court arose after them and saw reason to disagree with that judgment, it may do so and judge according to its own sights, as is said, *to the judge in charge at the time*, we are bound to follow the decisions of the Court of our own generation."[48] In certain areas of Jewish Law which we shall discuss later, this was true only if the latter Court was greater than the earlier one in both wisdom and numbers.[49]

Expounding and interpreting the Torah could come about only through intensive study and a teaching process. Indeed, the sessions of the Sanhedrin were conducted as if it were a college, where members of the faculty would gather to discuss the Biblical text among themselves and with the students. "Three rows of disciples would sit before the members of the Sanhedrin; each disciple recognizing his particular seat."[50] The opinions of the disciples were regarded very seriously, as reflected in this statement, "Every interpretation that an advanced disciple would propose in the presence of his master was already revealed to Moses at Sinai."[51] One Sage even remarked, "I have learned much from my teachers; more from

---

46   *Eruvin* 13b. See Rashi's explanation, *Ketubot* 51a *s.v., ha*, "...Sometimes this opinion pertains and sometimes the other opinion pertains, for the opinion is reversed when there is even a slight change in the circumstances."
47   See below, p. 64 for these rules.
48   *Hilkhot Mamrim* 2:1. Cf. Mishnah *Rosh Hashanah* 2:9 and Talmud *ad loc.*
49   Mishnah *Eduyot* 1:5 and *Avodah Zarah* 36a.
50   Mishnah *Sanhedrin* 4:4.
51   J.T. *Pe'ah* 2:6 (17a).

my colleagues; and most from my disciples."[52] Thus the Sanhedrin in effect was an Academy, a *Bet ha-Midrash*, a "House of Study for the Exposition of Torah," for this is the meaning of *Midrash*.[53]

Midrash: Rules of Interpretation

In Chapter Three[54] we spoke of Ezra and his colleagues, the *Soferim* or Scribes, as guardians of the text of the Torah. However, their seminal contribution to Torah also lay in their *teaching* of the Torah, which — as we have just indicated — implies the *midrash* or expounding of Torah, as is written, *...and the Levites explained the Torah to the people...and they read in the Book, in the Torah of God, distinctly, given the sense, so they understood the reading* (Neh. 8:7–8). Thus, halakhic rulings derived from an exposition of the text are called *divrei Soferim* in the generations after Ezra. The Sages attributed to these teaching the force of Mosaic Law, even according them greater importance. "More precious than *divrei Torah* are *divrei Soferim*; the penalty for disregarding them is greater than that for disregarding *divrei Torah*."[55]

Most of this Midrash was not taught in order to create new Halakhah, but rather to substantiate Halakhah which was part of the oral tradition of Torah she-b'al-Peh. Thus, for example, when Hillel wanted to prove that the Passover sacrifice is offered even when the fourteenth of Nissan falls on Shabbat, he argued from certain methods of Midrash. These arguments, however, were not

52   *Taanit* 7a.
53   Cf. Ezra 7:10 *For Ezra set his heart to expound* (lidrosh) *the Torah of the Lord, and to do it, and to teach in Israel statute and judgment.* Cf. the expression, "This verse says "expound me" (*darshuni*)" in *Tanḥuma Vayeshev* 13, quoted several times by Rashi.
54   Above, p. 45.
55   J.T. *Sanhedrin* 11:4 (30a); *Avodah Zarah* 35a. Also, Mishnah *Sanhedrin* 10:4. The term *divrei Soferim* is used ambiguously, sometimes denoting a law of Biblical force (*d'Oraita*) and sometimes a law of Rabbinic force (*d'Rabbanan*). See, e.g. *Rosh Hashanah* 34a, where *divrei Soferim* denotes a Biblical law derived from a method of interpretation; whereas in *Rosh Hashana* 19a, where the Talmud distinguishes between *Divrei Torah* and *divrei Soferim*, the latter undoubtedly referring to a law of Rabbinic force. See also *Kelim* 13:7 and *Tevul Yom* 4:6, where R. Yehoshua characterizes certain rulings as "innovations" of the Soferim. Maimonides occasionally employs the term divrei Soferim for a law

accepted by the Bnei Bethira, who were the heads of the Sanhedrin at the time. Finally, Hillel said, "So I have heard from Shmaya and Avtalyon (the previous heads of the Sanhedrin) that the Passover offering sets aside the (restrictions of the) Sabbath." Whereupon the ruling was immediately accepted.[56]

Another example of this method of exposition, taught in order to substantiate an oral tradition, is found in connection with the ruling that a *hakham*, a recognized scholar, may absolve a person from his vow on the grounds of his being unaware at the time of making the vow of some of its undesirable consequences. The Mishnah states that this absolving of vows "hovers in the air and has nothing (in Scripture) to support it." Whereupon several Sages aver that there is Scriptural basis for it, and proceed to expound verses to substantiate it.[57]

Hillel, we are told, expounded (*darash*) seven methods of interpretation before the Bnei Bethira.[58] As time went on, other methods of interpretation were introduced in order to derive from them the increasing number of *halakhot* that were being taught. Two early Tannaim, Nehunia b. Hakaneh and Nahum Ish Gimzu,[59] introduced respectively the methods of *k'lal u'prat* (a general statement followed by one or more particulars, implying additional unstated particulars) and *ribah u'mi'et* (the general statement including all similar particulars and the particular excluding only the least similar).[60] Two outstanding disciples of these teachers developed these

of Biblical force, e.g. *Hilkhot Ishut* 1:2. In his Introduction to Sefer ha-Mitzvot, Second Principle, he states that laws derived from methods of interpretation are either D'Oraita or D'Rabbanan, depending upon their categorization by the Talmud. See Y.Y. Neubauer, *Ha-Rambam al Divrei Soferim*, Mossad Harav Kook, Jer. 5717.

56   J.T. *Pesahim* 6:1(33a); a slightly different version is given in the Bavli, 66a.
57   Mishnah *Hagigah* 1:8; Talmud *ad loc*. Cf, Ramban, *Hilkhot Shevuot* 6:2, "This (absolving of an oath) has no source whatsoever in the Written Torah. However, it was learned from Moshe Rabbenu through an oral tradition that that which Scripture says, *He must not break his pledge* (Num. 30:3) means that he himself should not slightly and contemptuously break his pledge... but if he regrets and recants, a hakham releases him."
58   *Tosefta Sanhedrin*, end of Chap. 7.
59   The Talmud (*Taanit* 21a) would have it that he was called Ish Gam Zo because no matter what tragedy befell him he would say, *Gam Zo l'Tovah*, "This is also for the good."
60   *Tosefta Shevuot* 1:7; *Shevuot* 26a.

methods even further, R. Akiva following the method of R. Neḥu-nia and R. Yishmael following that of R. Naḥum.

R. Yishmael formulated thirteen methods (*middot*, hermeneutic principles).[61] The two best known are *kal va-ḥomer, the inference from minor to major, and gezerah shavah*, the inference from a similarity of expression. There is, however, a significant difference between them; a scholar may infer a ruling by means of a *kal va-ḥomer* on his own, since it is a purely logical principle, but he may not expound a *gezerah shavah* on his own; all he may do is transmit such an exposition already taught by his master. Apparently, some curb had to be placed upon the use of these methods of Biblical exegesis.[62]

Disputation and Decision

No body of intelligent and learned men, though all honoring the same tradition and motivated by the same ideals, think exactly alike. "Just as persons' features are unlike, so is their thinking unlike."[63] The same law, the identical verse, may convey a different nuance of meaning or imply a different scope of application to different minds. Where the Oral Tradition was clear and precise there was no room for disagreement among the masters,[64] but where no precedent opinion could be cited differing points of view would naturally ensue. Indeed, the expression of differing points of view was encouraged, for only through discussion and disputation could the Halakhah be established.[65] R. Yannai said, "If the Torah

61 Introduction to *Sifra*; added to daily prayer service. For explanation and examples, see *Siddur* of P. Birnbaum. (I do not understand why *middot* is translated in the Rabbinical Council Siddur as "principles of logic." Not all the principles are logical).

62 *Niddah* 19b. See *Arukh, s.v. Gezer* 3; Rashi, *Pesaḥim* 66a, *s.v. vekhi; Tosafot Shabbat* 97a, *s.v. Gezerah.*

63 J.T. *Berakhot* 9:2(13c); cf. *Berakhot* 58a.

64 Cf. Mishnah *Yevamot* 8:3, "If this is Halakhah (i.e. a traditional ruling), we will accept it." See also *Eduyot* 1:3 and *Pesaḥim* 66a for instances of such acceptance. Cf. *Tosefta Sanhedrin* 7:1 (*Bavli* 88b), "When the disciples of Hillel and Shammai did not attend sufficiently to their masters disputes increased in Israel."

65 Cf. statement of Rabbi A.I. Kook (*Olat Re'iyah*, Jer. 5699, p. 330), "Some people erroneously assume that world peace will come about only through sameness of opinion and characters, and therefore when they see that intensive Torah-study leads to a multitude of positions and opinions they think that it is the opposite of peace. The truth, however, is otherwise; true peace can come only when all positions and opinions are brought to light."

had been given clear-cut, no opinions would be countenanced in the halls of learning."[66] The process of argumentation to determine the Halakhah was considered a process of judging; in Talmudic parlance the verb describing it is *don*, to judge.[67] The same verb also describes the process of inferring a law from the midrashic method of Scriptural interpretation, the *middot*.[68] Just as in a case before a court of law we are told that the judges would "thrust and parry" (*nos'im ve-notnim*, literally, "take and give") before arriving at a decision,[69] so do they thrust and parry in the Halakhah in order to arrive at a *pesak Halakhah*, a final ruling. Thus we designate Halakhic argumentation, especially as found in the Talmud, as *massa u'mattan*, or in the Aramaic as *shakla ve-tarya*.[70]

Important as controversy is, the Sages insisted that it be conducted in a "civilized" manner. One tradition states that even though Bet Shammai and Bet Hillel disagreed in questions concerning marital status — a serious matter indeed — they conducted themselves with each other "in affection and comradeship," in accord with the verse *Love truth and peace* (Zach. 8:19).[71] The Talmud explains why it was Bet Hillel that merited to have the Halakhah decided in its favor, because "they were soft-spoken and patient; they would study both their own and Bet Shammai's opinions, even citing Bet Shammai's opinion before their own."[72] Commenting upon the verse *I took two staffs, one I called Graciousness* (no'am) *and the other I called Binders* (ḥovlim, literally, "destroyers"; Zech. 11:7), R. Oshiya says, "*Noam* refers to the scholars in Eretz Yisrael, for they are pleasant one to another; *Ḥovlim* refers to the scholars in Babylonia, who are harsh one to another."[73] Only

---

66 J.T. *Sanhedrin* 4:2(22a). See the commentaries *ad loc.* for different interpretations of R. Yannai's statement.

67 Cf. *Eduyot* 1:10, *ha-danim lifnei ḥakhamim*.

68 Cf. *Rosh Hashanah* 7a, *danim shanah...mi-shanah*.

69 Mishnah *Sanhedrin* 3:6. This requirement of argumentation prior to arriving at a decision may explain the ruling in capital cases that "if all (the judges) agree that the accused is guilty, he is set free;" *Sanhedrin* 17a. Cf. Rambam *Hilkhot Sanhedrin* 9:1.

70 *Sotah* 7b, "How did he know how to argue (*mishkal u'mitra*) with the Rabbis in halakhic statements."

71 *Yevamot* 14b; cf. *Tosefta ibid.* 1:10.

72 *Eruvin* 13a.

73 *Sanhedrin* 24a.

disputation conducted with mutual respect and courtesy, and a willingness to listen carefully to the opinion of one's opponent, can lead to the emergence of truth.

Disputation is the means; the goal is decision. When confronted with a practical problem which cannot be set aside indefinitely — in halakhic problems, how to fulfill a mitzvah or religious obligation — an authoritative answer has to be forthcoming. Thus the Torah has commanded, *If there rise a matter too hard for you in judgment ....matters of dispute in your courts; then you shall arise... and appear before the judge in charge at the time* (Deut. 17:8–9). For questions involving all Israel the "judge in charge" is none other than the Great Court, the Sanhedrin. The members of the Court could well be divided amongst themselves, but a decision would be forthcoming after a poll of opinions was taken and the majority opinion was ascertained. *Incline* (the law) *after the majority* (Exod. 23:2), says the Torah, in establishing the principle of majority rule in Jewish Law.[74]

Pharisees and Sadducees

Not all controversies were settled in one session of the Sanhedrin, or even in one generation. We are told that for almost a century (c. 150–50 B.C.E.)[75] the heads of the Sanhedrin were divided as to whether the ritual of *semikhah*, the laying of hands on a sacrificial animal, is performed on a Festival.[76] However, a more fundamental controversy raged at the time, dividing the people into two camps. The masters of the Halakhah, the teachers of the *Torah she-b'al-Peh*

---

74 *Tosefta Sanhedrin* 7:1. In capital cases, a majority of two was required in order to convict; Mishnah *Sanhedrin* 4:2. For the ordinary meaning of the verse in Exodus, see Rashi *ad loc.*

75 This was the period of the *Zugot*, or "Pairs," when there were two chief officials in the Sanhedrin, the *Nasi* and the *Av-Bet Din*. In the later period, there is mention only of the Nasi but not of the Av-Bet Din. However, mention is made of a *mufla she-b'Bet Din*, "the distinguished" member, though his actual function is not clear; see *Tsafot Sanhedrin* 16b, *s.v. eḥad*, and S.B. Hoenig, *The Great Sanhedrin* (Phila. 1953), p. 61.

76 Mishnah *Ḥagigah* 2:2–3. See Hoenig, *op. cit.* p. 48 for an explanation of the controversy.

were known as the *P'rushim*, or Pharisees, most probably because they were "explainers" or commentators of the Written Torah.[77] Many questioned the validity and authenticity of the whole concept of Torah she-b'al-Peh, halakhic rulings based upon hermeneutic interpretation of Scripture. These opponents of the P'rushim were the *Tsaddokim*, or Sadducees, who asserted that Mosaic law is inferred only from a literal interpretation of the Bible. Thus, for example, the Sadducees insisted that the Festival of Shavuot must always fall on a Sunday, since Scripture says that it is celebrated on the fiftieth day counted from *the morrow of the sabbath* (Lev. 23:15), taking *ha-Shabbat* to mean Saturday. The P'rushim, however, insisted that *ha-Shabbat* here refers to the first day of Passover, which occurs not only on a Saturday but on other days of the week as well.[78] The Sadducees attracted mainly the priestly and aristocratic class, and had little influence among the people at large. They ceased to exist as a force in Jewish life after the destruction of the Temple, and thus was established for all time the preeminence of the Halakhah as interpreted by the P'rushim — later on the Sages of the Talmud — as the unifying and preserving force of the Jewish people.

Halakhah and Theology

It was not only a matter of Scriptural interpretation which divided the Sadducees from the Pharisees; there was an underlying division concerning the theodicy of Judaism. We read in *Avot d'R. Nathan* (chapter five): "Antigonus of Sokho had two disciples who used to study his word...They proceeded to examine his teaching (i.e. Be not like slaves that serve your Master for the sake of compensa-

---

77 For explanations of the name "Pharisees" see S.W. Baron, *Social History of the Jews*, (Phila. 1952), Vol. 2, p. 342.

78 *Menaḥot* 65a. For other controversies, see *Yadayim* 4:6–8; *Menaḥot* 10:3; *Makkot* 1:6; *Yoma* 19b. For a bibliography on the controversies, see V. Tcherikover, *Hellenistic Civilization and the Jews* (Phila. 1959), p. 491. See also S. Zeitlin, *The Rise and Fall of the Judean State* (Phila. 1962), part 3. It is interesting to note that Rambam, *Hilkhot Temidim U'Musafin* 7:11, still found it necessary to argue this point concerning Shavuot, apparently against the Karaites of his day, who were in a sense the reincarnation of the Sadducees of Second Temple days.

tion... and let the fear of Heaven be upon you, so that your reward may be doubled in time to come)[79] and asked, 'Why did our forefathers[80] see fit to say this? Is it possible that a laborer should do his work all day and not take his remuneration in the evening'? ...So they arose and withdrew from the Torah and split into two sects, the Sadducees and the Boethusians, named after (the two disciples) Zadok and Boethus." Ever since, the epithet Tsaddokim and/or Boethusim in Talmudic parlance refers to those heretics who deny the basic principles of Judaism as taught by the Sages.[81]

The founding of these sectarian groups prompted the Sages to institute certain regulations and codify certain principles in order to incorporate their theology as an integral part of traditional Judaism. "Originally, the closing phrase to all benedictions recited in the Temple was *ad ha-olam* (i.e. Blessed art Thou...for everlasting); but since the Sadducees[82] corruptly taught that there is only one world, the Sages instituted that the closing should be *min ha-olam ad ha-olam*, "from everlasting to everlasting."[83] They also denied a portion in the bliss of *olam ha-ba*, the world-to-come, to those who deny that the Torah indicates that there will be a Resurrection of the Dead[84] or that the Torah was given from Heaven.[85]

Unity and Division in Jewish Life

We have said that disputation is a good thing, leading to the clarification of the Halakhah. However, this is so as long as it is

---

79   Cf. *Eruvin* 22a, "*Today to perform them* (the mitzvot; Deut. 7:11); tomorrow to receive their reward." See also the discussion in *Kiddushin* 39b.

80   Some read "our teachers" for our forefathers.

81   *Menaḥot* 65a, quoting *Megillat Taanit*, reads (in the first instance there) "Tsaddokim", though Megillat Taanit itself reads "Boethusin."

82   A variant reading, *minim*, i.e. heretics.

83   Mishnah *Berakhot* 9:5; a reminder that there are two worlds, the present one (*ha-olam ha-zeh*) and the world-to-come (*ha-olam ha-ba*). Cf. *Parah* 3:7; *Zevaḥim* 21a, "to expunge from the mind of the Sadducees (their opinion)."

84   Mishnah *Sanhedrin* 10(11):1. Some explain *olam ha-ba* as referring to life here on earth after the Resurrection of the dead; others as the life of the soul after it departs from the body at death; see the commentaries *ad loc.*

85   See Rashi *ad loc.*, "He denies the midrashim ... and even if he believes that the dead will be resurrected but it is not indicated in the Torah he is a heretic. Since he denies the principle who needs his belief; how does he know that it is so."

continued on a theoretical or ideological level; but as soon as it is translated to the practical level, where each side puts into practice its particular teaching and conducts itself accordingly, we are creating divisiveness and schism in Jewish life, a most undesirable phenomenon. The Sages, basing themselves on a phonetic similarity, interpreted the verse *You shall not gash yourselves* (Deut. 14:1) as an admonition against creating sects, each with its distinctive practice.[86] Even more so was the individual admonished against following a practice deviant from that of the community in which he finds himself, lest it lead to contention and divisiveness.[87]

Already prior to the destruction of the Second Temple in the year 70 C.E., controversy in Jewish Law had been growing keener and more widespread with the increase in the number of disciples attached to the two schools of Torah-study, *Bet-Shammai* and *Bet Hillel*.[88] One cannot help but see in the division between these two schools the natural division between a liberal or less stringent interpretation of the Law and a conservative and more stringent interpretation.[89] This was no doubt a reflection of the contrasting characters of the respective founders of the schools, Hillel being of a more gentle and lenient disposition and Shammai more impatient and strict.[90] But it is folly to contend that these disputes were primarily due to the different economic positions of the disputants.[91] The masters of Jewish Law, though indeed mindful of the social and economic needs of their times, were not motivated by personal considerations.[92] Their exclusive concern was the applica-

---

86 *Yevamot* 13b. From the discussion there and from its codification in Rambam *Hilkhot Avodat Kokhavim* 12:14, it seems that this is not an aggadic midrash but an halakhic inference; see M. Lewittes, *Sefer Tzemihat Ge'ulateinu* (Jer. 5744), pp. 173 ff. As we point out below, the restrictions of this admonition became extremely limited. In fact, in our times the stress is upon the preservation of distinctive local custom, rather than the integration of the several communities into a uniform practice.

87 Mishnah *Pesahim* 4:1.

88 *Sanhedrin* 88b; J.T. *Shabbat* 1:4(3c); *Bavli* 17a.

89 See, however, *Eduyot* 4:1–3 for instances where Shammai maintained the more lenient position.

90 *Shabbat* 30b.

91 As does, e.g., L. Finkelstein in "The Pharisees."

92 See *Eduyot* 5:6, where Akavyah b. Mehallalel refused to compromise his opinion even though it cost him the position of *Av Bet Din*. See further, where he supposedly accused Shemayah and Avtalyon of having personal motives in carrying our a certain law and how he was condemned for such accusation.

tion of the laws of the Torah to daily life in order to sanctify the people and make them both capable and willing to bear the burden of living a Torah life.[93]

When the division between the schools of Shammai and Hillel threatened a breach in the unity of the people — so much so that "the Torah became like two Torahs"[94] — it was decreed that the Halakhah is according to the teachings of Bet Hillel.[95] One distinguished Sage, R. Eliezer b. Hyrcanus, refused to accept this decision and was excommunicated.[96] Nevertheless, his disciples continued to communicate with him, and in his community they continued to follow his teachings. Eventually it was conceded that each community may continue to practice its distinctive custom, except that within the same community the people should not be divided into groups following differing practices.[97] Furthermore, a scholar, when visiting the community of a colleague who differs from his teaching, must follow the practice of the local scholar in order to avoid strife and contention.[98]

Semikhah in the Diaspora

The Sages ruled that Semikhah could be conferred only in Eretz Yisrael, probably in accord with the verse *For out of Zion will go forth the Torah* (Isaiah 2:3).[99] This of course did not mean that communities outside Eretz Yisrael would be deprived of recognized halakhic authorities. It did imply, however, the absence in the Diaspora of two major prerogatives enjoyed by those upon whom had been conferred the traditional Semikha "person from person,

---

93   Cf. *Keritot* 1:7, where Rabban Shimon b. Gamaliel reduced the required number of offerings in order to reduce the price.

94   *Sanhedrin* 88b.

95   *Yevamot* 14a, ascribed to a *bat kol*, a heavenly voice. See however *Baba Metzia* 59b, "we do not pay attention to a *bat kol*." In J.T. *Yevamot*, end of chap. 1, (3c) this decision is ascribed to the Sanhedrin in Yavneh, at the end of the 1st Cent. C.E.

96   *Baba Metzia* 59b. Though a disciple of Rabban Yoḥanan b. Zakkai, who was a Hillelite, R. Eliezer was called a Shammaite (J.T. *Sheviit* 9:6(39a), see *Gilyon ha-Shas ad loc.*), probably because of his adamant nature.

97   *Yevamot* 14a.

98   *Ḥullin* 53b, 57b.

99   *Sanhedrin* 14a.

from Moshe Rabbenu." The right to constitute themselves as a Sanhedrin with the power to rule for all Israel on the basis of Scriptural interpretation and to regard it as a command of the Torah is exclusive to those having the proper Semikhah; no group of Rabbinic leaders not possessing such Semikhah, whether residing in or outside Eretz Yisrael, could arrogate to themselves such power. Secondly, only those with the proper Semikhah could, in their capacity as judges (*dayyanim*), impose a fine (*k'nas*) prescribed by the Torah; for example, the double payment extracted from a thief.

To insure the proper administration of justice with officially authorized dayyanim in accord with Jewish Law — and for centuries most communities in the Diaspora were autonomous as far as this is concerned — a corresponding form of Semikhah was instituted. It was called *Reshut* (the right to govern). The Sages in Eretz Yisrael distinguished between Semikhah and Reshut, giving each its proper name; but the Rabbis in Babylonia would call the conferring of Reshut, Semikhah.[100] Indeed, the Talmud would have it that the Reshut given by the Babylonian authorities conferred the right to judge even in Eretz Yisrael; whereas Reshut given by the Palestinian authorities was effective only in Eretz Yisrael and not in Babylonia.[101] The conferring of Semikhah in subsequent generations, up to and including the present, was also a sort of *reshut*, the recognition by a superior authority that the conferee *higi'a l'hora'ah*, i.e. his knowledge of Talmudic law was sufficient to allow him to render halakhic decisions.[102] The Talmud emphasized this status of *higi'a l'hora'ah*, stating that he who has not reached this status and renders decisions is "foolish, wicked and arrogant;" but one who has attained it yet refuses to render decisions places obstacles in the path of those who wish to observe the law.[103]

Later we shall have the occasion to discuss the scope of authority in the post-Talmudic era exercised by those who received Semikhah and enjoyed the title "Rabbi."

100 J.T. *Sanhedrin* 1:2(19a); cf. *Sanhedrin* 5a, "What is *reshuta.*"
101 *Ibid.*
102 Rema, *Yoreh De'ah* 242:14
103 *Avot* 4:7; *Avodah Zarah* 19b; *Sotah* 22a.

Dissolution and Reestablishment of the Sanhedrin

The Mishnah states, "When the Sanhedrin ceased, singing ceased at feasts."[104] This ceasing most probably occurred shortly before the destruction of the Temple in 70 C.E.[105] Thus the Talmud says, "From the day that the Bet ha-Mikdash was destroyed, even though the Sanhedrin ceased, the four methods of execution did not cease."[106] Even before that — according to one version, forty years before — the Sanhedrin removed itself from its seat in the Chamber of the Hewn Stone so as not to deal with capital cases.[107] From the statements of R. Akiva and R. Tarfon, "Had we been in the Sanhedrin no one would have been executed,"[108] it appears that the reconstituted Sanhedrin in Yavneh did not consider itself competent to execute criminals. The last seat of the Sanhedrin before its final dissolution was in Tiberias, and there — assures us the Amora R. Yoḥanan — it is destined to be reestablished.[109] From there, adds Maimonides, it will move back to its ancient seat in the Temple.[110] And it is Maimonides who suggests how the Sanhedrin with all its ancient prerogatives can be reestablished even though the chain of traditional Semikhah "person to person, from Moshe Rabbenu" has long been broken. He says, "It seems to me that if all the scholars in Eretz Yisrael were to agree to appoint *dayyanim* and confer upon them Semikhah, their ordination would be valid... However, this matter requires careful reflection."[111] Much later we shall see how this suggestion of Maimonides was rejected, the very notion of the revival of the Sanhedrin through human initiative dismissed from contemporary Rabbinic polemic.

---

104 *Sotah* 9:11; cf. *Gittin* 7a and *Tosafot ad loc., s.v. zimra.*
105 See Hoenig, *op. cit.* chap. XII.
106 *Sanhedrin* 37b.
107 *Ibid.* 41b.
108 Mishnah *Makkot* 1:10.
109 *Rosh Hashanah* 31b.
110 *Hilkhot Sanhedrin* 14:12.
111 *Ibid.* 4:11.

5

From Oral Tradition to Written Text

אכתוב לו רובי תורתי: מרובין הדברים הנדרשין מן הכתב
I write for him many teachings (Hosea 8:12):
Many are the things expounded from Scripture*

The Tannaim

"Ten times the Sanhedrin was driven from place to place,"[1] yet it
continued to function as the generating source of Torah she-
b'al-Peh for a century or more after the destruction of the Second
Temple. Despite the Hadrianic decrees against the study of the
Torah, leading members of the Sanhedrin defied the Roman per-
secutors and continued to expound Scripture and "raise up many
disciples." Most prominent among them was Akiva ben Yosef,[2]
who is reputed to have had twenty-four thousand disciples.[3] In a
simple but captivating parable, Rabbi Akiva explained his determination to teach Torah publicly even at the threat to his life. "To
what is our situation compared," he said to someone who questioned his seemingly reckless action, "to a fox walking by the bank of
a stream who noticed the fish jumping to and fro. When the fox
asked them why they are running away, they replied, 'From the nets
spread by the humans.' 'Then why not come up to live with me on
dry land,' suggested the fox. 'Fool that you are,' countered the fish,

---

*   J.T. *Peah* 2:6(17a); J.T. *Hagigah* 1:7 (76b).
1   *Rosh Hashanah* 31a–b.
2   Cf. *Yevamot* 16a, "You are Akiva ben Yosef whose name spreads from one end
    of the world to the other."
3   *Ketubot* 63a.

' if we are afraid for our lives in our natural habitat; how much more so are we doomed in the place we face certain death.' "So it is with us," continued Rabbi Akiva. "If presently, studying the Torah of which it is said *For it is your life and your length of days* (Deut. 30:20) we are in danger, how much more so are our lives in danger if we abandon the study of Torah." Not long afterwards, the Talmud informs us, Rabbi Akiva was seized by the Romans, who combed his flesh with iron combs until he expired.[4]

Rabbi Akiva attracted many disciples because he was an excellent teacher; his lessons were well organized. The basic text studied was the Pentateuch, particularly those sections dealing with the mitzvot, but the bulk of the teaching consisted of rulings handed down orally from previous teachers and from the schools of Shammai and Hillel. These Rabbi Akiva examined to make sure there was no error in transmission, added his own rulings based on his own method of Scriptural interpretation, then organized the material according to subject matter. His work is described as follows:[5] "To what might Rabbi Akiva be likened? To a laborer who took his basket and went forth. When he found wheat, he put some in his basket; when he found barley, he put that in; spelt, he put that in; lentils, he put them in. Upon returning he sorted out the wheat by itself, the barley by itself, the beans by themselves, the lentils by themselves, arranging the whole Torah in rings." He assigned to four distinguished disciples different compilations which became the basis for all subsequent Rabbinic teaching. R. Meir was given the Mishnah; i.e. rulings not attached to any Scriptural phrase (before the term "Mishnah" came into general usage, these were known as *halakhot*); R. Nehemiah, the *Tosefta*, i.e. addendums to the Mishnah; R. Yehudah (b. Ilay'i), the *Sifra*, i.e. the halakhic commentary to Leviticus, also known as *Torat Kohanim*; R. Shimon (b. Yohai), the *Sifre*, the halakhic commentary to Numbers and Deuteronomy.[6] (The commentary to Exodus was compiled by R. Akiva's colleague, R. Yishmael, and is called *Mekhilta*).[7] Two other noteworthy disciples of R. Akiva whose opinions are often cited in

---

4   *Berakhot* 61b.
5   *Avot d'R. Natan*, chap. 18; cf. Rashi *Gittin* 67a.
6   *Sanhedrin* 86a.
7   There is also a Mekhilta compiled by R. Shimon b. Yohai; see M. Kasher, *HaRambam ve-HaMekhilta etc.* (N.Y. 5703).

the Mishnah, were R. Yose b. Ḥalafta and R. Eleazar b. Shamua.[8]

Smaller compilations of halakhic material were extant before R. Akiva, some of them dating back to Temple days and dealing with Temple procedures.[9] These are referred to as *Mishnah Rishonah*, the First Mishnah, and record the opinions of Bet Shammai and Bet Hillel. Later teachers of these *halakhot* were R. Eliezer b. Hyrcanus,[10] R. Yehoshua b. Hananiah, R. Tarfon; R. Akiva and his disciples, though there were many others.[11] They are the *Tannaim*, which is the Aramaic for "teachers," and their rulings comprise what is now known as "the Mishnah."

The Mishnah

The Hadrianic persecutions and the ill-fated rebellion led by Bar Kokhba had their negative repercussions on the study of Torah in the second half of the second century. The bulk of Jewish Law, transmitted mainly by the disciples of R. Akiva, had become so voluminous and disorganized, and the conflicting opinions so numerous, that Jewish life could easily become fragmented. R. Shimon, son of R. Gamaliel of Yavneh, against the opposition of R. Meir and R. Natan,[12] reasserted — more successfully than his father[13] — the dominant position of the Nasi of the Sanhedrin, thus laying the foundation for its complete dominance by his son and successor, R. Yehudah ha-Nasi, also known by the simple title "Rabbi" or "Rabbenu ha-Kadosh." By the latter's time the political situation vis-a-vis Rome had eased considerably. R. Yehudah established very cordial relations with the Roman governor Antoninus, and the harsh decrees against the practice of Judaism were no longer in effect. This "breathing spell" — unfortunately not of too long a duration — gave R. Yehudah the opportunity to collect

---

8   *Yevamot* 62b.
9   For a description of these, see Y.N. Epstein, *M'vo'ot l' Sifrut ha-Tannaim*, Part One, chaps. 2 and 3.
10   Cf. *Sanhedrin* 68a.
11   For a listing of Tannaim, see Rambam, *Intro. to Mishneh Torah*, and the many standard works on the Mishnah and Talmud.
12   *Horayot* 13b.
13   *Berakhot* 27b.

the numerous opinions handed down from preceding generations and arrange them in proper order, preserving them for future generations. Rashi describes this undertaking as follows: "He sent for and gathered together all the scholars in Eretz Yisrael. Until his time, the tractates (*mesikhtot*, see below) were not arranged in order; rather, each scholar who heard something from his superior repeated it, saying 'This particular ruling I heard from this teacher.' When all were gathered, each one said what he had heard; then they discussed the reasons for the different opinions and whose opinion should be followed. They arranged the tractates; matters of torts separate and matters of levirate marriage separate and matters of the holy sacrifices separate. Those opinions that R. Yehudah saw fit to accept were repeated without stating the name of the author (*s'tam*) so that they would be estalished as the Halakhah."[14]

Thus was born the Mishnah, the basic text of Torah she-b'al-Peh, the complement to the word of God as recorded in the Torah she-bikhtav. Commenting upon the verse *For after the tenor* (al pi) *of these words I have made a covenant with you and with Israel* (Exod. 34:27), R. Yoḥanan said, "The Holy One, blessed be He, made His covenant with Israel only with the Torah she-b'al-Peh."[15] It is a moot question how long the Mishnah remained Torah she-b'al-Peh, i.e. not committed to writing. From the fact that in the period following the generation of R. Yehudah ha-Nasi we still find students whose special function was to repeat the Mishnah for the scholar,[16] it is apparent that it did not become a written text till much later.[17] In any event, it was now the Mishnah which became the subject studied in the Yeshivot headed by the disciples of "Rabbi" both in Palestine and in Babylonia. Its language commended it to all, written in Hebrew, the *lingua franca* of all Jews.[18]

---

14   *Bava Metzia* 33b.
15   *Gittin* 60b.
16   *Ḥullin* 15a. A repeater was also called a *Tanna*, but he should not be confused with a Tanna whose views are recorded in the Mishnah.
17   Cf. *Yevamot* 64b, where it says, "Rabbi (Yehudah ha-Nasi) ordered (*tikken*) the Mishnah," and not "wrote" the Mishnah. *Iggeret Rav Sherira Gaon*, on the other hand, several times says that Rabbi "wrote" the Mishnah.
18   Cf. *Baba Kamma* 82b–83a, Rabbi said, "In Eretz Yisrael why the Syrian (i.e. Aramaic) tongue; speak either the Holy Tongue (Hebrew) or Greek." See also *Rosh Hashanah* 26b, where Rabbi's housemaid enlightened some of his disciples as to the meaning of certain Hebrew terms.

Mishnaic Hebrew is a natural linguistic development from Biblical Hebrew, enriched by words of Greek and Latin origin, especially for the many technical terms and the *realia* of second century life in Palestine. Though comprehensive, covering the vast range of Jewish Law both practical and theoretical, it is concise, easily learned by rote.[19]

By including in this *magnum opus* opposing and contradictory opinions as well as his own, R. Yehudah ha-Nasi apparently did not intend the Mishnah to serve as a definitive legal code, such as the Mishneh Torah of Maimonides or the Shulḥan Arukh of Yosef Karo. It did however serve as a source book of legal precedents for the Rabbinic jurist, the dayyan. The Mishnah itself offers several reasons why opposing and unaccepted opinions were included. "Why do they mention those views of Shammai and Hillel which were not accepted? To teach future generations that a person should not persist in his opinion, seeing that "the fathers of the world" did not persist in their opinion. And why do they mention the views of the individual opposed by the majority, when the halakhah follows the majority? Because if a Bet-Din will find acceptable the views of an individual it can depend upon them, provided it is greater than the previous Bet-Din in wisdom and numbers. Furthermore, if a person will say, 'This is my tradition,' he will be told that it is only an indivudal opinion."[20]

The Six Orders

The Mishnah enables us to see at a quick glance the comprehensive range of Jewish Law. It comprises six Orders (*Sedarim*) or major divisions, each of which is divided into Tractates called *Masekhtot* (singular, *Masekhet*), as follows:

Seder Zeraim (Seeds):

Berakhot, Prayers and Benedictions

Pe'ah, Corner of the Field (Lev. 19:9)

---

19 Cf. *Pesaḥim* 3b, "One should always teach his student in a brief way."

20 *Eduyot* 1:4–6. See supplements to the Mishnah in H. Albek's ed. (Mossad Harav Kook, Jer. 5713) p. 475–6.

D'mai, Doubtful (if tithed)[21]
Kilayyim, Mixed seeds (Lev. 19:19)
Sh'vi'it, Seventh Year (Lev. 25:1–7)
Terumot, Priestly Portions (Num. 18:8–20)
Ma'asrot, Tithes (Num. 18:21–24)
Ma'aser Sheni, The Second Tithe (Deut. 12:6–18)
Ḥalah, The Dough Portion (Num. 15:17–21)
Orlah, Forbidden Fruit (Lev. 19:23)
Bikkurim, First Fruits (Deut. 26:1–11)

Seder Mo'ed (Appointed Times; Lev. chap. 23).
Shabbat
Eruvin, Mingling and Consolidating Domains
Pesaḥim, Passover
Shekalim, Shekels for the Temple Service
Yoma, Day of Atonement
Sukkah, Tabernacles
Betzah: Yom Tov, Festivals
Rosh Hashanah, New Year
Ta'anit, Fast Days
Megillah, Purim
Mo'ed Kattan, Intermediate Festival Days
Ḥagigah, Festival Offerings

Seder Nashim (Marital Laws):
Yevamot, Levirate Marriage, Spouses rights to the Priestly Portion, Missing Husbands
Ketubot, Dower Rights, Rape, Joint Property
Nedarim, Vows (Num. 30:27)
Nazir, Vow to abstain from wine (Num. 6:1–21)
Sotah, Suspected Adulteress (Num. 5:11–31)
Gittin, Bills of Divorcement (Deut. 24:1)
Kiddushin, Contracting Marriage, Prohibited Marriage

---

21 The average peasant — the so-called *am ha'aretz* — was suspected of not having set aside from his produce the required tithes (Num. 18:21–24; Deut. 14: 22–29).

Seder Nezikin (Damages: Exod. chaps. 22–23)

> *Bava Kamma*, (First Gate), Principal Torts (Exod. chaps. 21–22)
> *Bava Metzia* (Middle Gate), Lost and Found, Employers-Employees, Bailees (*ibid.*)
> *Bava Batra* (Last Gate), Partners, Neighbors, Claims to Ownership, Acquisition of Property, Loans
> *Sanhedrin*, Courts of Law, Capital Offenses
> *Makkot*, Penalty of Stripes (Deut. 24:1–3)
> *Shevuot*, Oaths (Exod. 22:10; Lev. 5:4; Num. 30:1–3)
> *Eduyot*, Testimonies (concerning *halakhot*)
> *Avodah Zarah*, Idolatry (Exod. 20:2–5; Deut. 12:2–3)
> *Avot*, Ethics of the Fathers
> *Horayot*, Decisions of the Court (Lev. 4:3–26)

Seder Kodashim (Consecrated Objects):

> *Zevahim*, Animal Sacrifices (Lev. chaps 1–7)
> *Menahot* Meal Offerings (Lev. chaps 2 and 6)
> *Hullin*, Dietary Laws (Exod. 22:30; 23:19; Lev. chap. 11)
> *Bekhorot*, The First-Born (Exod. 13:2)
> *Arakhin*, Vows of Persons (Lev. chap. 27)
> *Temurah*, Changing Sacred Objects (Lev. 5:15–16)
> *Me'ilah*, Use of Sacred Objects (Lev. 5:15–16)
> *Tamid*, Daily Temple Service
> *Middot*, The Temple Structure
> *Kinnin*, Bird Offerings (Lev. 1:14–17; 12:6–8)

Seder Tohorot (Cleanness):

> *Kelim*, Utensils (Lev.11: 24–47)
> *Oholot*, Tents (Num. 19:14–22)
> *Nega'im*, Skin Plagues (Lev. chap. 13)
> *Parah*, The Red Heifer (Num. 19:1–13)
> *Tohorot*, Cleanness
> *Mikvaot*, Pools for Cleanness
> *Niddah*, The Menstruant (Lev. 15:19–30)
> *Makhshirin*, Disposition to Uncleanness (Lev. 11;34,38)
> *Zavin*, Men and Women with an Issue (Lev. 15:1–15)
> *Tevul Yom*, Who Immersed Themselves
> *Yadayim*, Hands that cause Uncleanness
> *Uktzin*, Stems that transmit Uncleanness

Commentaries to the Mishnah

The Mishnah has remained to this day a basic text of halakhic Judaism. It has been published in numerous editions, together with commentaries that provide the student with the accepted Halakhah. The classic commentary is that of Maimonides, written in Arabic but translated into Hebrew by several medieval and modern scholars.[22] It is included in standard editions of the Talmud. The most popular commentary is that of R. Ovadiah of Bertinoro (c. 1445–1510), usually published with the commentary of R. Yom Tov Lipman Heller (*Tosafot Yom Tov*, 1579–1654). More recent commentaries worth mention are those of R. Yisrael Lifshitz (*Tiferet Yisrael*, 19th cent.), H. Albeck (published with vowelization) and Pinḥas Kahati. There are several translations of the Mishnah into English, the best-known being that of H. Danby.

Tosefta-Baraita

The Mishnah, as a systematic collection, is an anthology, and as such is selective, which means exclusive. Consequently, many halakhic statements of the Tannaim are not to be found in the Mishnah. Furthermore, the language of the Mishnah is concise and at times elliptical. To fill in these lacunae and to add some explanations, two disciples of R. Yehudah ha-Nasi, R. Ḥiyya (the greater) and R. Oshiya (also Hoshiya), decided to compose a supplement to the Mishnah.[23] It follows the order of the Mishnah, and is called *Tosefta*, i.e. "Addendum." An interesting story illustrating the

---

22 The most recent and probably the most accurate, that of Yosef Kapaḥ (Mossad Harav Kook, Jer. 5721).

23 Cf. *Ḥullin* 141a–b, "Any *matnita* which was not learned in the schools of R. Ḥiyya and R. Oshiya (Rashi, "they arranged the baraitot") is corrupt." See also Rambam's Introduction to his Commentary to the Mishnah (Kapaḥ ed. p. 18), "...therefore one of his disciples, R. Ḥiyya, saw fit to compose a book, following in the footsteps of his teacher, to explain that which is not clear in the words of his teacher, and this is the Tosefta. R. Oshiya also did this." Y.N. Epstein, *M'vo'ot l'Sifrut ha-Tannaim*, p. 243, asserts that the assumption by the Rishonim that R. Ḥiyya composed the Tosefta is erroneous. R. Ḥiyya composed a Mishnah which was complementary to that of Rabbi in that it is more elaborate and states the Halakhah, i.e., the accepted ruling.

importance of this collection is related in the Jerusalem Talmud.[24]
R. Abbahu (of Caesarea) went down to Tiberias. The disciples of R.
Yoḥanan saw that his face was shining, so they said to R. Yoḥanan,
"R. Abbahu must have found a treasure." R. Yoḥanan said, "Per-
haps he heard some new (interpretation of) Torah." So the disciples
went to R. Abbahu and asked him what new Torah he had heard.
He said to them, "I have found an old Tosefta." Whereupon they
applied to him the verse *A man's wisdom lights up his face* (Eccl. 8:1).

The statements found in the Tosefta are referred to in the Talmud
as *Baraita*, which means "outside," i.e. outside the Mishnah. The
latter term is also applied to statements found in the halakhic
midrashim, i.e. *Mekhilta, Sifra, Sifre*. When quoting an halakhic
statement, the Talmud differentiates between a Mishnaic one and a
Baraita; the former is *matnitin*, *our* Mishnah, and the quotation is
preceded by the word *t'nan*, we have learned; whereas a Baraita is
matnita, a learning, and the preceding word is either *tanya*, it was
learned, or *tanu rabbanan*, the Rabbis have learned, or, in the
Jerusalem Talmud in particular, *tani*.[25]

The Amoraim

The most extensive, as well as the most authentic, commentary to
the Mishnah was composed in the schools founded and conducted
by the disciples of R. Yehudah ha-Nasi, and by their disciples in
turn. In Palestine in the third century the prominent centers of
learning were in Sepphoris and Tiberias in the Galil, though there
were also schools and scholars in Caesarea and in the southern
coastal area called *Darom*, the South.[26] Most prominent among the
scholars was R. Yoḥanan (199–279, occasionally referred to by his
patronym, Bar Nafḥa). He laid the foundation for the Palestinian

---

24 Cf. *Shabbat* 8:1(11a). Our faces also may light up upon the publication by the
     Jewish Theological Seminary of New York of the critical edition of the Tosefta
     by the late Prof. Saul Lieberman together with an extensive commentary
     entitled *Tosefta Kip'shuta*. So far, only the first three *Sedorim* have been pub-
     lished. It is to be hoped that scholars will be found to continue this work and
     cover the last three Sedorim.
25 See, however, Y.N. Epstein, *Mehkarim b'Sifrut ha-Talmud* (Jer. 5744), p. 93, for
     exceptions.
26 See *Encyclopedia l'Geographia Talmudit* (Tel Aviv 5732), pp. 348–349.

Talmud, which was finally composed towards the end of the fourth century.[27] Meanwhile schools were founded in Babylonia which flourished and served as centers of halakhic study and decision for well nigh a millennium. Most prominent among these was the one established by Abba Arikha, more familiarly known as Rav, in the town of Sura. His colleague Shmuel, noted physician and astronomer, established a Yeshiva in his native city Nehardea, which was later transferred to Pumbedita. The discussions in these schools, over a period of three centuries, constitute the bulk of the Babylonian Talmud.

During this period there was a constant interchange of scholars between Palestine and Babylonia, so that the opinions of the Babylonians are referred to in the Palestinian Talmud, and the opinions of the Palestinian scholars form the basis of discussion in the Babylonian schools. In fact, there were certain scholars from Babylonia who were assigned the task of going to Eretz Yisrael to learn the views of the Palestinian scholars and bring them back to Babylonia.[28] These scholars of the post-Mishnaic period are the *Amoraim*, to distinguish them from the Tannaim of the Mishnah and Baraita.[29]

Though the devotion to Torah study was equal in these two conters of Jewish life, their systems of learnig differed. The Babylonians engaged in much discursive and hair-splitting arguments, described in one place as "putting an elephant through the eye of a needle."[30] These rabbis did not hesitate to restrict the ruling of the

---

27   In the immediate post-Talmudic period, the Palestinian Talmud was called, "the Talmud of the West (*ma'arav*)", Palestine being west of Babylonia. It was also referred to as "the Talmud of Eretz Yisrael." The later designation, "Talmud Yerushalmi," came about when Jerusalem often denoted the entire land of Israel (cf. the use of the name Zion), even though this Talmud was not composed in the city of Jerusalem.

28   They were called, *nehutei*, i.e. those who went down from Eretz Yisrael to Babylonia; cf. *Ḥullin* 124a. Prominent among them were Dimi of Nehardea (called Abudimi in J.T.), Rabin (contraction of R. Abin) and Ulla.

29   Technically, the Amora was the spokesman of the Rosh Yeshiva; the latter would whisper his instruction to the former, who would deliver it out loud to the assemblage. Cf., for example, *Taanit* 8a, "Shmuel set up over himself an Amora and lectured."
     Another designation for such a spokesman was *Turgeman*.

30   *Bava Metzia* 38b.

Mishnah to a rare instance, or declare it as only an individual — and thus, not binding — opinion, if they found a Baraita that ruled otherwise, or if it did not agree with the ruling of their esteemed teachers, R. Ḥiyya and Rav.[31] They took such pride in their institutions of learning that one of their scholars declared that he who leaves Babylonia for Eretz Yisrael transgresses a positive commandment.[32] The Palestinians, however, looked askance at the excessive argumentation of the Babylonians, and applied to their Talmud the verse *He has made me dwell in darkness like those long dead* (Lam. 3:6).[33] And they had fulsome praise for their own system of learning, asserting, "One small group (of scholars) in Eretz Yisrael is more precious than a great Sanhedrin outside Eretz Yisrael."[34]

The Talmudim

The teachers in both centers did agree that their discussions and conclusions replaced the Tannaim as the source of halakhic rulings, saying that "we do not learn (the law) from the halakhot (i.e. the mishnayot) or the haggadot or the tosafot; only from the Talmud.[35] And they criticised those who would rule only on the basis of the Mishnah without taking into account the discussions of the Amoraim.[36] They laid down certain principles as to whose opinion should be followed in case of a conflict of views.[37] They stressed the overwhelming importance of the study of Torah, elaborating upon the statement of the Mishnah that "Talmud Torah is above all else" by asserting that it is greater than saving life, or building the Bet ha-Mikdash, or honoring parents.[38] When finally arranged in the

---

31 Cf. *ibid.* 5a, "R. Ḥiyya is a Tanna and disagrees:" *Ketubot* 8a, "Rav is a Tanna and disagrees." See *Tosafot ad loc.* that R. Yoḥanan did not accept this.

32 *Ketubot* 110b. See Rashi *ibid.* 111a, *s.v. kakh*, "Because there are Yeshivot there that are constantly spreading Torah."

33 *Sanhedrin* 24a.

34 J.T. *Nedarim* 7:13(40a). See also Lewittes, *Tzemiḥat Ge'utateinu* (Jer. 5744), pp. 83 ff.

35 J.T. *Pe'ah* 2:6(17a); cf. Rashbam, *Bava Batra* 130b, *s.v. ad she-yomru*.

36 *Sotah* 22a; *Bava Metzia* 33a–b.

37 See *Arukh ha-Shalem s.v. halakh* (Vol. 3, p. 208 in Shilo ed. 5730) for references.

38 *Megillah* 16b.

two Talmudim to follow the relevant Mishnayot (called Halakhot in the Jerusalem Talmud) these discussions of the Amoraim constituted the *Gemara.* Mishnah and Gemara together constitute the Talmud.[39] Another designation for Talmud, invariably employed in popular parlance, is *Shas,* an acronym for *Shishah Sedorim,* the Six Orders of the Mishnah.[40]

It should be noted that there is no Gemara in the Babylonian Talmud for Seder Zeraim except for Tractate *Berakhot,* nor for Seder Tohorot except for Tractate *Niddah,* since the laws in these Sedorim — with several exceptions — were not observed outside of Eretz Yisrael. Nevertheless, there is Gemara for Seder Kodashim even though its laws had no practical significance, for the study of these laws in itself was deemed a practical substitute for the actual offering of the sacrifices.[41] The Jerusalem-Palestinian Talmud has Gemara for Seder Zeraim, since agricultural laws had practical significance in Eretz Yisrael, though only to a limited extent after the destruction of the Temple. There is no Gemara, however, for Seder Kodashim and Seder Tohorot — except for Tractate *Niddah* — since these laws had no practical significance even in Eretz Yisrael.

In addition to the Tractates mentioned above (Pages 79 to 81), standard editions of the Babylonian Talmud include fifteen treatises known as *Mesikhtot Ketanot* (Minor Tractates).[42] We have had occasion to quote from the two largest, *Soferim* and *Avot d'R. Natan.* Modern scholars disagree as to the provenance of these works, and whether they are Talmudic or post-Talmudic in origin.[43] It should be noted, however, that in some instances of ritual observance the accepted practice is that of *Soferim* even though it differs from that of the Talmud.[44]

---

39 For the use and explanation of these terms, see H. Albeck, *Mavo l'Talmudim* (Tel Aviv, 1969), Chap. 1.

40 Printed editions of the Talmud in some instances write *Shas* in place of Talmud; see *Arukh ha-Shalem s.v. Talmud.*

41 *Menahot* 110a.

42 They are printed at the end of Seder Nezikin, most probably because of the first, *Avot d'R. Natan,* which is a Tosefta on Mishnah *Avot,* which is in Seder Nezikin.

43 See the preface to the English translation, Soncino Press, London, 1965.

44 See *Tosafot Megillah* 31b, *s.v. Rosh Hodesh.*

Exactly when the Jerusalem Talmud (*Yerushalmi*) was composed, and by whom, has not been established,[45] though it was sometime towards the end of the 4th Century, after Rome became Christian and Jewish life in Palestine became increasingly difficult, and the schools in Sepphoris and Tiberias were closed. Most of the extant text is Tiberian in origin, though there are sections composed in the school of Caesarea.[46] The language is Palestinian Aramaic, much less familiar than the Babylonian Aramaic which was a spoken language for centuries after the Talmudic period.[47] It contains a substantial amount of Greek and Latin terms, unfamiliar to the standard commentators of the Yerushalmi. Though it is quoted fairly often by the Rishonim of the Middle Ages, it was not studied regularly in their schools, and therefore few copies existed. As a result, the printed text as it appears today is full of scribal errors, ommissions and transpositions, making its study a difficult undertaking. Nevertheless, a select group of scholars today are devoting more and more attention to this Talmud, which it may be assumed transmits the view of its Sages more faithfully than as found in its Babylonian counterpart.[48]

Fortunately conditions in Babylonia in the post-Mishnaic period were quite different from those in Palestine. There, Jewish life was well organized and the Jewish people enjoyed a great deal of autonomy, allowing the continuation of the Yeshivot and the exercise of halakhic authority. Though there was no Sanhedrin there, certain of its prerogatives which required properly ordained masters of the halakhic tradition were assumed by the Amoraim on the basis that "we are acting as their agents."[49] Though the gates of direct Scriptural interpretation by means of the hermeneutic principles which had been open to the Tannaim were now closed, the interpretation of the Halakhah transmitted by the earlier authorities did not cease, and the chain of authority originating with Moshe Rabbenu was maintained.

45   Cf. S.W. Baron, *Social and Religious History*, Vol. II, p. 195, and Y,N, Epstein, *Mavo l'Sifrut ha-Amoraim*, p. 274.

46   See S. Lieberman, *Talmudah shel Kesarin* (Tarbitz Supplement, Jer, 5691). See, however, Y.N. Epstein, *op. cit.*, pp. 282 ff.

47   See Y.N. Epstein, *Peirush ha-Geonim etc.* (Jer.-Tel Aviv 5742), pp. 48–49.

48   See L. Greenwald, *Did the editors of the Bavli see the Yerushalmi* (Hebrew, N.Y. 1954).

49   *Bava Kamma* 84b.

A Babylonian scholar of the 5th Century made the following statement, "From the days of Rabbi (Yehudah ha-Nasi) to the days of Rav Ashi we do not find Torah and high office combined in the same person."[50] Two centuries separated these two rabbinic giants, and the time had come to collect and organize the halakhic traditions which had accumulated in the interim. Rav Ashi, who led the Yeshiva in Sura for almost sixty years, commenced this task, but had to leave it to others to complete. By the middle of the 5th Century the situation in Babylonia changed radically, as the local rulers began to persecute the Jews, giving added impetus to the need for consolidating the teachings of the Amoraim and recording them for posterity. The man who led this effort, resulting in the production of Talmud Bavli, was Rabina (d. 499), and thus it was said by the final redactors of the Talmud, "Rav Ashi and Rabina are the end of instruction."[51] The final redactors, a generation after Rabina, were a group of scholars called *Rabbanan S'vorai*.[52] They put the finishing touches to what for centuries had been *Torah-she-b'al-Peh* and now became *Torah-she-bikhtav*, the Written Law for all Israel to heed and practice.

Though the Palestinian authorities, as we have pointed out above, considered their Talmud superior, it is the Babylonian Talmud which was accepted as the authority in halakhic questions and gained the attention of succeeding scholars. This was largely due to historical circumstance, the dwindling of the Jewish community in Palestine as against the continued vitality of Jewish life in Babylonia in the post-Talmudic period. Rav Hai Gaon and Isaac Alfasi (the Rif) maintain that the Babylonian Talmud is decisive because of its later redaction, following the rule that the Halakhah is according to the later authority.[53] Maimonides was most emphatic about this. He says,[54] "All Israel is obligated to follow everything in the Babylonian Gemara; and every city and province is to be compelled to practice all the customs of the Sages of the Gemara...since all

50   *Gittin* 59a.
51   *Bava Metzia* 86a.
52   See *Iggeret Sherira Gaon* (Kiryat Ne'emanah ed., Jer. 5727), p. 84, n. 29.
53   *Eruvin*, end. of chap. 10.
54   Introduction to *Mishneh Torah*. Cf. statement of R. Yosef ibn Migash (*Hiddu-shim* to *Bava Batra*), "Our Talmud (i.e. the Bavli) is accepted Halakhah, for it was written only after critical examination of many generations and many editions... it was written so that it be followed in actual practice."

Israel agreed to follow everything found in the Gemara. They are the Sages...who heard the tradition of all the Torah's principles, generation after generation, till Moshe Rabbenu."

Verily, we may paraphrase the Biblical affirmation and declare with reference to the Babylonian Talmud, "This is the Torah which the Sages of the Talmud put before the children of Israel." It remains for us to examine the essential features of Talmudic law as opposed to Mosaic law, how the former both expanded and limited the scope of the latter, and why.

6

A Hedge Around The Law

ושמרתם את משמרתי (ויקרא יח, ל): עשו משמרת למשמרתי
And you shall keep My charge (Lev. 18:30):
"Make a charge for My charge"*

D'oraita and D'Rabbanan

Twice Israel was enjoined by Moses not to add to nor subtract from the mitzvot of the Torah, as is written *You shall not add to that which I command you nor subtract from it* (Deut. 4:2; 13:1). Nevertheless, the masters of Jewish Law, in particular the Sages of the Talmud, did not hesitate to add new legislation to the corpus of Jewish Law. They interpreted the Biblical injunction quoted above to apply to each mitzvah in itself; i.e. not to add to a mitzvah a feature not prescribed for it by the Torah. Thus they learned from this injunction that it is forbidden to add to or subtract from the number of species (four) prescribed for the mitzvah of Lulav; or for the kohen to add his own blessing to those prescribed in the Torah in the mitzvah of *birkat kohanim* (Num. 6: 22–26).[1] Furthermore, it was not considered a violation of this injunction if the additional legislation was clearly denoted as Rabbinic and not Biblical in origin. Maimonides offers the following example: "It is written *You shall not seethe a kid in its mother's milk* (Exod. 23:19; 34:26; Deut. 14:21).[2] Now it was learned from an oral tradition that this prohibi-

---

*   *Yevamot* 21a

1   *Sifre* to Deut. 13:1. See the discussion in *Rosh Hashanah* 28b. and *Tosafot ad loc.*

2   See *Ḥullin* 115b for an expanation of the repetition three times.

tion includes flesh of both a domestic and an undomesticated animal, but does not include the flesh of fowl. If a Bet Din were to declare that the flsh of an undomesticated animal is permitted (to be seethed in milk), it is subtracting from the mitzvah. If it were to declare tht the flesh of an undomesticated animals is permitted (to be term "kid," it is adding. But if the Bet Din declares that the flesh of fowl is permitted by the Torah but we forbid it, and the people are told that this is an added restriction (*gezerah*) ...this is not adding to the mitzvah but making a fence around the Torah."[3]

The Halakhah did attempt to specify which Talmudic injunctions are Biblical (*min ha-Torah* or *d'oraita*) and thus have the force of Biblical legislation, and which are Rabbinic (*mid'rabbanan*) and possess only the force of Rabbinic legislation. There is ample reason to maintain this distinction, for it is vital for halakhic decision. When two opinions are expressed concerning a certain matter but there is no statement as to which is the Halakhah, then if a Mosaic law is involved we are obliged to follow the more stringent opinion, whereas if only a Rabbinic law is involved we follow the less stringent opinion.[4] Similarly, if a doubt exists as to the facts in a case, then if the case is governed by Mosaic law we assume that the law does apply, but if it is governed by Rabbinic law we assume that the law does not apply.[5]

There is much Talmudic legislation where authorities both early (*Rishonim*) and late (*Aharonim*) differ as to whether it is *min ha-Torah* or *mid'rabbanan*. Such a fundamental practice in Jewish life as daily prayer is in dispute. Maimonides maintains that the recital of one prayer a day is obligatory by Scriptural command; while Nahmanides maintains that any and all prayer is only a Rabbinic requirement.[6] A dispute whether the laws of Shemitta (the Sabbati-

3   *Hilkhot Mamrim* 2:9; see stricture of Ravd *ad loc.*
4   *Avodah Zarah* 7a.
5   *Niddah* 7a; *Pesaḥim* 10a; *Bava Batra* 66a. Cf. *Tohorot* 4:11.
6   Rambam, beg. of *Hilkhot Tefillah*, see *Kesef Mishnah ad loc.* See also *Tosafot Ḥagigah* 18a, different opinions concerning labor on Ḥol ha-Mo'ed. I have explained the different views of Maimonides and Nahmanides re the obligation to pray as stemming from their different views concerning sacrificial worship. Maimonides (see above p. 27) regards it as a mode of worhip inferior to prayer, and since the Torah commanded sacrificial worship it no doubt commanded worship through prayer. Nahmanides' attitude towards sacrificial worship was totally different; he saw it as a symbol of man's willingness to self-sacrifice (Ramban to Lev. 1:9), and hence superior to prayer. Nahmanides suggests that

cal year) nowadays, i.e. after the destruction of the Temple, are *d'oraita* or *d'rabbanan* arose among the Rishonim,[7] and is still a matter of controversy among the Aḥaronim of our own times.[8] Another dispute among medieval Rabbis which was resumed with added vigor after the establishment of the State of Israel concerns the question of *Aliyah*, i.e. Jews coming to settle in Eretz Yisrael. Is the mitzvah of *yishuv Eretz Yisrael* as indicated in the verse *You shall drive out the inhabitants of the land and settle in it, for I have given the land to you to possess it* (Num. 33:53)[9] applicable even today? Nahmanides says "Yes," but Maimonides does not include it in his *Sefer ha-Mitzvot*.[10]

The Benediction Recited Over Mitzvot D'Rabbanan

There are mitzvot which all agree are Rabbinic in origin — such as kindling lights on Sabbath eve and Hanukkah, or reading the Megillah on Purim — and yet the obligation to observe them is based upon Scriptural command. When observing them we recite the benediction "Who has sanctified us by His commandments and has commanded us etc." "Where have we thus been commanded?" asks the Talmud, and replies, "In the verse *You shall not depart from the instruction which they* (the judges, i.e. the Sages) *shall declare unto you* (Deut. 17:11).[11] This is not to imply, as Maimonides was careful to point out,[12] that therefore these mitzvot are subject to the

prayer for salvation in a time of distress may be a mitzvah *min ha-Torah*. For further discussion see H. Heller's ed. of *Sefer ha-Mitzvot* (Mossad Harav Kook, Jer. 5706), p. 5, n. 4.

7 Cf. *Tosafot Gittin* 36a, *s.v. bizman*, and Meiri *ad loc.* See also *Mo-ed Kattan* 2b.
8 See below, p. 235; also Z. Yaron, *Mishnato shel Harav Kook* (Jer. 5734), p. 14, n. 8.
9 See below, p. 234. I have translated *vehorashtem* "to drive out," following Targum and Rashi. J.P.S. translates "You shall take possession," following Ramban and Malbim. All would agree that "to drive out" applied only in the days of Joshua with reference to "the seven nations" and not to the present-day Palestinians.
10 Ramban *ad loc.* See *Megillat Esther*, commentary to *Sefer ha-Mitzvot*, for this and other differences between Rambam and Ramban.
11 *Shabbat* 23a. See also *Yevamot* 20a, "It is a mitzvah to heed the words of the Sages."
12 Introduction to *Sefer ha-Mitzvot*, 1st Principle.

same stringency as *mitzvot min ha-Torah*. They are Rabbinic in origin and remain subject to the rules governing *mitzvot d'Rabbanan*.

Reciting a benediction prior to performing a mitzvah is in itself a Rabbinic regulation,[13] another ritual obligation that has occasioned halakhic disputation to this very day. Women are exempt from certain *mitzvot min ha-Torah*;[14] nevertheless they have voluntarily accepted to observe many of them. The question arose, Are they permitted to recite the blessing over the mitzvah, or would they be taking the name of God in vain?[15] Generally speaking, the Ashkenazic authorities say "Yes," and the Sephardic authorities say "No."[16] Also in dispute is the reciting of a blessing over a practice which is not a statutory obligation but merely a matter of custom (*minhag*), such as reciting Hallel on Rosh Ḥodesh.[17] In such disputed matters we have no alternative but to follow the advice of the Sages, "Go out and see how the people conduct themselves."[18]

Rabbinic Legislation is divided into three main divisions: 1. *Gezerah*; 2. *Takkanah*; 3. *Minhag*.

Gezerah[19]

Gezerah is a restriction added by the Sages in order to safeguard the observance of Scriptural Law. "Make a hedge around the Torah," admonished the men of the Great Assembly,[20] and they found support for such added restrictions in Scripture itself. We read in *Avot d'R. Natan*, "What is the hedge which the Torah made about its words? Lo it says, *Do not approach a woman during her period of uncleanness etc.* (Lev. 18:19). May then her husband embrace her or

---

13 See *Pesaḥim* 7b. According to many authorities, the blessing recited before the study of Torah (*birkat ha-Torah*) is *d'oraita*; see *Megillat Esther, op. cit.*

14 Mishnah *Kiddushin* 1:7.

15 Cf. *Rosh Hashana* 33a and *Tosafot ad loc., s.v. ha* .

16 See E.G. Ellinson, *Ha-Ishah ve-Hamitzvot* (Jer. 5742), Vol. I, pp. 54 ff.

17 *Tosafot Berakhot* 14a *s.v. yamim*. Authorities differ whether reciting Hallel on Festival Days is *d'oraita* or *d'rabbanan*; see *Megillat Esther, op. cit.*

18 *Eruvin* 14b. Cf. *Pesaḥim* 66a, "Leave it to the Israelites; if they are not prophets they are the sons of prophets."

19 For an extensive treatment of *gezerah*, see *Encyclopedia Talmudit*, Vol. V, pp. 529 ff.

20 *Avot* 1:1.

kiss her?...No, for it says, *Do not approach*"[21] In addition to safe-guarding sexual morality, other significant restrictions (*gezerot*) were instituted to safeguard the observance of the laws of cleanness (*tum'ah ve-taharah*),[22] the laws of the Sabbath,[23] and the dietary laws, especially against the mixing of meat and milk.[24] These *gezerot* were considered so important as to even override a positive commandment of the Torah. Thus, for example, we do not sound the shofar on Rosh Hashanah when it occurs on a Sabbath lest it lead to an infraction of a Sabbath ordinance.[25] Another gezerah which has led to the cancellation of a Positive Precept of the Torah is the ban against attaching a blue thread of wool (*tekhelet*) as a fringe (*tzitzit*) to a linen garment.[26] The Sages invested their decrees

---

21 *Avot d'R. Natan* 2:1; cf. *Sifra ad loc.* Maimonides (*Hilkhot Issurei Bi'ah* 21:1) rules that embracing a woman forbidden by the Torah "through lust" is a Biblical offense for which one incurs the penalty of stripes. Ramban disagrees; see his strictures to *Sefer ha-Mitzvot*. See also discussion in *Shabbat* 13a.

22 *Shabbat* 13b ff. Cf. *Yoma* 23a that "they were more concerned about the cleanness of vessels than the spilling of blood."

23 These are called *shevut*; see Mishnah *Betzah* 5:2, Maimonides (*Hilkhot Shabbat* 21:1) seems to imply that they are Biblical restrictions, except that the Torah left it up to the Sages to decide which to adopt.

24 *Hullin* chap. 8. See especially *ibid.* 105a re the time that must elapse after eating meat before eating dairy. In this aspect customs vary from one to six hours.

25 *Rosh Hashanah* 29b. The same applies to the taking of the Lulav and the reading of the Megillah on a Sabbath. Only the Babylonian Talmud ascribes the non-performance of these mitzvot on Shabbat to this *gezerah*. J.T. allows the taking of the Lulav on Shabbat (the practice in Eretz Yisrael then); ascribes the non-performance of shofar to Scripture, and postpones the reading of the Megillah to Sunday so that it should not interfere with the Sabbath meal (J.T. *Megillah* 1:6, 70b). For other instances of non-performance of shofar because of *gezerot*, see Mishnah *Rosh Hashana* 4:8.

26 *Menahot* 40a–b. Incidentally, the ruling of the Sages that the dye for the blue thread must come only from a certain urchin called *hilazon* that arises from the sea only once in seventy years (*ibid.* 44a) has led to the obsolescence of the mitzvah of tekhelet. A century ago R. Yeruham Leiner (Hassidic rabbi of Radzin) wanted to revive the mitzvah, but the rabbinate did not accept it. The late Chief Rabbi Isaac Herzog also identified the *hilazon* and suggested that it can be employed once again for the making of tekhelet, but it is almost impossible today to revive something in Jewish life which has been dormant for centuries. See full discussion by M. Kasher in Leo Jung Jubilee Volume (N.Y. 1962), Hebrew section, pp. 241–258.

with such authority and force as to brand one who dare defy them as deserving of death.[27]

Not all the Sages regarded the adding of restrictions as an unmitigated blessing. *Avot d'R. Natan* already indicates how adding an unnecessary restriction can actually lead to the violation of the basic law, citing the example of Adam and Eve. God had told Adam not to *eat* of the tree of knowledge, but Adam said to Eve, *But of the fruit of the tree.... God said 'You shall not eat of it nor shall you touch it'* (Gen. 3:3).[28] From this incident the conclusion is derived that if a person puts a hedge about his words he won't be able to stand by them. Similarly, R. Yehoshua asserts that on the day Bet Shammai instituted by force eighteen *gezerot* they acted excessively.[29] In another context another Sage said, "Is it not enough for you what the Torah has forbidden, that you go and forbid yourself additional things!"[30]

Accordingly, the Sages did impose some restriction against the making of restrictions. "We do not decree a gezerah unless the majority of the community is able to stand it."[31] Nor do we add a restriction merely in order to buttress a previous restriction.[32] However, once a gezerah is adopted by the proper authorities and accepted and observed by Jewry at large, it can never be rescinded.[33] And to this categorical statement is joined another, "One Bet Din cannot annul the decree of another Bet Din unless it is greater in both wisdom and numbers;"[34] and the assumption is that every later court is inferior to an earlier one.[35]

---

27 *Eruvin* 21b; *Berakhot* 4b. Cf. *Tosefta Makkot* 4(3):17. Lashes for transgressing a Rabbinic ordinance are administered until the culprit relents or perishes.

28 Actually, this was said by Eve to the serpent, but *Avot d'R. Natan* 1:5 attributes the admonition not to touch to Adam, who wanted to make sure that they would not come to eat of the fruit.

29 *Shabbat* 153b. See the different interpretations of Rashi and Tosafot.

30 J.T. *Nedarim* 9:1 (41b), quoted by Maimonides in his Intro. to *Avot*.

31 *Avodah Zarah* 36a.

32 *Betzah* 3a. Additional references are noted there.

33 *Avodah Zarah* 36a.

34 *Ibid.* and *Eduyot* 1:4.

35 *Shabbat* 112b, "If the early ones are angels, we are human; if the early ones are human, we are like asses etc."

These statements and their application to gezerot mentioned in the Talmud are subject to a great deal of discussion and argument among both earlier and later halakhic authorities, and their elucidation is vital for much of the actual practice of Jewish Law in our day. Especially since many authorities rule that even if the reason which prompted the earlier Bet Din to adopt the gezerah no longer applies, the decree is not cancelled without a specific act of annulment by a later Bet Din,[36] an almost impossible contingency in view of the restraints mentioned above. If such is the case, argues Maimonides, then the gezerot of the Sages would be more severe than Torah Laws, which — if the existing situation warrants it — may be suspended temporarily by a Bet Din.[37]

Actually, the Sages themselves as well as later authorities found the key to unlock the gates of burdensome restriction. Thus, Rabban Gamaliel and his Bet Din cancelled the pre-Sabbatical-year restrictions imposed by Bet Shammai and Bet Hillel. When some Amoraim questioned this cancellation, it being contrary to the principle of non-cancellation mentioned above, the answer — given after a moment's hesitation — was that those who made the gezerah originally did so on condition that if a later authority sees fit to cancel it they may do so.[38] Another method of easing the burden of a gezerah was to limit the scope of its application. Thus Rava excluded a "noble person" from the gezerah against reading by the light of a lamp on Friday night since such a person does not adjust the light by himself even on a weekday.[39]

Post-Talmudic authorities recognized that many gezerot which applied to the situation existing when they were adopted were not meant to apply to a changed situation. They permitted, for example, reading by the light of a wax candle on Friday night, arguing that the reason for the gezerah against reading; i.e. adjusting the wick, does not apply to a wax taper.[40] Many restrictions imposed by

36   *Betzah* 5a–b.
37   *Hilkhot Mamrim* 2:4.
38   *Mo'ed Kattan* 3b.
39   *Shabbat* 12b and Rashi *ad loc*.
40   *Sh. A. Orah Hayyim*, sec. 275, *Mishnah B'rurah ad loc*. No recent authority has questioned the permissibility of reading by the light of an electric bulb; however a question was raised about a 3-way bulb, where one may be inclined to switch the bulb to a higher wattage.

the Talmud against dealing with non-Jews are not considered as applying to the Christian or Moslem of today — who cannot be placed in the same category of the heathen of old — in view of the compelling fact that we live amongst them and depend upon dealing with them for our livelihood.[41] Meiri maintains, though with some hesitation, that we cannot waive a restriction already in force only if the decreeing Bet Din felt that the circumstances prompting their decree would be permanent, but if the circumstance was one subject to change then as soon as it is changed the restriction becomes void without a special act on the part of a contemporary Bet Din.[42]

Many decrees were promulgated in Talmudic times banning food prepared by non-Jews lest it contain some prohibited ingredient; i.e. milk milked by a non-Jew without a Jew being present (to see that there is no admixture of milk from a non-kosher animal).[43] Later authorities limited this ban against non-Jewish milk (*halav akum*) "now that milk from non-kosher animals is not found amongst us;" and some would permit it entirely while others are adamant in insisting that once the Sages forbade it we cannot rescind their ban.[44] From the discussion in the Talmud,[45] it would seem that the gezerot against non-Jewish food were not made — as most gezerot are — in order to add a restriction to a Biblical law, but rather to make people aware of certain facts; namely the addition by non-Jews of non-kosher ingredients in their food. Hence, it is reasonable to assume that the intention was not to ban a product forever if it can be ascertained that it no longer contains a non-kosher element.[46]

---

41 *Tosafot Avodah Zarah* 2a, *s.v. assur* and 57b, *s.v. la'afukei*. See below 125. See also Meiri, *Bet ha-Behira, Bava Kamma*, chap. 4 (p. 122 in K. Schlesinger ed. Jer. 5721), who provides a different reason; see below p. 137.

42 *Bet ha-Behirah, Betzah* 5a; *Encyclopedia Talmudit*, Vol. VI, pp. 703–4.

43 Mishnah *Avodah Zarah* 2:3.

44 *Sh. A. Yoreh De-ah*, sec. 115, *Pri Ḥadash and Pitḥei Teshuvah ad loc.*

45 Case of *murayas, Avodah Zarah* 34b.

46 Remarkably enough, the gezerah against bread baked by a non-Jew (*pat akum*), a real restriction in order to forestall intermarriage ("they banned their bread lest they drink their wine, and they banned their wine lest they become involved with their daughters") was lifted because of the practical difficulties involved; *Avodah Zarah* 36b and *Sh. A. Yoreh De'ah* 112.

There are other gezerot of the Sages which — at least, to the mind of this author — were adopted when the circumstances were radically different from those of today, and it is reasonable to assume that the gezerot were not intended for the contemporary situation. For example, the Sages banned all therapeutic measures on Shabbat for a person whose ailment does not endanger his life, lest one grind the herbs used for the medication.[47] It is obvious that nowadays one does not prepare medications at home, and by no stretch of the imagination could the ingesting of medication lead to a labor prohibited on the Sabbath.

Some Middle Ages authorities (Rishonim) restrict the making of gezerot to the Rabbis of the Talmud, denying themselves the right to incorporate new restrictions in their halakhic rulings.[48] Nevertheless, there exist today in the corpus of Jewish Law many gezerot which arose after the close of the Talmud. Best known are the so-called *Ḥerem d'Rabbenu Gershom*, such as the ban against polygamy or divorcing a woman without her consent.[49] These latter-day restrictions, then, would be in the category of *takkanah* or *minhag*, where — as we shall see —local authorities of all times and places could exercise their authority almost without restraint. Thus the bans of Rabbenu Gershom were accepted only in Ashkenazic communities, but not amongst the Sephardim. Similarly, the gezerah against eating *kitniyot* (legumes, such as peas and beans) on Passover is observed only by Ashkenazim.[50] Furthermore, the adoption by a community of a more stringent ruling (*ḥumra*) where the Halakhah favors the lenient position is in the category of *minhag*, and its compelling force will be discussed under that rubric.

Takkanah

The mitzvot of the Torah were given to the people of Israel in the wilderness; but their essential purpose was to regulate both the civil and the religious life of the people in the commonwealth about to be

---

47 Mishnah *Shabbat* 14:3,4; 22:6. See I. Jakobovits, *Jewish Medical Ethics* (N.Y. 1959) chap. 6 for details.
48 *Encyclopedia Talmudit*, Vol. V, p. 540.
49 *Ibid.* VOl. XVII, Appendix.
50 See *Sefer Ma'adanei Shmuel* to the *Kitzur Shulḥan Arukh*, Sec. 117, subsec. 2:23.

established in the Promised Land.[51] However, no basic code of law can cover all contingencies; there has to be an instrument for the issuing of additional regulations for those aspects of society not covered by the basic code. Furthermore, history moves on, circumstances change, habits and customs evolve, and the need for new regulations for adjustment to these novel situations arises. These regulations are called *takkanot* (singular: *takkanah*). They are not added *mitzvot*, mitzvot are permanent; takkanot are for a given situation which may change in the course of time and create the need for new regulations superseding the old ones. Furthermore, mitzvot obligated the people as a whole; whereas the number of people made subject to takkanot varied according to the scope of authority exercised by the regulating authority. Thus, municipalities or labor guilds or merchant leagues are empowered by the Halakhah to adopt takkanot which become incumbent upon the respective members of these groups. Indeed, communal elders are obliged to regulate commercial practices, weights and measure, the collection and distribution of charity, and to adopt sanctions against those who defy their regulations.[52]

A brief review of some noteworthy takkanot adopted for *klal yisrael* (the entire people) in the course of its history, from the days of Moses to the close of the Talmudic period, will illustrate the many purposes for which they were instituted. Moses instituted (*tikken*) that lectures dealing with the laws of a Festival be given on the day of the Festival, "the halakhot of Passover on Passover, the halakhot of Shavuot on Shavuot, the halakhot of Sukkot on Sukkot."[53] Moses' successor Joshua decreed ten "conditions" for the new settlers in Eretz Yisrael, primarily in order to avoid clashes between public interest and individual property rights, thus attempting to establish a peaceful and productive society.[54] Based on the verse (Eccl. 12:9) *Kohelet was wise...he pondered and searched out, he set in order* (tikken) *many maxims*, the Sages ascribed to King Solomon several takkanot, among them the washing of hands before a meal (*netilat yadayim*).[55]

51   See Ramban to Deut. 4:5.
52   Mishnah *Bava Batra* 1:5, *ibid.* 8b, "Citizens of a town may make certain conditions regulating measures and prices and workmen's wages, and to punish violators."
53   *Megillah* 32a. See *Tzemihat Ge'ulateinu, op. cit.* pp. 235 ff.
54   *Bava Kamma* 80b–81a.
55   *Eruvin* 21b.

When the Temple built by King Solomon was destroyed (586 B.C.E.), the prophets of the time (Jeremiah and Ezekiel) instituted four fast days, commemorating the tragic events of the period.[56] Seventy years later, when Jews returned from the Babylonian Exile to resettle in Eretz Yisrael, the need for takkanot again arose, and Men of the Great Assembly and Ezra the Scribe rose to the occasion and instituted many takkanot, mainly in the field of religious ritual and prayer.[57] Several centuries later, when Hillel the Elder saw that people were refusing to extend loans to the poor because of the Biblical law of *Shemittah* which cancelled all loans after the Sabbatical year (Deut. 15:1–11), he instituted the use of the document (*prosbul*) which transferred the collection of loans to the court, thus making them collectible even after the year of Shemittah.[58]

A radical change in Jewish life took place a century after Hillel with the destruction of the second Temple (70 C.E.), and again it became necessary to institute many new regulations. Rabban Yoḥanan b. Zakkai, who saw to it that the Sanhedrin should be transferred to the town of Yavneh, was the initiator of many takkanot, some to transfer to the reconstituted Sanhedrin prerogatives of the Jerusalem Sanhedrin, and some for the people to continue to practice outside of Jerusalem certain ceremonies which hitherto were practiced only in the Bet ha-Mikdash.[59] A little later Rabban Gamaliel of Yavneh, and still later his son Rabban Shimon, found it necessary to institute many takkanot dealing with social and economic affairs, all of them for the purpose of *tikkun ha-olam*; i.e. the welfare of society.[60] Rabban Gamaliel also commissioned Shimon of Pekuliy to rearrange the Eighteen Benedictions (*Shemoneh Esreh*) to conform to the new post-Ḥurban situation, and Shmuel ha-Kattan offered to compose an additional benediction, against the sectarians (*minnim* and Zadokim, most probably the new Christians).[61] To this day, this is the central prayer of our liturgy. Some-

---

56 Zechariah 7:5; 8:19. See discussion in *Rosh Hashanah* 18b and *Tzemiḥat Ge'ulateinu*, pp. 20 ff.
57 See Lewittes, *Religious Foundations etc.*, pp. 58 ff, for details.
58 Mishnah *Gittin* 4:3, See Mishnah *Arakhin* 9:4 for another takkanah of Hillel.
59 Mishnah *Rosh Hashanah* 4:1–4.
60 Mishnah *Gittin*, chap. 4.
61 *Berakhot* 28b. Cf. *Tur Oraḥ Ḥayyim*, Sec. 188, "They instituted the version (of *birkat ha-mazon*) according to the good which had been added to Israel; for

what later, after the defeat of Bar Kochba and the transfer of the Sanhedrin to a new seat in Usha, new conditions made necessary the adoption of new regulations, primarily concerned with economic and domestic affairs.[62]

Some takkanot went through various stages of development, each bet din assessing the effectiveness of a previously made takkanah, and if they found that it is not achieving its purpose they would make a new takkanah. Thus we are informed of the developments in dowry agreements or *ketubah*, at each stage affording more protection to the woman in the event of the termination of a marriage either through divorce or demise of the husband.[63] A series of takkanot were made in order to provide for an orphaned daughter, and to ensure that she be married off in a befitting manner.[64]

The Penal Code as a Hedge

Most takkanot and gezerot were hedges set up by the Sages in order "to keep a person far from a transgression;" i.e. to insure that a person would not inadvertently lapse into committing a violation of a law of the Torah. Typical of these is the one described in the following Baraita: The Sages made a hedge about their words, so that a person should not come from (working in) the field in the evening and say, "I'll go home and have a bite and some drink and take a nap, and then I will recite the Shema and pray (the evening prayer)." Doing so, sleep will overcome him and he will sleep through the night (thus missing his prayers). Rather, a man coming from the field in the evening first enters the synagogue, studies a chapter, recites the Shema and prays, (then goes home and) eats his meal and recites the grace after meals.[65]

certainly they did not recite the same prayer before the conquest and building up of the Land as after, etc." Also *Bet Yosef*. Sec. 187, quoting Ramban, "Prayers are recited according to the times." Do we have to wait for the reestablishment of the Sanhedrin before the religious authorities of our day follow the example of their predecessors and adjust some of our prayers in the light of the establishment of the State of Israel!

62 See *Religious Foundations etc.* p. 100 for references.
63 *Ketubot* 82b and *Tosafot ad loc. s.v. Bithilah*. See *Tzemihat Ge'ulateinu*, p. 223.
64 Mishnah *Ketubot* 4:11 and Talmud *ibid*. 52b.
65 Mishnah *Berakhot* 1:1 and Talmud *ibid*. 4b.

101

What hedge, however, did the Sages make to insure a person should not deliberately violate a Biblical or Rabbinic injunction? The hedge of dire punishment. Thus R. Eliezer b. Yaakov (1st Century Tanna) reports, "I have heard that a Bet Din administers physical punishment (Rashi, "lashes and execution") not prescribed by the Torah... in order to make a hedge about the Torah. It happened in the days of the Greeks that someone who rode a horse on Shabbat was brought before the Bet Din and they stoned him; not that the law prescribed such a punishment, but the times required it. It also happened that a man who had intercourse with his wife under a fig tree (Rashi, "an exposed place") was brought before the Bet Din and they whipped him... the times required it."[66]

Incidentally, this statement of R. Eliezer b. Yaakov that a court may administer punishment not prescribed by the Torah is the halakhic sanction for the penal code adopted nowadays by the Knesset. When "the times require it" for the security of its citizens, the authorities are empowered to punish the violators of its code. Whether strict punishment, particularly capital punishment, is desirable or achieves its purpose as a deterrent, was already debated by the Tannaim as it still is today. R. Tarfon and R. Akiva contended that if they were in the Sanhedrin no one would ever be put to death; but R. Shimon b. Gamaliel countered, "If so, they would increase the number of murderers in Israel."[67] As far as whipping in order to force compliance with the law is concerned, a person who refused to observe a positive commandment of the Torah was to be whipped "until his soul departs from him."[68]

A further means of enforcing compliance with the law was the court's power to confiscate a delinquent person's property. This is the principle — first proclaimed by Ezra though in different language — of *hefker bet din hefker*; a court's decree that a person's property is no longer his gives to the court the right to assign his property to whomsoever or for whatever purpose it sees fit.[69] A favorite weapon employed by the Sages to enforce compliance with

---

66 *Sanhedrin* 46a. Riding an animal on Shabbat is not a Biblical restriction; see Mishnah *Betzah* 5:2.
67 Mishnah *Makkot* 1:10.
68 *Ḥullin* 132b. See also *Kiddushin* 81a, "A person is whipped for a bad report (of his conduct)."
69 Ezra 10:8; *Gittin* 36b.

a court order or to uphold the dignity of the Torah scholars was a form of excommunication, either *shamta* or *nidui*. Some considered this punishment to be more severe than whipping.[70] Another form of excommunication was called *ḥerem*, a powerful weapon of the Jewish community employed till modern times.[71] The Sages also did not hesitate to levy fines (*k'nas*) for infractions of its gezerot and takkanot.[72].

Minhag

Minhag is a customary practice which came about not as a result of a specific halakhic ruling or takkanah, but because of a spontaneous desire of the community to adopt a certain ritual. It was assumed that the ritual had probably been sanctioned by the Hakham of the community; and indeed only such customs that received such sanction were regarded as binding.[73] Minhag, however, does not have the same force as takkanah, and therefore no benediction is recited before its performance.[74] The Sages placed a great deal of confidence in popular practice, relying upon it when the Halakhah was in doubt. They said, "Leave it up to (the people of) Israel; if they are not prophets they are the sons of prophets."[75] Often the popular practice would determine the Halakhah when the Rabbis were undecided as to which opinion should prevail. Thus, when the

---

70 *Mo'ed Kattan* 17a.
71 See S.W. Baron, *The Jewish Community* (Phila. 5702), Vol. II, pp. 30 ff. and Vol. III, pp. 111–112; A.A. Neuman, *The Jews in Spain* (Phila. 5705), Vol. I, chap. 4.
72 The instances are numerous, scattered throughout the Talmud, Cf. J.T. *Avodah Zarah* 1:6 (39d), "Fines are levied for transgressing a minhag."
73 Cf. *Tosafot Pesaḥim* 51a, *s.v. Iy Atta*.
74 Rashi *Sukkah* 44a, *s.v. minhag*. See, however, *Tosafot ibid*. 44b, *s.v. kan* and *Ta'anit* 28b. *s.v. amar*. See also A.I. Kook, Responsa *Da'at Kohen*, no. 84.
75 *Pesaḥim* 66a.

Rabbis were asked whose opinion should be followed in a dispute concerning the benediction to be recited for drinking water, the answer was, "Go see what the people do."[76] The minhag of the people would even clarify a tradition which seemed to have been recorded incorrectly. Though the Mishnah stated that in the Saturday night Havdalah service one first recites the blessing over the candle and then over the spices, the custom was to first recite the blessing over the spices, and this became Halakhah.[77]

Minhag ha-Makom

More often, when the Talmud speaks of minhag, it refers to a local custom that is not observed universally. The Sages laid great stress upon the obligation to conform to local custom. They even found confirmation in Scripture for the popular saying, "When in Rome do as the Romans do." R. Tanḥum said, "A person should never differ from the local custom, for did not Moses refrain from eating when he ascended to heaven (whose inhabitants, the angels, do not eat), and did not the angels eat when they descended to earth (to visit Abraham)."[78] Many practices not required by Jewish Law arose in various localities, yet once accepted and followed in that locality they acquired the force of Halakhah obligating not only the citizens of that community but also visitors to the community. This ruling was made in order to avoid divisiveness and conflict. Thus the Halakhah provided that one may not engage in any labor the afternoon of Passover Eve, but in some communities they would not work even in the forenoon.[79] More often, in a matter under dispute, where one opinion would permit a certain practice and another opinion would forbid it, a community would accept the more stringent view even though the Halakhah did not declare it universally binding. There are recorded several reverse instances, where a stringent ruling was declared by most Rabbis to be binding but the local Rabbi favored the lenient ruling; in the latter's com-

---

76   *Berakhot* 45a.
77   *Ibid.* 52a.
78   *Bava Metzia* 86b; cf. *Bereshit Rabbah* 48:16.
79   Mishnah *Pesaḥim* 4:1.

munity the people continued to follow his ruling.[80] Thus there arose in the course of time differences in ritual and other observances between Palestinian and Babylonian Jewries, in Babylonia itself between the two Yeshivot, Sura and Pumbeditha, and later on between Ashkenazic and Sephardic Jewries.[81]

Jewish Law laid down the following rules regarding minhag: One is obliged to follow the stringencies of the place whence he came (if he left his home temporarily) and of the place to which he came. Furthermore, the force of minhag was such that it carried over from one generation to another; if the fathers had decided to observe a certain stringency then its practice devolved upon the children.[82] *Minhag ha-Makom* was a determinant in economic affairs; local custom fixed the terms of employment as far as hours of work and fringe benefits were concerned.[83] This latter ruling moved R. Hoshiah to make an oft-quoted, though often misunderstood, statement that "minhag cancels Halakhah." What R. Hoshiah meant, as explained by R. Ami in the Jerusalem Talmud, was that an employee who makes a claim against his employer for more money than the local customary arrangements provide, must bring witnesses that his employer agreed beforehand to such favorable conditions.[84]

By its very nature, minhag is restricted to its locale; one is not justified in performing in his town a ritual which is customary only in another town.[85] However, one is cautioned not to advise a

---

80   *Yevamot* 14a.
81   Differences between Eretz Yisrael and Babylonia, already recorded in the Geonic period, were published by M. Margaliot, Jer. 1938, and B.M. Levin, Jer. 1942. Between Sura and Pumbeditha, see S. Assaf, *Tekufat ha-Geonim*, pp. 261 ff. Differences between Ashkenazim and Sephardim, are largely recorded in the Shulḥan Arukh.
82   *Pesaḥim* 50b; *Betzah* 4b. In the Epilogue I discuss the advisability of retaining this ruling even in the face of radically changed circumstances.
83   Mishnah *Bava Metzia* 7:1.
84   J.T. *ibid*. (11b). We find this expression once more, in J.T. *Yevamot* 12:1 (12c) with reference to the ceremony of Halitzah. There it means that once *minhag* has established the Halakhah, a teacher cannot come subsequently and declare the Halakhah to be contrary to the minhag. One cannot use this expression as a sweeping principle of the Halakhah, as does Prof. E.E. Urbach in his recent work on the Halakhah, p. 31.
85   *Bava Batra* 100b. Cf. *Megillah* 22b, conduct of Rav.

community to abandon a certain minhag on the grounds that it is not required by the Halakha.[86] If, however, an individual or a community adopted a certain practice because they were under the mistaken impression that it is required by the Halakhah, they may be relieved of the obligation to continue that practice upon the advice of a scholar. Not every minhag acquires the approval and sanction of the Halakhah; if it is a "foolish" minhag a scholar may allow the disciples to ignore it.[87]

Zedakah and Mishpat : Righteousness and Justice

The twin pillars of Biblical Judaism, spanning its history from beginning to end, are Zedakah and Mishpat. Of the first Jew, Abraham, God said, *For I have singled him out that he may instruct his children and his posterity to keep the way of the Lord by doing Zedakah and Mishpat* (Gen. 18:19). The prophet Isaiah, foretelling the future Redemption of Israel, says, *Zion shall be redeemed by Mishpat and her returnees by Zedakah* (1:27). Corresponding to these two terms, illuminating for us the distinction between them, are two other terms, *Emet*-Truth and *Hesed*-Kindness. God reveals Himself as *abundant in Hesed and Emet* (Exod. 34:6), and the Psalmist, combining all attributes, praises Him by saying, *Zedek and Mishpat are the base of Your throne; Hesed and Emet stand in Your presence* (89:15). Upon these pillars of justice and truth, righteousness and kindness, the Sages of the Talmud built their system of jurisprudence.

A substantial part of Halakhah is concerned with the adjudication of litigation between two parties in civil matters. The underlying principle of such Halakhah is Mishpat and Emet, i.e. justice based upon the law of the Torah, which is a *Torat Emet*, and its impartial and unprejudiced application without regard to the parties involved, as is said, *You shall not do unrighteousness in judgment; do not favor the poor or show deference to the rich; judge your neighbor justly* (Lev. 19:15). From this last phrase our Sages deduced that it is forbidden to have one of the contestants stand

---

86   *Pesaḥim* 50b–51a.
87   *Tosafot ad loc. s.v. Iy Atta.*

while the other one sits; or to allow one to speak as much as he wants and tell the other to be brief.[88]

On the other hand, the Sages realized that on occasion strict adherence to the law (*Din*) may result in undue hardship to one of the parties, and therefore they provided that the judge may, with the consent of the parties involved, decide the case not on the basis of the rigid dictate of the law but by a *pesharah*, a sort of compromise which takes into account the situation of the parties.[89] Since the parties agree to such arbitration, the Rabbis felt that any judgment rendered will be readily accepted by the parties and they will resolve their differences peacefully. It is interesting to note that the Sages found this flexible approach to the Law in the term Zedakah — usually translated "righteousness" — as opposed to Mishpat or Din. Zedakah is thus that part of righteousness which takes into account a person's need for special consideration because of his difficult situation, and hence the ordinary use of this term to denote charity and almsgiving. In such an arrangement the Sages saw the fulfillment of the prophetic exhortation, *Truth and a judgment of peace shall you judge in your gates* (Zech. 8:16).[90]

In order to further facilitate the adjudication of disputes the Sages made certain takkanot. For example, they provided that a tribunal can be composed by having each party appoint one of the judges, someone who he felt will listen sympathetically to his complaint, and the two judges thus appointed agree upon the third member of the tribunal.[91] The parties were even allowed to appoint a relative as one of the judges if the contesting party agreed.[92] Nor were witnesses in civil cases subjected to the same thorough examination as required in criminal cases.[93]

---

88 *Shevuot* 30a.
89 *Sanhedrin* 6a–b.
90 *Ibid.*; cf. *Avot* 1:18.
91 Mishnah *Sanhedrin* 3:1. This procedure is known as *Zabla*, the acrostic for "this (party) selecting one (arbitrator)." *Rosh ad loc.* is quick to point out that this does not mean — as erring individuals understood it — that in such case each judge would arbitrarily favor in judgment the party who selected him without regard to the law. Rather, the selectee is better able to understand his party's case and thus present it more clearly to the other judges. Ultimately, however, it is the law which decides.
92 *Ibid.* 3:2.
93 *Sanhedrin* 32a.

Ha-Yashar ve-ha-Tov : The Right and the Good

The Scriptural basis for *pesharah* or arbitration is also seen in the verse *Do what is right and good in the eyes of the Lord* (Deut. 6:18).[94] Another Talmudic principle based upon this verse is called *lifnim mishurat ha-din*; i.e. doing more than the Law requires. If, for example, you find something that belonged to a person who had given up hope of recovering it, though the law says that you may keep it; a moral imperative calls upon you to do *lifnim mishurat ha-din* and return it to its erstwhile owner.[95] Another example of this principle was given above (p. 5) in the case of the poor porters. An extension of this principle is found in the law of *bar metzra*, the adjoining property owner. If someone wishes to sell his field and there are two persons willing to buy it at the asking price, one who already owns an adjacent field and another who does not, it must be sold to the neighboring owner.[96] The Sages also ruled that where another can benefit from the use of our property at no cost to us, we are compelled to allow him to benefit.[97]

In the same spirit of good neighborly relations, the Sages laid down many rules *mipnei darkhei shalom*, for the sake of promoting peace. In order to avoid contention, they regulated, among other similar instances, the order in which people are to be called up for the Torah-reading, and ruled that the farmer whose cistern is nearest to the irrigation channel fills his cistern first.[98] This principle of *darkhei shalom* was extended to include our non-Jewish neighbors; and therefore non-Jewish poor are supported together with Jewish poor; we greet our non-Jewish neighbors, visit their sick and bury their dead.[99] Furthermore, regulations were designed *mishum eivah*, to prevent disharmony and resentment in family relations.[100] In general, he is praiseworthy "who speaks gently to all creatures."[101]

---

94 Rashi *ad loc*. See the discussion on this verse by N. Leibovitch *Studies in Devarim*, Jer. 5744.
95 *Bava Metzia* 24b.
96 *Ibid*, 108a–b; cf. Rambam *Hilkhot Shekhenim* 12:5.
97 *Bava Kamma* 21a.
98 Mishnah *Gittin* 5:8; *ibid*. 60a.
99 *Ibid*. 61a.
100 *Ketubot* 47a, 58b; J.T. *Yoma* 8:1 (44d).
101 *Yoma* 86a.

In the verse *that you do the good and the right in the eyes of the Lord your God* (Deut. 12:28), the Sages saw the obligation to respect the opinion of one's fellowman, as the *Sifre*[102] explains, "*The good* in the eyes of Heaven, and *the right* in the eyes of man." Thus Rabbi (Yehudah ha-Nasi) advises in Ethics of the Father,[103] "Which is the right path that a man should choose for himself? That which is honorable both in his estimation and in the estimation of mankind." [104]

Talmud Torah k'neged Kulam : The Study of the Torah above all Else

We began this chapter with the Rabbinic exhortation to make a hedge about the Torah, to safeguard its charge. The strongest and most effective hedge is the constant study of the Torah, study that leads to practice. It says, *Hear O Israel the statutes and the judgments which I proclaim to you this day. Study them and keep to do them* (Deut. 5:1); and wherever it says *You shall keep the mitzvot* (*ibid.* 5:29, 11:22; 12:28) *keep* refers to study of the Law.[105] One of the most interesting discussions ever held by the Sages is reported as follows: R. Tarfon and the Elders were gathered in the upper-story of the house of Nitzeh in Lod, and this question was put before them, "Is study greater, or is practice greater?" R. Tarfon said, "Practice is greater;" R. Akiva said, "Study is greater." Then they all responded, "Study is greater because it leads to practice."[106]

There is no nation on the face of the earth that has urged study of the Law as the Israelite nation. "As soon as a child learns to talk, his father teaches him Torah."[107] Maimonides reflects Talmudic tradition when he states in his Code, "Every man in Israel is duty-bound to study Torah, the poor and the rich, the healthy and the sick, the young and the old weakened by age...Till when is one duty-bound to study Torah, till the day of his death."[108] This is no mere rhetoric.

102 Quoted by Rashi *ad loc.*
103 *Avot* 2:1.
104 I.e. it satisfies his own conscience.
105 *Sifre ad loc.*
106 *Kiddushin* 40b.
107 *Sukkah* 42a.
108 *Hilkhot Talmud Torah* 1:8, 10.

The Jewish people were the first to set up a system of universal education.[109] No other people until most recent times could boast of the absence of illiteracy and general ignorance of the law as could the people of the Torah, who strove to fulfill the prophetic ideal, *And all thy children shall be taught of the Lord* (Isaiah 54:13). The distance of time did perhaps lend some enchantment to the Sages of the Talmud when they asserted that in the days of King Hezekiah "a survey was made throughout the length and breadth of Eretz Yisrael and a single ignoramus was not to be found; neither any boy or girl, man or woman, who was not familiar with the (complicated) laws of cleanness and uncleanness."[110] Nor was Josephus exaggerating overmuch when he asserted that "should anyone of our nation be questioned about the laws, he would repeat them all more rapidly than his own name."[111]

This universal devotion to Torah-study has preserved Israel's devotion to Torah-practice throughout the generations; verily the Torah is *our life and the length of our days* (Deut. 30:20). It remains for us to examine in the following chapters how this was accomplished in the days following the period of the Talmud.

---

109 See *Bava Batra* 21a, and N. Drazin, *History of Jewish Education*, Baltimore 1940, esp. chap. 3.
110 *Sanhedrin* 84b.
111 *Against Apion*, Book II, Sec. 18.

7

From Geonim to Rishonim

שאל אביך ויגדך, זקניך ויאמרו לך (דברים לב, ז)
Ask your father and he will tell you;
your elders and they will inform you (Deut. 32:7)*

She'eilot u'Teshuvot : Questions and Answers

Moses, in charging newly-appointed judges, concluded his charge
with these words, *And any matter that is too difficult for you, you
shall bring to me and I will hear it* (Deut. 1:17). Herein lies the
precedent for that important phenomenon in the history of the
Halakhah known as *She'ilot u'Teshuvot*, "Questions and Answers,"
comprising the contents of that vast literature spanning millenia,
the Responsa. Why and how did this phenomenon develop.

We have spoken above of the universality of Torah-education for
every Jewish child, whereby he would become familiar with his
religious responsibilities, especially as regards the observance of the
mitzvot of the Torah. This in addition to his being reared in a
Torah-observant environment, and his being inducted, while still a
minor and statutorily exempt from all mitzvah observance, into
their actual practice by virtue of the obligation of his father to train
him for his role as a practicing Jew.[1] However, the Halakhah which
determines so much of Jewish practice is too all-encompassing, and
much too complex and detailed — especially as it was developed
and expanded by the teachings of the Tannaim and Amoraim — for

---

*   Cf. *Shabbat* 23a.
1   This is the obligation of ḥinukh; see *Sukkah* 42a, and *Encyclopedia Talmudit*,
      Vol. XVI, for details.

even an adult to familiarize himself with it in all its entirety. Not every child possessed the intellectual capacity or strong desire to continue his formal education throughout his adolescent years. The vast majority of Jewish children were taught on the elementary level alone, the sole text being Scripture, with the teacher supplying the interpretation of the text according to the Oral Law. Approximately ten percent continued their studies throughout their early adolescence, concentrating on the teachings of the Tannaim whose opinions are recorded in the Mishnah and the halakhic midrashim.[2] Those who aspired to attain a degree, to be ordained as a *hakham* or rabbi[3] and receive the authority to decide questions of Jewish Law, would sit at the feet of the great scholars, members of the Sanhedrin or heads of the Academies (Yeshivot or Metivtot), and join in their discussions.[4] This pattern of study led to a three-fold division in Jewish life as far as learning is concerned: *ba'alei Mikra, ba'alei Mishnah, and ba'alei Gemara*[5]. Mikra[6] is the designation by the Rabbis of the Talmud for the three components of Scripture: the Pentateuch, the Prophets, and the Writings; *Tanakh* for short (Mishnah and Gemara have been described in a previous chapter). The Sages cautioned against deriving an halakhic directive from the Mishnah alone; only the ba'alei Gemara who attained the status of a hakham were considered competent to determine the halakhah in each particular case.[7]

Thus it was to the hakham of his community that a Jew would turn, not only when he was involved in litigation with his fellow Jew and required a judge to settle his dispute, but more often when he sought an opinion in ritual matters. Even for the average Jew who knew Scripture with its rabbinic commentaries and was familiar with ordinary religious practice and requirements, it was a commonplace occurrence to ask a *she'ilah* of his rabbi. The response to his query, the *teshuvah*, constituted a *pesak halakhah*, a binding

---

2   *Avot* 5:21; *Kohelet Rabbah* 7:49.
3   *I.e. Semikhah*; see above p. 58.
4   Mishnah *Sanhedrin* 4:4.
5   *Bava Metzia* 33a–b; cf. *Sotah* 44a, commentary to Prov. 24:27.
6   Literally, "Reading", probably because quotations from Scripture had to be read from the scroll, and not orally; cf. *Gittin* 60b.
7   *Niddah* 7b and *Bava Batra* 130b; cf. commentaries *ad loc.* who explain the word "Talmud" as referring to Mishnah and Baraita.

decision. In fact, once having received a decision from one rabbi, a person was not permitted to solicit an opinion from another rabbi.[8] Rabbis themselves were admonished not to reverse an opinion already expressed by a colleague;[9] and were advised against setting themselves up as halakhic authorities in their own teacher's community or where a hakham of equal eminence had already established himself.[10] Though students who had not yet received the authority to decide questions of Jewish Law were cautioned against arrogating themselves to a position of authority, those who did receive the authority were urged to exercise it and overcome any inhibition because of an exaggerated sense of modesty.[11]

Questioning was by no means confined to the layman. Because of the diverse opinions recorded in the Talmud, or because of novel situations not mentioned specifically in the halakhic sources, the hakham himself was often faced with the need to consult a more learned colleague, or one whose position as head of an Academy or whose reputation for scholarship and piety gave his response greater weight. When the greater authority resided in another city, questions could be transmitted either orally by colleagues traveling from the one city to the other or by submission in writing. For almost a century after the founding of the Academies in Babylonia, the superior authority of the Palestinian teachers was recognized, and there was a steady flow of both scholars and correspondence between the two centers of Jewish life, the questions coming from Babylonia and the answers from Eretz Yisrael. Thus, Shmuel of Pumbeditha sent loads of questions in Jewish Law to R. Yoḥanan in Tiberias,[12] or, in a later period, we find Abbaye saying to Rav Safra, "When you go to Eretz Yisrael, ask them how they prepare the liver."[13] Many Babylonian scholars who went to study in Palestine, particularly under R. Yoḥanan, would send to their colleagues back home the rulings and practices they found in Eretz Yisrael.[14]

The superiority of the teachers in Eretz Yisrael lasted for about two generations after R. Yoḥanan (3rd cent.). In fact, in Eretz

---

8 *Avodah Zarah* 7a; see *Tosafot ad loc. s.v. hanishal.*
9 *Ibid., Ḥullin* 44b.
10 *Berakhot* 63a; *Eruvin* 62b, 63a.
11 *Sotah* 22a.
12 *Ḥullin* 95b.
13 *Ibid.,* 110b. The question was if the liver may be boiled even though it is bloody.
14 E.g. *Rosh Hashanah* 20b; *Mo'ed Kattan* 18a.

Yisrael they looked with disdain upon the scholars coming from Babylonia, even referring to them as *tipsha'i*, fools,[15] but the situation changed in the first half of the 4th Century with the decline of the Yeshivot in Eretz Yisrael. Thus, to the comment of Abbaye that "one scholar in Eretz Yisrael is smarter than two of us" his colleague Rava countered, "But one of us when he goes to Eretz Yisrael is smarter than two of them."[16] Indeed, it was due to the eminence of Rava as the head of the Yeshiva he founded in his home town Maḥoza that now Babylonia was taking the place of Eretz Yisrael as the halakhic authority because of the well-organized structure of the community there, headed by an official recognized by the Persian government, the *Resh Galuta*, the Chief of the Exile.

The Geonim

It should be noted that she'eilot were addressed to great scholars not only because of their personal reputation as such, but primarily because of their position as heads of Yeshivot. The institutional authority which had resided in the Sanhedrin in the days of the Tannaim was now transferred to the Roshei yeshivot — *Metivtot* in Aramaic — so that an halakhic responsum from a Resh Metivta carried with it the institution's seal of authority.[17] Though the Babylonian Talmud received its final editing in the generation following R. Ashi and Rabina,[18] and these scholars were declared to be "the end of instruction," the chain of halakhic authority was not broken as the Yeshivot in Babylonia continued to flourish. The heads of these Academies were now given the title *Gaon*,[19] perhaps to mark the transition from the Talmudic to the post-Talmudic era

15   *Yoma* 57a.
16   *Ketubot* 75a.
17   Cf. statement of Rav Sherira Gaon (*Likutim l'Iggeret R.Sh.G.*, p. xxviii). "The Yeshiva is in place of the Sanhedrin, and its head is in place of Moshe Rabbenu." See also S.K. Mirsky, *Bein Shekiah Lizriḥah* (N.Y. 1951), Chap. 1.
18   See above, p. 88.
19   For the meaning of this title, see *Arukh Completum*, ed. Kohut, *s.v. gaon*. Meiri (Intro. to *Bet ha-Beḥirah Avot*) advances the opinion that the title was conferred upon scholars versed in 60 tractates of the Talmud, 60 being the numerical value of the word *gaon*. Regrettably, the value of this title has been cheapened in recent times by its indiscriminate use.

and to retain the authority exercised by their predecessors. The Babylonian Academies continued to flourish — with some closings of short duration — for some 500 years, into the 11th Century, and therefore this period is designated in the history of the Halakhah as the period of the Geonim.

Teshuvot ha-Geonim

It was during the earlier half of this period that the rise of Islam took place. The followers of Mohammed swept from the Arabian desert all through the Middle East, conquering all of North Africa and crossing over into Spain. Jews were swept along with this movement, establishing new communities in these lands and adopting Arabic as their household language. Uncertain as to the religious practices which should be instituted in these new settlements, and no longer conversant with the Aramaic of the Talmud, the leaders of these communities addressed their questions to the Geonim, inquiring after the exact manner in which to perform a ritual, or the exact text of a prayer, or the precise meaning of a Talmudic statement. In fact, the very first *siddur* (Prayer Book), *Seder Rav Amram Gaon*, was a teshuvah to an inquiry from the community in Barcelona, Spain. But it was not only to the communities in Islamic lands, with which the Gaonate maintained frequent contact, that these teshuvot were addressed. Even the relatively new settlements in the Rhine region — the founding fathers of Ashkenazic Jewry — also relied upon Gaonic teachings for halakhic instruction.[20]

An interesting description of how many of these teshuvot were composed we find in the words of R. Natan ha-Bavli: "Every day during the month of Adar the Gaon would produce for the scholars (gathered for the *Kallah*)[21] all the questions addressed to him. He would give permission for them to respond. Each one would speak according to his opinion and wisdom, raising and answering questions, arguing pro and con, while the Rosh Yeshiva would listen... After weighing their words until he arrived at the truth, he would order the scribe to write the responsum. This was their custom every

20 See A. Grossman, *Ḥakhmei Ashkenaz ha-Rishonim* (Jer. 5741), p. 19.
21 For an explanation of this word, see Y.N. Epstein, *Meḥkarim b'Sifrut ha'Talmud* (Jer. 5744), pp. 128–129.

day until they would write an answer to all the questions that had been received during the year from the communities in Israel. At the end of the month they would read the questions and answers in the presence of the entire gathering; the Rosh Yeshiva would sign them, and then they were sent to the respective questioners."[22] These teshuvot are distinguished by their terseness; the Geonim responded directly and to the point, invariably stating that "this is the practice or custom of our Metivta," and occasionally adding, "As they have shown us from heaven."[23]

In the course of the centuries these teshuvot must have numbered in the thousands, and frequent reference is made to them by the *Rishonim*, the halakhic authorities of the period succeeding that of the Geonim. With the passage of time, with the decimation and dispersal of so many communities due to persecution by both Moslem and Christian rulers, the bulk of these teshuvot in their original form were lost to halakhic scholars until recent times. The expedition by the late Solomon Schechter to the Genizah in Cairo,[24] a repository of nigh one hundred thousand fragments of Hebrew manuscripts mainly from the early Middle Ages, led to the discovery of many hundreds of these teshuvot, grist for the painstaking scholarship of many savants engrossed in ancient and medieval Jewish literature. As a result, many restorations of these teshuvot, together with scholarly annotations, have been edited and published. Prominent among the early scholars — and the research of Geonic material is an ongoing process — are Jacob Mann,[25] B.M. Levin, who arranged and edited the teshuvot according to the tractates of the Talmud (Otzar ha-Geonim),[26] Professors S. Assaf[27] and Y.N. Epstein[28] of the Hebrew University and Professor Levi Ginzberg of the Jewish Theological Seminary.[29]

22 Quoted by S. Assaf, *Tekufat ha-Geonim* (Jer. 5715), p. 214.
23 For the significance of this phrase, see I. Twersky, *Rabad of Posquieres* (Phila, 5740) pp. 293–4.
24 S. Schechter, *Studies in Judaism*, Second Series (Phila. 1908), "A Hoard of Hebrew Manuscripts," esp. p. 28.
25 Responsa of the Babylonian Geonim as a source of Jewish History.
26 For a negative reaction on the part of an eminent Rabbinic authority to this work, and his attitude to modern halakhic research in general, see Z.A. Yehuda in *Tradition*, Vol. 18, No. 2 (Summer 1980).
27 S. Assaf, *op. cit.*
28 *Mehkarim etc. op. cit.*
29 Geonica. See also essay on Palestinian Talmud in *On Jewish Law and Lore*, (J.P.S. Phila. 1955), pp. 3–57.

Piskei Halakhot : Halakhic Digests

Teshuvot are not the only literary heritage of the Geonim. The all-encompassing character of Jewish Law, directing one's daily activity from rising to retiring, made necessary another genre of halakhic literature for the Jews living in the new far-flung settlements, a concise and systematic arrangement of the Halakhah to serve as a handy reference for the observant layman. The first of these halakhic digests in the *Halakhot Pesukot* of Rav Yehudai Gaon (middle of the 8th Century). Despite his blindness, he was able to dictate to his students briefly stated rulings of the Talmud confirmed as Halakhah by his teachers. He was opposed to innovation, and therefore ruled against the introduction of prayers and benedictions not mentioned in the Talmud. Not much later, Rav Shimon Gaon Kiara[30] basing himself on the *Halakhot Pesukot*, composed a larger digest called *Halakhot Gedolot*, which became widely circulated and frequently cited by the Rishonim as absolutely reliable. Not everybody was happy with these digests. Rav Paltoi Gaon, for example, when asked what is preferable, studying the Talmud or these abridged (*ketuot*) halakhot, replied, "It is not right (to study these piskei halakhot), for it is a diminution of Torah." We shall see later how the various Codes of Jewish Law met with even stronger opposition, but to no avail.

Several decades prior to the appearance of *Halakhot Pesukot* apeared the *She'iltot* of Rav Aha[30a] of Shivha, a compilation of sermons delivered at Sabbath morning services and dealing with the mitzvot mentioned in the weekly Torah-reading. Thus the first She'ilta, spoken on Shabbat Bereishit, begins: "That the House of Israel is obligated to rest on the Sabbath day, for when the Holy One, blessed be He, created His world He did so on six days and rested on the Sabbath day... and it is forbidden to fast on it. Rather, an Israelite has to enjoy it with eating and drinking." And it goes on to quote from the Talmud what may and may not be done on the Sabbath, weaving into the sermon many aggadic tales and statements concerning the importance and beauty of the Sabbath. According to one modern scholar who published a critical edition

---

30 For the meaning of *Kiara*, see S. Assaf, *op. cit.* p. 69.
30a Some call him *Ahai*.

of the *She'iltot*, some of these sermons were originally delivered in the days of the Talmud.[31]

Two centuries later there appeared upon the horizon of Jewish life a great luminary who not only composed *piskei halkhot,* but practically all other types of rabbinic literature.[32] He is none other than Rabbenu Saadia Gaon (882-942). He wrote a *Siddur*, and we must bear in mind that a Siddur contained not only the text of the prayers, but also *hilkhot tefillah*, the laws concerning prayer. Saadia's Siddur, as well as that of Rav Amram Gaon mentioned above, served the Rishonim as an important source book for their own digests of Halakhah. His piskei halakhot were in the form of separate treatises, each dealing with the laws of a specific subject; such as the Book of Legal Documents (*Sh'tarot*), of Inheritance, of Dietary Laws, etc. His best-known work is his *Emunot ve-De'ot*, the Book of Beliefs and Opinions, a seminal opus on Jewish Philosophy. Though not specifically halakhic in character, we have already indicated above[33] that Jewish philosophy — particularly its theology — is the underpinning of the Halakhah. Halakhic in character, and very significant for the preservation of the Halakhah as the norm in Jewish life, are Saadia's writings against the Karaites, who like the Sadducees of Second Temple days, denied the authenticity of the Oral Law as taught by the Sages.

The review of Saadia's literary legacy includes an item which is an outstanding example of how discoveries of musty fragments from the Genizah can resurrect an event which had long been obliterated from the memory of our people. This is by now the well-known controversy between Saadia and a Palestinian teacher by the name of Ben Meir. The latter had presumed to rule in a matter concerning all Israel by virtue of his being the head of a Yeshiva in Eretz Yisrael and a descendant of the patriarchal House of Hillel. The controversy revolved around the fixing of the day Rosh Hashanah of the year 4684 (923 C.E.) was to fall. It was more than this one halakhic question that was involved; it was the more general question of

---

31 S.K. Mirsky. Four volumes published by Sura, Yeshiva University, with the cooperation of Mossad Harav Kook. Rav Aḥa in later life left Babylonia for Eretz Yisrael, and modern scholars are divided as to where the She'iltot were written; see Y.N. Epstein, *op. cit.* pp. 85–86.

32 See H. Malter, *Saadia Gaon* (Phila. 5702).

33 See above, p. 3.

whose halakhic authority was to prevail, that of the Babylonian Gaonate which had held full sway for centuries, or that of a scholar from Eretz Yisrael where religious hegemony had long been surrendered. Saadia's superior skill in halakhic dispute won the day for the Babylonian point of view and its acceptance by all Jewish communities, and the attempt by Ben Meir to act independently was thwarted.[34]

The Last of the Geonim

About sixty years after Saadia, Shmuel ben Hofni, scion of the Geonim from Pumbedita, was appointed head of the Academy in Sura, thus acquiring the title Gaon. Like his illustrious predecessor, he was a prolific writer in all branches of Rabbinic literature, but unfortunately most of his writings have been lost.[35] His son-in-law, Hai ben Sherira, acceded to the Gaonate in Pumbedita shortly before the year 1000, a year which — as we shall see — marks a turning point in the history of the Halakhah. Hai Gaon, due to his commanding personality and erudition, raised the prestige and influence of the Gaonate before it gave way to the vicissitudes of history. From all points she'ilot were addressed to Hai, and his teshuvot numbered in the thousands. Students flocked to his Yeshiva from the various countries of the Diaspora, and then brought back his teachings to the respective communities. Following the style of Saadia, he composed separate halakhic treatises for specific subjects, most prominent among them his *Sefer Mekah u'Memkar*, the Book of Buying and Selling.

The halakhic legacy of the Geonim includes many other works that have been lost to posterity; their existence is known because they are quoted by the Rishonim, and from these quotations scholars have been able to restore some of them.[36] One that deserves mention since it is published in many editions of the Talmud,[37] is called *Shimusha Rabba* and deals with laws concerning Tefillin. It is a source of significant rulings carried out to this day.

34   See H. Malter, *op. cit.* for details of the controversy.
35   See A. Greenbaum, *Pirush ha-Torah l'R. Shmuel b. Hofni*, (Jer. 5739).
36   E.g. *Basar al gabei Gehalim*; see Y.N. Epstein, *op. cit.* p. 274.
37   Appendix to Hilkhot Tefillin of Rabbenu Asher (Rosh) in Tractate *Menahot*. See S. Assaf, *op. cit.* p. 209, for explanation of name.

Takkanot Ha-Geonim

As the halakhic heirs of the Amoraim, the Geonim did not hesitate to exercise their authority to institute new regulations to comply with the needs of the times, primarily in economic and domestic affairs.[38] One of the perennial and vexing problems Rabbis have to deal with — and our times are no exception — is that of the woman who petitions the court for a divorce. The Mishnah already speaks of an earlier ruling and a later one,[39] and the Talmud discusses the case of the reluctant or rebellious wife (*moredet*) from various angles.[40] Whereas the Talmud prescribed a wait of twelve months before compelling the husband to divorce his wife, the Geonim decided that she should be divorced right away. Whereas in the days of the Talmud a woman would collect her dower rights (*ketubah*) only from real property, the Geonim instituted — due to a shift from a mainly agricultural economy — that she can collect from portable goods as well. Though the Talmud ruled that judges who did not possess the authentic semikhah could not impose fines (*k'nas*), the Geonim ruled that they could enforce payment for bodily damages and rape. These and other takkanot became the rule for later authorities in most cases. Jewish life in Babylonia during the period of the Geonim was conducted almost on an imperial scale, with pomp and circumstance, and thus its hegemony was accepted for nigh five centuries far beyond its borders.[41]

We must now proceed to examine how the halakhic heirs of the Geonim, Rishonim, preserved this legacy of religious authority and assured the continued dominant rule of the Halakhah in the communities of the Dispersion.

38   H. Tikuchinsky, *Takkanot ha-Geonim* (Tel Aviv-N.Y. 5720).
39   Last mishnah in *Nedarim*.
40   *Ketubot* 63a.
41   See S. Assaf, *op. cit.* p. 62, and *Religious Foundations etc.,*. p. 114.

8

From Rishonim to Aḥaronim

מימיהן של אבותינו לא פרשה ישיבה מהם
*From the days of our Fathers (the Patriarchs) Yeshiva
did not depart from them**

Hakhmei Ashkenaz[1]

The Talmud, in listing the heads of Yeshivot in the days of the
Tannaim, mentions R. Mattia (b. Ḥeresh), head of the Yeshiva in
Rome.[2] When R. Shimon b. Yoḥai and R. Eleazar B. Yose went to
Rome to plead for the abolition of decrees against religious observance by the Jews in Eretz Yisrael, R. Mattia took advantage of
their presence to ask them questions in Jewish Law.[3] Another
leader of the Jewish community in Rome at that period was Todos,
who made a certain ruling concerning the Seder meal contrary to
the opinion of the Sages.[4] Already in the days of the Talmud
differences in custom between the Jewish communities in Eretz
Yisrael and Babylonia had developed;[5] the Jews in Rome, who had
come there directly from Palestine and maintained contact with the
Homeland, in the main followed Palestinian custom. In time, there

---

* *Yoma* 28b
1 Ashkenaz is mentioned in Gen 10:3 among the families of the Grecian Isles.
   For the application of this name to Germany and German Jewry, see S.W.
   Baron, *Social and Religious History*, Vol. IV, p. 235 (n.1).
2 *Sanhedrin* 32b.
3 *Me'ilah* 17a.
4 *Pesaḥim* 53a.
5 Cf. *Berakhot* 44a and other instances noted there.

emerged a distinctly Italian Jewish custom, especially in liturgical practice.[6]

In the course of time, Jews followed the expansion of the Roman Empire, and already in the 9th and 10th centuries we find Jewish settlements in Northern Italy (Lombardy) and the Rhine region of Germany (contiguous with Northern France) — the region known in Rabbinic parlance as *Ashkenaz* — with distinguished scholars and schools of learning. Tradition has it that Charlemagne encouraged the migration of the famous Kalonymos family from Lucca to Mayence (Mainz or *Magentza* in halakhic literature), where soon a renowned Yeshiva, the fountainhead of Ashkenazic Halakhah, was established.[7] Ashkenazic migration reached as far as England, the family of the scholars Eliyahu Menaḥem of London and his brother Berakhyah of Lincoln (early 13th Century) having settled in London from Mayence around the year 1000.[8] These countries fell under the hegemony of the Roman Catholic Church, its adherents instigators of the Crusades which took such a heavy toll of Jewish lives in these settlements, and subsequently led to a series of expulsions and the migration of Ashkenazic Jewry to Central and Eastern Europe.

Despite persecution and enforced migration, Torah flourished in Ashkenaz. A younger contemporary of Hai Gaon[9] was Rabbenu Gershom b. Yehudah (c. 955–1028), entitled *Me'or ha-Golah*, Light of the Exile, head of the Yeshiva in Mayence. He was the author of a comparatively new division in halakhic literature, *peirushim* or commentaries to the Talmud, paying particular attention to the proper *girsa* or correct textual reading, so important for the determination of the Halakhah. R. Gershom's commentaries are extant today only in fragments, which are published in the Vilna-Rom edition of the Talmud. His fame is enduring because of his well-known takkanot against polygamy and divorcing a woman without her consent. These and others are known as *ḥerem d'Rabbenu*

---

6 For a description of early Roman Jewry, see H.J. Leon, *The Jews of Ancient Rome* (Phila. 1960). For a discussion of the influence of the Palestinian versus the Babylonian tradition in Ashkenaz, see A. Grossman, *Ḥakhmei Ashkenaz ha-Rishonim* (Jer. 5741), pp. 424 ff.

7 For a discussion of this tradition, see A. Grossman, *op. cit.* pp. 29 ff.

8 Cf. M. Zaks, *Peirushei R. Eliyahu of Londres* (Jer. 5716), pp. 21 ff.

9 See above, p. 119.

Gershom because the means of enforcing such regulations was the *herem* or excommunication, and they were accepted by Ashkenazic Jewry for all time.[10]

Rashi and the Ba'alei Tosafot

A disciple of a disciple of Rabbenu Gershom is the commentator *par excellence* R. Shlomo b. Yitzhak (1040–1105), familiar to all as *Rashi* (acronym of R. Sh'lomo Y'itzhaki). His commentary to the Pentateuch, a blend of the simple interpretaion of the text with both halakhic and aggadic exegesis, has become so basic a text in Jewish life that it replaces the Aramaic of Onkelos in fulfilling the obligation to review the weekly portion of Torah-reading with the Targum.[11] His commentary to the Talmud Bavli, with its frequent rendering of material objects into colloquial French, made the Talmud accessible to all. Occasionally Rashi would include a statement of the Halakhah or actual practice where such is not clear from the discussion in the Talmud, even citing the Jerusalem Talmud for support. Thus in the very first Mishnah of the first Tractate Rashi explains why it was customary to recite the evening Shema earlier than the time specified in the Mishnah.[12] Needless to say, Rashi fulfilled the dictate of the Men of the Great Assembly to "raise up many disciples," two of them in particular who edited his many writings, Rabbis Shemayah and Simhah of Vitry. To the latter we are indebted for his edition of *Mahzor Vitry*, a comprehensive prayer-book that includes, in addition to the order and text of the prayers, the halakhic rulings concerning prayer. A contemporary of Rashi,[13] whose work also served to clarify many obscure statements in the Talmud, was R. Natan b. Yehiel of Rome, known as the *ba'al ha-Arukh*. The Arukh is a lexicon of the Talmud, both Bavli and Yerushalmi, the Targumim and the Midrashim. It is

10 See *Encyclopedia Talmudit*, Vol. 17, esp. subsections 3 and 4, and appendix. Cf. Sh. A. *Even ha-Ezer* 1:10 and *Rema ad loc.*
11 Sh. A. *Orah Hayyim* 285:2.
12 For a full discussion of this problem, see Y. Katz, *Halakhah ve-Kabbalah* (Jer. 5744), pp. 175 ff., and my *Tsemichat Ge'ulateinu* (Jer. 5744), pp. 4143.
13 Rashi sent a *she'eilah* to R. Natan inquiring when to perform a *brit milah* on Rosh Hashanah; see *Teshuvot ha-Rid* (Jer. 5727), p. 21.

especially helpful in establishing the etymology of words of foreign origin, such as Arabic, Greek, Latin and Persian. Most of the Arukh's explanations were derived from the Geonim, transmitted by R. Ḥannanel and by R. Natan's teacher R. Mazliaḥ, who was a disciple of Hai Gaon. The Arukh is frequently cited by the Tosafists as well as Sephardi scholars; and continues to serve students of the Talmud to this very day. About a century ago a critical edition was published by Dr. Alexander Kohut, who for a time was rabbi in New York, and is called *Arukh ha-Shalem*, the Complete Arukh.

Among Rashi's disciples were his two sons-in-law and his grandsons, who studied his commentary to the Talmud critically and added their own comments. This gave rise to a super-commentary that finally developed into a compilation of the comments of over a score of scholars over a period of two centuries (1100–1300 C.E.). This compilation appears in most editions of the Talmud opposite Rashi's commentary and is designated *Tosafot* or Additions; and the scholars are designated the *Ba'alei Tosafot* or Tosafists.[14] Most of them lived in various cities in Northern France or in the famous three cities of the Rhine: Speyers (Shapira), Worms (Vermaiza), and Mayence (Magentza) or *Sh'u'm'* for short. It may be said that the Tosafists introduced a new dimension in the study of the Talmud; their work is not merely commentary, it is critical analysis. They not only advance novel interpretations of the text; they establish the correct reading and they reconcile its seeming contradictions by positing new assumptions and distinguishing between cases which at first glance appear to be identical. This gave rise to a new *genre* of Halakhic literature, *ḥiddushim*[15] and *ḥillukim*, Novellae and Distinctions, which in a later period develped into a system of *pilpul* or sophistical argument which had no direct bearing on halakhic decision. The reasonings of the Ba'alei Tosafot, however, had practical significance; later authorities found support in them for their halakhic decisions.[16]

---

14 The handiest one-volume reference to the lives and works of these scholars can be found in E.E. Urbach's *Ba'alei ha-Tosafot* (Jer. 5715). A new edition of this work has been published recently: our references are to the first edition.

15 The term *ḥiddush* is already found in Tannatic literature; cf. *Hagigah* 3b. *ein bet midrash belo hiddush.*

16 See Urbach, *op. cit.* pp. 566 ff.

Reconciling Law with Life

A major contribution of the Ba'alei Tosafot to the continuity of the halakhic tradition despite changes in life-style consisted in their reconciling practices dictated by Talmudic prescription with the actual custom followed in their day. A whole series of restrictions against Jews engaging in commerce with pagans — for example, selling them cattle or handling their wine — is laid down in Tractate *Avodah Zarah*, the tractate dealing with idolatry and idol-worshippers. At the very beginning of the tractate Tosafot asks, "How come we deal with them on days prohibited by the Talmud?" A tentative answer says, "Because of *eivah*," i.e. in order to prevent hostility (on the part of our non-Jewish neighbors if we refuse to deal with them). But then a more fundamental answer is given which removes practically all the restrictions; to wit, "We know for certain that the pagans among us do not worship idols."[17] R. Yaakov b. Meir (c. 1100–1171), better known as Rabbenu Tam, grandson of Rashi and most outspoken of the Ba'alei Tosafot, displayed his dialectical ingenuity by arguing that the Talmud refers only to matters that are offered as sacrifices to the idols, things which do not exist in our times. Another tosafist went further and argued that even lending a Gentile money so that he can bring it as an offering to the Church is not forbidden, "for what they give to their priests is not really for idol worship but for the personal benefit of the priests." An even further extenuation of the common practice to sell cattle to non-Jews was found in this argument: "Certainly the prohibition against selling an animal applied only in their days when many Jews lived together, and if someone had an animal he didn't need he could sell it to his (Jewish) friend and would suffer no loss; but nowadays, what he can do; if he can't sell it he will lose it."[18] However, Rabbenu Tam refused to rule leniently in connection with wine handled by a non-Jew, though there were sufficient grounds for doing so.[19] Wine was in a separate category; drinking a non-Jew's wine would lead to too much familiarity,

---

17 Whether Christians were regarded as idolators was a matter of controversy among the Halakhic authorities in the Middle Ages; see above, chap. 2, n. 17. Also, Y. Katz, *op. cit.*, pp. 291 ff.

18 *Tosafot Avodah Zarah* 15a, *s.v. eimor*.

19 *Ibid.* 57b, *s.v. la'afukei*; 64b, *s.v. ein*.

which in turn might lead to intermarriage, an eventuality to be avoided at all costs.[20]

Justification was also found for the fact that many customs prevalent in Talmudic times which became requirements of the Halakhah were no longer practiced by Ashkenazic Jewry. Due recognition was given to the change in life-style which rendered ancient practices obsolete, such as mourners covering their faces and overturning the beds in their homes.[21] Here the tosafists displayed a sensitivity to the opinion of their non-Jewish neighbors, that if we were to follow these alien customs we would become an object of derision. They also were aware of their dependence upon the good will of the rulers to whom they were subject, and they explained the Talmudic principle "the law of the kingdom is law"[22] on the basis that the land belongs to the ruler who can say to his subjects, "If you do not obey my commands I will expel you from the land."[23]. At the same time they did not hesitate to assert that only if the law is applied to all subjects equally and without discrimination is it to be honored, but if the ruler seizes a Jew's property unlawfully "this is not the law of the land, but robbery."[24]

Ḥasidei Ashkenaz

As in the days of the Geonim,[25] many concise digests or handbooks of Jewish Law were composed by the Ḥakhmei Ashkenaz in order to give halakhic guidance in matters of daily ritual and halakhic sanction to many new customs. However, a new element was introduced into many of these new works, adding moral and pietistic exhortations to strictly legal directives. This was the nightmare period of the Crusades, when Jewish martyrdom reached a new peak with Jews slaying their beloved ones for the sake of *Kiddush*

---

20 *Avodah Zarah* 36b; *Tosafot ibid.* 29b, *s.v. yayin.*
21 *Tosafot Mo'ed Kattan* 21a, *s.v. elu.* For other examples, see *Megillah* 22a, *s.v. ein*; *Betzah* 30a, *s.v. tenan*; *Avodah Zarah* 35a, *s.v. hada*; *Bekhorot* 2b, *s.v. shema.*
22 *Bava Batra* 55a. For a full treatment of this principle, see S. Shilo, *Dina D'Malkhuta Dina* (Jer. 5735).
23 *Ran* to *Nedarim* 28a.
24 *Tosafot Bava Kamma* 58a, *s.v. Iy Nami.*
25 See above, p. 117.

Hashem.[26] Such tragedies, paradoxically enough, led to a plea for more intense devotion in prayer and practice and an emphasis on the aggadic and mystical elements in Jewish tradition. Foremost expression to this tendency was given in the *Sefer Ḥasidim* of R. Yehudah ha-Ḥasid, whose teachings influenced such halakhic works as *Sefer ha-Roke'ah* of R. Eleazar of Worms and *Sefer Yera'im* of R. Eliezer b. Shmuel of Metz, a disciple of Rabbenu Tam. Other works of this period worthy of mention are the *Even ha-Ezer* of R. Eliezer b. Natan of Mainz, *Sefer ha-Terumah* of R. Barukh b. Yitzḥak of Worms, and the *Avi ha-Ezer* (also known as *Sefer Raviyah*) of R. Eliezer b. Yoel ha-Levi. The last and most comprehensive of this series is the *Or Zaru'a* of R. Yitzḥak b. Moshe of Vienna, a staunch defender of the earlier authorities.

Second only to Rabbenu Tam among the Ba'alei Tosafot is his nephew R. Yitzḥak b. Shmuel of Dampierre, known by his initials *R'iY'* or *R'iY' ha-Zaken.* Less harsh than his uncle in halakhic dispute, he said, "It is a mitzvah to listen to one's colleague and deal with him fraternally."[27] He also was influenced by the pietistic tendencies of Ḥasidei Ashkenaz, his devotions in the synagogue prolonged beyond those of others. His halakhic decisions are recorded in the Tosafot and Responsa of his many disciples. Most prominent among the latter is R. Shimshon of Sens, whose collection of Talmudic comments included in the Tosafot is the largest. He is also distinguished in that he was the first among these medieval scholars who wrote a commentary to the Mishnah of Seder Zeraim and Seder Tohorot, both of which deal with laws not operative in the Diaspora. Another cluster of the R'iY's disciples studied in Paris. Of them, mention should be made of R. Moshe of Coucy, known for his *Sefer Mitzvot Gadol (S'M'aG')*, an halakhic and homiletic treatment of the Taryag (613) mitzvot. Head of the Yeshiva in Paris was R. Yeḥiel, known for his defense of the Talmud against its Christian detractors. He argued that the anti-Gentile statements in the Talmud refer only to the ancient idolators and not to the Christians. Nevertheless, Pope Gregory banned the Talmud, and in the year 1242 twenty-four wagon-fulls of the Talmud were burned in a public bonfire in Paris. Eventually, R. Yeḥiel and his

---

26   See S. Spiegel, *The Lst Trial* (Phila. 1967), esp. pp. 18–19.
27   Urbach, *op. cit.*, p. 199.

disciples left France for Eretz Yisrael, and thus began the decline of the Yeshivot in France.

A similar decline because of persecution had taken place in southern Italy during the 10th Century, but experienced a revival during the 11th, to such an extent that Rabbenu Tam remarked, "For the Torah goes forth from Bari and the word of the Lord from Otranto."[28] A disciple of Rabbenu Simḥah of Speyers who had also studied with some of the French Tosafists headed a Yeshiva in the city of Trani,[29] and produced noteworthy comments to the Talmud. He was R. Yeshaya ha-Zaken, known as the *Rid* (acronym of *R. Y'eshaya D'Trani*). His *Tosafot Rid* have been published in some editions of the Talmud. His *Piskei Rid* and Teshuvot have recently been published in critical editions by the Institute of the Israeli Talmud, together with the Talmudic commentary of his grandson R. Yeshaya the Second, known as *Ri'az* (acronym of *R. Y'eshaya ha-A'ḥaron Z'ikhrono Livrakhah*).[30]

In Germany, Torah learning continued all through the 13th Century. Bringing this period to a close was the distinguished R. Meir b. Barukh (c. 1215–1293), familiarly known as *Maharam mi'Rothenburg*. He studied in some of the Yeshivot in France and brought back their teachings to Germany, where he was recognized as the outstanding spiritual leader of his day. He was independent of mind, maintaining his views despite critical opposition. His teachings are mainly recorded in the works of two of his disciples; the oft-quoted *Sefer ha-Mordekhai* of R. Mordekhai b. Hillel ha-Cohen and the *Hagahot Maimuniyot* of R. Meir ha-Cohen of Rothenburg, published as a commentary to the Mishneh Torah of the Rambam. Maharam mi'Rothenburg was invincible in spirit. He was jailed in Italy after leaving Germany because of the hostile attitude of the ruler, but he continued his Torah activity during the seven years of his imprisonment. Though he marks the close of a period, his decisions, primarily of Ashkenazic custom, were transferred by his disciples to two new centers of Jewish learning, Central Europe and Spain.

28 *Sefer ha-Yashar*, end of no. 46. Cities on the Adriatic coast. Otranto should not be confused with Taranto on the gulf of Taranto, nor with Trani, which is some 35 miles north of Bari. Re Bari, see below, p. 129.

29 See above, n. 28.

30 *Makhon ha-Talmud ha-Yisraeli ha-Shalem*, with Mossad Harav Kook (Jer. 5724–36).

Ḥakhmei Sepharad[31]

Parallel with the trek of Palestinian-Roman Jewry northward into Ashkenaz, was the trek of Babylonian Jewry westward into North Africa and Spain (Sepharad), swept along by the fiery spread of Islam which brought in its wake the Arabic language and culture. Here also, Torah and Yeshivot accompanied the wandering Jews, and by the year 1000 Jewish communities had developed to such an extent that they could boast of famous schools of Torah learning of their own, with noted scholars as their religious leaders. It should be noted that during the entire period of this development of Sephardic-Arabic-speaking Jewry, in the 9th and 10th Centuries, close ties were maintained with the Yeshivot headed by the Geonim in Babylonia, and hence the continuation of the influence of the Babylonian Talmud among Sephardic Jews.

If we are to believe the story told by the Spanish-Jewish philosopher Abraham ibn Daud (middle of 12th Century) — though some of the details are questionable, the core of the story is undoubtedly true[32] — much of this development was due to the stranding of four distinguished Babylonian scholars in North African and Iberian communities. Briefly, the story recounts how these four scholars embarked at Bari, southern Italy, to attend a wedding of a colleague's daughter in Siponto. While at sea they were captured by a Moslem naval officer out to capture Christian vessels. He sold the scholars as slaves, each in a different city. In each city the captive was redeemed by the local Jewish community, which then took note of his excellence in Talmudic lore and appointed him head of the local academy. Rabbi Shemariah was redeemed in Alexandria, whence he made his way to Fostat, the old Jewish neighborhood of Cairo where later Maimonides settled. Rabbi Ḥushiel was redeemed by the community of Kairouan, Tunis, which had long depended upon the Babylonian gaonate for religious guidance but now found an authoritative scholar in its midst.

---

31   *Sepharad* is a city in Asia Minor mentioned in Obadiah 1:20 as a community of the Diaspora, and adopted by Spanish Jewry because they were one of the furthest outposts of the Diaspora. Similarly, French Jewry called France *Zerephat*, mentioned in the same verse.

32   For a full discussion of this tale, see Z. Yavetz, *Toldot Yisrael* (Tel Aviv 5692), Vol. X, pp. 238 ff.

And Rabbi Moshe ben Ḥanokh was redeemed by the thriving and influential community of Cordova in Moorish Spain. His superior understanding of the Talmud was recognized by the local spiritual leader, who yielded his office to Rabbi Moshe. (The teller of this tale says that he does not know the name of the fourth scholar).

In this condensed survey of the development of the Halakhah it is impossible to list all the bright stars whose brilliance illuminates the myriad facets of Jewish Law to this day; let alone discuss the main features of their respective works. We can record only those outstanding teachers whose works served as the core — we might say, as the bright suns — of numerous satellite works, and are the main links in the chain of the halakhic tradition. Among the early ḥakhmei Sepharad is Rabbenu Ḥannanel, son of the aforementioned R. Ḥushiel, and a younger contemporary of Hai Gaon. He wrote a commentary to the Talmud similar to that of Rabbenu Gershom, fragments of which are published in many editions of the Talmud. His colleague in Kairouan was Rabbenu Nissim b. Yaakov. (It was to this R. Yaakov that the famous *Iggeret Rav Sherira Gaon*, recounting the history of the Babylonian scholars of the Talmud (the Amoraim) and the Geonim, was addressed). Rabbenu Nissim's most important work was entitled *Sefer ha-Mafte'aḥ*, the Key, and was written originally in Arabic but has been translated into Hebrew. As the title indicates, it is the key to the understanding of many Talmudic statements which require explanation.

Rif and Rambam

With the death of Hai Gaon in 1038, the period of the Gaonate with its centralized halakhic authority came to an end. Now, to take its place, was not an institution but a person, a commanding figure whose authority would be acknowledged by the scattered communities of the Sephardic Diaspora. Such a figure emerged in the person and writings of R. Yitzḥak b. Yaakov ha-Kohen, better known as the Rif or Alfasi.[33] Born in a small town in Algeria in 1013, he studied in Kairouan under R. Ḥannanel, and then settled in Fez in Morocco, from which he acquired the name Alfasi. At the age of 75,

---

33 A most appreciative summary of his role in the spreading of Torah study can be found in I.H. Weiss, *Dor Dor ve-Dorshav* (Berlin 5684), Vol. IV, pp. 281 ff.

he had to leave Fez for some obscure reason and he settled in Lucenna, near Cordova in Spain. Here he again became head of the community and raised up many disciples. His major work is *Hilkhot ha-Rif*, a digest of those sections of the Talmud that had practical significance (i.e. excluding *Seder Zeraim* except *Berakhot*, and *Sedorim Kodashim* and *Tohorot* except *Niddah*) and including the post-Talmudic decisions of the Geonim. Of this work Maimonides wrote: "The Halakhot which the great R. Yitzḥak composed....include all the necessary decisions and judgments required in our time...In them he rectified all the errors found in the decisions of his predecessors, and we can question only a few of his decisions, not even ten."[34] Indeed, these Halakhot became a prime source of later halakhic discourse, and most printed editions of the Rif are surrounded by the commentaries of later scholars, reminiscent of the commentaries of Rashi and Tosafot which surround the Talmud.

In Lucenna, one of the Rif's disciples and his successor as head of the local Yeshiva, was R. Yosef ibn Migash (1077–1141), esteemed by his contemporaries as the greatest teacher of his time. Unfortunately, most of his writings — Responsa and Commentary to the Talmud — have been lost, but there is one extant comment of his worth recording. He writes, "This Talmud of ours (i.e. Talmud Bavli) is actual Halakhah to be carried out in practice, for it was written only after scrutiny and examination of generations and after many revisions; it was written so that we follow it in actual practice."[35] Ibn Migash's renown, however, is the influence — albeit indirect — he had upon that master of all masters, Maimonides. The latter writes of him as follows: "This man's understanding of the Talmud is staggering to everyone who examines his words and their profundity. One may verily say of him, 'There was none before like unto him.'"[36] Though Maimonides refers to him as his teacher, he was such only through his writings or through Maimon the father who presumably did study under Ibn Migash.[37]

---

34   Intro. to *Commentary to the Mishnah*, Kapah ed. (Jer. 5723), p. 25.

35   Comment to *Bava Batra* 130b.

36   *Commentary etc. op. cit.*, p. 25.

37   Cf. Graetz, *History of the Jews* (JPS English ed.), Vol. 3, p. 447. Though the historians accept that Maimonides was born in the year 1135 (even the day and the hour of the birth is noted), a foremost scholar of Maimonides' writings, Y. Kapah, insists that he was born in 1138.

"From Moshe (Rabbenu) to Moshe (b. Maimon=Rambam=-Maimonides 1135–1204) there arose none like (the latter) Moshe."[38] So much has been written about Maimonides, there is nothing that this survey can add;[39] yet to pass over him with only a perfunctory reference would be unconscionable. Towering high above all others in the history of the Halakhah, the contributions of Maimonides to Jewish thought in general and to the Halakhah in particular are almost without par. His monumental Code of Jewish Law, the *Mishneh Torah* or *Yad ha-Hazakah*, stands out as preeminent because of both its comprehensiveness and its systematic arrangement, in addition to its lucid style. Many editions of this *magnus opus* have been published, and even now two Institutes are engaged in combing all manuscripts and references in order to publish yet another critical edition. These, as well as previous editions, show that much of the pilpul surrounding the Mishneh Torah's rulings are based upon faulty texts. I must also add that some of the misunderstandings of the Rambam on the part of the traditional halakhists are due to their failure to take into account Maimonides' rational approach to Talmudic law. Attempts have even been made to read into the Rambam an acceptance of some Kabbalistic premises — a subject we shall refer to later — without any real foundation.[40] Maimonides' Code is surrounded by a host of commentaries, second in number only to those which surround the Talmud itself, and to this day most halakhic discourses contain one or more references to its rulings.

Perhaps more amazing, because of the conditions under which it was composed, is Maimonides' *Commentary to the Mishnah*. While still in his twenties, and while he with his family were still trying to

---

38 A popular saying. During his lifetime the Jews of Yemen added his name to the Kaddish in the phrase "In your lifetime and in your day and in the lifetime of Rabbenu Moshe." Yemenite Jews would study the *Mishneh Torah* by rote, and thus they have preserved an authentic text. This special connection was a result of Maimonides' famous *Iggeret Teiman*.

39 A brief biography in English can be found in Yellin and Abrahams, *Maimonides* (Phila. 1944). I. Twersky has published an *Introduction to the Code of Maimonides* (New Haven 1981). Unfortunately, Maimonides' popularity has attracted other writers whose knowledge of his works is rather superficial. Yale University Press has published an English translation of the *Mishneh Torah* (Yale Judaica Press, New Haven).

40 See *Migdal Oz* to *Hikhot Yesodei ha-Torah*, chap. 1. For other references, see S.W. Baron, *Social and Religious History* (*op. cit.*), Vol. VIII, p. 293.

find a place of permanent settlement after their forced departure from Spain, Maimonides undertook to write, in Arabic, an explanation of the entire Mishnah which included chapters of Jewish Theology and Ethics. Herein we find his Thirteen Principles of Faith, which despite cogent criticism of subsequent Jewish philosophers have become the accepted creed and dogma of believing Jews. His Introduction to Tractate Avot, the *Shemonah Perakim* or *Eight Chapters*, is a review of his Ethics, with the emphasis on the Aristotelian doctrine of the mean and its denigration of extremism and addition of supererogatory restrictions. And herein also are his first thoughts concerning the reconstituting of the Sanhedrin. We see already the boldness and uninhibited self-confidence of this great mind, which came to full expression in his Introduction to the Mishneh Torah when he wrote, "I have called this work Mishneh Torah because a person first reads (i.e. studies) the Written Torah and then reads this and knows the entire Oral Torah without any need to read any other composition in between." Though many have criticised this self-confidence as exaggerated, the tendency among later halakhic authorities is to the opposite extreme of self-denigration and powerlessness to take the bold decisions necessary to continue the process of halakhic development and vitality.

As we move from the 12th to the 13th Century we move from Moorish to Christian Spain, where the two main centers of Torah learning were in Gerona and Barcelona. The outstanding scholar in this region, though his influence spread far and wide, was R. Moshe b. Naḥman, the *Ramban*, or Nahmanides (1194–1270). Like the other great halakhic personalities we have been discussing, Nahmanides was distinguished both by the keenness and independence of his mind as exhibited in his writings, and by the transmission of his erudition to his disciples. His commentaries (*ḥiddushim*) to many Talmudic tractates have been recently published in critical editions by the Israeli Institute of Talmud, while many other of his works have been published by Mossad Harav Kook in critical editions of the late Rabbi H.D. Chavel. Foremost among the latter is Ramban's commentary to the Pentateuch, a blend of Talmudic interpretation and the mysticism of the Kabbalah. A most trenchant observation in this important work is his comment to Lev. 19:2, *Speak to the entire congregation of the Children of Israel and say to them, 'You shall be holy, for I the Lord your God am Holy.'* Ramban writes, "This means, since the Torah admonished against

133

incest and forbidden food but permitted intercourse within marriage and the consumption of meat and wine, a glutton might find permission to wallow in sex with his wife or many wives, or be a guzzler of wine and a glutton for meat, or speak pornography as much as he desires since these things are not expressly forbidden by the Torah, and thus this person will be *obscene with the Torah's permission*; therefore Scripture gave a general command that we should abstain from excessive indulgence."

Though Ramban greatly respected Maimonides, he wrote strictures to the latter's *Sefer ha-Mitzvot*. One stricture of great significance for our own time is the Ramban's contention that there is an ongoing mitzvah for Jews to settle in and rebuild Eretz Yisrael. In fact, Ramban intimates that all the mitzvot were given primarily to be observed in Eretz Yisrael.[41] Ramban also recorded for posterity his arguments in the public debate he was compelled to hold with the apostate Jew Pablo Christiani.[42] Like R. Yeḥiel of Paris mentioned above, Ramban had to leave his native country and settle in Eretz Yisrael, where he spent the last three years of his life.

A cousin of the Ramban, R. Yonah of Gerona, is known primarily for his fierce opposition to the philosophical writings of Maimonides, and for his popular pietistic work *Sha'arei Teshuvah* (Gates of Repentance). In his latter years, R. Yonah became head of the Yeshivah in Barcelona, attracting many students. Among them was the distinguished R. Shlomo b. Aderet, the *Rashba* (1235–1310), who also studied under the Ramban. Rashba is primarily known for his voluminous number of Responsa, remarkable for their clarity and conciseness, addressed not only to communities in Spain, but also to France and Germany, Bohemia and North Africa. He was a staunch defender of the right of a community to enforce its takkanot, regulating the economic as well as the religious affairs of its members. Thus the Rashba confirmed, though evidently with some hesitation, that if a person contracted a marriage in a manner contrary to a takkanah which had received the sanction of the ḥakham of the community, that marriage is null and void.[43]

---

41 Cf. Ramban to Gen. 26:5. See also *Gittin* 7b, that Sages permitted requesting a non-Jew to write a bill of sale of property from a non-Jew to a Jew on Shabbat for *Yishuv Eretz Yisrael*.

42 See H.D. Chavel, *Kitvei ha-Ramban*, Vol. I, pp. 299 ff.

43 See M. Elon, *Ha-Mishpat Ha-Ivri* (Magnes Press), Vol. II, pp. 691–692.

Also living in Barcelona at this time was R. Aharon ha-Levi (*HaRa'ah*). Though also a prolific commentator to the Talmud, most of his writings have been lost. Strangely enough, he became known as the author of a most popular book *Sefer ha-Ḥinukh*, which deals with both halakhic and philosophic aspects of the Taryag Mitzvot, and is ascribed to him in error. The real author identifies himself as "a Jew from the House of Levi of Barcelona," but his exact identity is still in doubt.

We bring this period of Sephardic Jewry to a close with another native son of Gerona who became head of the Yehiva in Barcelona, R. Nissim b. Reuven (c. 1310–1375), the *Ran*. He is best known for his commentary to the Rif, most valuable for his analysis of the opinions of his predecessors. His commentary to Tractate Nedarim is the standard one, since Rashi's commentary to that tractate is incomplete. Two observations in Ran to Nedarim are worthy of mention because of their timely relevance. "It seems to me to imply (i.e., the statement there of Rav Dimi) that sometimes one has to pray for a sick person's death when he suffers greatly and it is impossible for him to live."[44] Again, quoting Tosafot, "The principle of 'the law of the kingdom is law'[45] applies only to non-Jewish kings...but not to Jewish kings, for all Jews are partners in Eretz Yisrael" (and therefore the Jewish King has no right to expropriate Jewish property).[46] Ran's heritage also includes *Derashot Ran*, in which he demonstrates his leanings towards the rational rather than the mystical in Judaism.[47]

Ḥakhmei Provence

A third center of Jewish law and learning, in addition to those of Ashkenaz and Sepharad, arose in Southern France. There is a long roster of distinguished halakhic scholars known as *Ḥakhmei Provence* who flourished in the communities of Narbonne, Lunel,

---

44 *Nedarim* 40a. From which it can be inferred that we may remove life-sustaining apparatus from the terminally ill; see below, p. 219.
45 See above, p. 79.
46 *Nedarim* 28a.
47 For a significant quotation, see Lewittes, *Religious Foundations etc. op. cit.*, p. 87.

Montpelier and Marseilles. The beginnings of this prolific Torah
center date back from the reign of the Emperor Carl, who invited R.
Makhir of Baghdad to become the spiritual leader of the Jewish
community in Narbonne at the close of the 8th Century. One of its
first renowned scholars was R. Moshe ha-Darshan, quoted so often
in Rashi's commentary to the Torah. Among the earliest halakhic
works produced in Provence is the *Sefer ha-Ittim* of Yehudah b.
Barzilai of Barcelona (d. 1158). A digest of laws on the Sabbath and
Festivals, it is distinguished by its many citations from the Geonim
and its influence upon succeeeding works. Thus the *Sefer ha-Eshkol*
of Avraham b. Yitzhak of Narbonne (1110–1179) is based upon the
Sefer ha-Ittim, and was followed by the *Sefer ha-Ittur* of Yitzhak b.
Abba Mari of Marseilles (1122–1193). All of these works are
referred to frequently by succeeding codifiers of the Halakhah.

A most illustrious son of Provence, a contemporary of Maimonides and his severest critic, was R. Abraham b. David of Posquieres (c. 1120–1198) known as the Ravad.[48] He shared Maimonides' boldness and self-confidence, adopting for himself the
Geonic phrase, "Thus have they shown me from Heaven."[49] His
important works, in addition to his *hasagot* (strictures) on the
Mishneh Torah, are a commentary to the halakhic Midrashim (only
the one on the *Sifra* has reached us in its entirety), *Sefer Ba'alei
ha-Nefesh* on *Hilkhot Niddah* and *Temim De'im*, a collection of
Responsa. His colleague and adversary in halakhic matters was R.
Zerahiah ha-Levi of Lunel, the city of *Hakhmei Lunel* with whom
the Rambam corresponded. R. Zerahiah is known primarily for his
commentary to the Rif entitled *Ha-Ma'or*. In this work we find an
important historical observation. In disputing the Rif's ruling that
Jews in Eretz Yisrael also have to observe Rosh Hashanah two
days, he writes, "They need observe only one day, and this was the
custom in Eretz Yisrael for generations before us, until now when
some Hakhmei Provence came there and made them follow the
Rif's ruling and observe two days." A half century later, another
son of Lunel, R. Aharon ha-Cohen, produced a popular digest of
Jewish Law entitled *Orhot Hayyim*. The works of these and other
medieval scholars of this region, long undisclosed in hidden manu-

48 A recent volume on the life and works of Ravad has been published by I.
Twersky, entitled *Rabad of Posquieres* (Phila. 5740).
49 See above, p. 116.

scripts, have now received the light of day in recent publications, especially those of Rabbi M.Y. Blau of New York, a series of volumes under the general title *Shitat ha-Kadmonim*, and another series published by the Israeli Institute of Talmud entitled *Ginzei Rishonim*.

Menaḥem Ha-Meiri

What may be regarded as the most important contribution to the history of the Halakhah made by modern research is the publication of the *Bet ha-Beḥirah* of R. Menaḥem b. Shlomo ha-Meiri. Flourishing in the second half of the 13th Century, head of the Yeshiva in Perpignan, Me'iri wrote a comprehensive and lucid commentary to thirty-seven tractates of Talmud Bavli, a worthy supplement to that of Rashi. Just as geographically Provence is situated between Ashkenaz and Sepharad, so is Me'iri the bridge between Ḥakhmei Ashkenaz and Ḥakhmei Sepharad of the 12th Century. In the early period of the Rishonim there was little contact between these halakhic authorities; Rashi did not know of the Rif; Rambam did not know of Rashi; and Rabbenu Tam did not know of the Ravad. It is Mei'iri who is constantly citing the opinions of these great masters and their contemporaries, after which he usually draws his own conclusions. One of his conclusions, vital for the continued development of the Halakhah, I have cited above (p. 00). Another of his important conclusions is his categorical ruling that Christians are not to be regarded as idolators, and hence the Talmudic restrictions against dealing with pagans does not apply to them. Though the *Ba'alei Tosafot* also arived at a similar conclusion, they did so for practical reasons, economic exigencies and the like; whereas Me'iri did so because he acknowledged Christianity's moral principles.[50]

Me'iri lived in a period when the Church was attempting to rid Europe of its Jewish inhabitants, whose very presence and vitality were a denial of the Christian premise that God had completely forsaken the Children of Israel. The attempt was made on two fronts: persuasion by means of theological argument, and physical expulsion. One of the Church's arguments reaching the ears of

---

50   See Y. Katz, *op. cit.*, for particulars.

Me'iri was that the Jews have abandoned the paths of penitence and that Judaism is a soulless legalism. To counter such argument, Me'iri wrote the *Hibbur ha-Teshuvah*, a thorough and systematic treatise on all the aspects of Repentance in Jewish sources, including the laws for the season of Repentance, Rosh Hashanah and Yom Kippur, as well as the related laws of fasting and mourning.[51] In his systematic approach we see the influence of the Rambam, whom Me'iri greatly admired. Another work important for the history of the Halakhah is Me'iri's *Magen Avot*, a defense of many local customs against the attacks launched by Hakhmei Sepharad. Also in his Introduction to Tractate Avot Meiri records for posterity the halakhic masters of the preceding generations, an important source for the history of the early Rishonim.

Philosophy, Mysticism, Pietism

Halakhah, by its very nature, is legalistic; its major concern is with the minutiae of *kiyyum ha-mitzvot*, ritual observance. Religious leaders in all ages have felt that Halakhah, in and of itself, is not the sum total of the religious experience, and hence not the sum total of Torah Judaism. Some, like Saadia Gaon and Maimonides, found the complement to the Halakhah in Philosophy, which includes both Theology and Ethics and gives to the mitzvot of the Torah their essential rationale and purpose. Others, like the Hasidei Ashkenaz or the opponents of Maimonides, could not accept Philosophy as a component of Judaism — the former because it was totally unfamiliar to them, and the latter because of its non-Jewish provenance — and therefore found the complement to the Halakhah in what is designated as *sod*, or mysticism, which they felt was imbedded in the very letters of the Torah (*notarikon* or acrostics) and their numerical value (*gematria*).[52] Since the words of the Torah were susceptible to more than one interpretation, each of which is valid, these mystic references to certain veiled but pro-

---

51 Published in critical edition by Yeshiva Univ. (N.Y. 5710).

52 See Ramban's Introduction to his Torah commentary. For an example of *notarikon* see *Shabbat* 104a = J.T. Megillah 1:11 (71d); for *gematria* see *Berakhot* 8a.

found truths and supernatural entities are also valid and sanctioned by the religious tradition.[53]

Ḥakhmei Ashkenaz, as a consequence of their particular environment, Medieval Christendom, were ignorant of classical philosophy.[54] and therefore found religious experience beyond the actual observance of the mitzvot in their exclusive devotion to the study of Talmudic law. Ḥasidei Ashkenaz heightened their religious experience in ascetic practices and the mysteries inherent in the composition of the prayers. Typical of the unsophisticated attitude of the *Ba'alei Tosafot* is the following reaction of Rabbenu Tam. The Talmud relates that the wise men of Israel maintained that the sun travels at night from West to East above the firmament, while the wise men of the Gentiles claimed that it travels below the earth. Whereupon Rabbi (Yehudah ha-Nasi) remarked that the Gentiles are right, proving their point from the fact that by day the springs are cold but at night they are hot. To this Rabbenu Tam is reported to have said, "Even though the Gentiles proved their point, this is so only in so far as argument is concerned, but the actual fact is according to the wise men of Israel, as we say in our prayers, "the sun splits open the windows of the firmament."[55]

In Sepharad the milieu was different. Arab scholars had translated the classical Greek philosophers into Arabic, making their teachings available to the Jewish scholars, who were impressed by their logic and apparent truth. "Accept the truth from whomever speaks it," was their guiding principle. Maimonides went much further than others by including in his Mishneh Torah, an halakhic work, a description of the universe more Aristotelian than particularly Jewish. His major philosophic work, the *Moreh Nevukhim* or Guide for the Perplexed, is a rational exposition of the mitzvot of the Torah and its anthropomorphic expressions. For those who objected to this grafting of non-Jewish thought onto the principles of Judaism, a ready substitute, the Kabbalah, was found. The roots of the Kabbalah are found in the Talmud, where such mystic lore is designated as *ma'aseh merkavah* or "the works of the Chariot," an exposition of the heavenly hosts as described in the first chapter of

---

53   See *Shabbat* 88b.
54   Cf. *Tosafot Shabbat* 116a, *s.v. Philosopha.*
55   *Gilyon ha-Shas* to *Pesaḥim* 94b.

Ezekiel.[56] In Talmudic times and until the 13th Century there was an esoteric lore confined to a few devotees and transmitted orally. However, with the publication of the Zohar — which is a sort of Bible of the Kabbalah — around the year 1280, the Kabbalah became a public doctrine accessible to all, especially for those seeking a religious experience beyond the fulfillment of the mitzvot. Ascribing its authorship to the Tanna R. Shimon b. Yoḥai made it acceptable to Rabbinic circles, and gradually some of its ideas and practical suggestions began to influence the decisions of the halakhists, a matter we shall discuss later.[57]

The Influence of the Environment

R. Yehudah ha-Hasid, in no approving tone, remarked, "In every city, as is the custom of the Gentiles, so in most places is the custom of the Jews."[58] Since custom soon becomes law, this means that the Halakhah — as Jewish life in general — was not immune or impervious to the influences of the non-Jewish environment. Thus the differences between Ashkenazim and Sephardim which are not due to their respective origins — Eretz Yisrael and Babylonia — are due to their respective milieu. The Ashkenazim living in Christian lands accepted quite readily the ban against polygamy since it was not in vogue in the general community;[59] whereas the Sephardim did not accept the ban since they lived amongst Moslems who sanctioned and practiced polygamy. Though Jews in the Middle Ages lived largely in self-contained communities and followed religious teachings and practices basically different from those of their neighbors, they nevertheless assimilated many features of the ambient culture, such as language and dress, and even modes of thinking. Parallels can even be found between the halakhic litera-

---

56   Cf. Mishnah *Hagigah* 2:1 and Talmud *ad. loc.*
57   For a full discussion of Jewish Mysticism, see G. Scholem, *Major Trends etc.* (N.Y. 1941; Paperback ed., 1961). See also Y. Katz, *Halakhah ve-Kabbalah.*
58   Quoted by E.E. Urbach, *op. cit.*, p. 17, from Sefer Hasidim.
59   According to R. Yaakov Emden, Rabbenu Gershom's ban against polygamy was due to the Christian ban against it, and it would be dangerous for Jews to have more than one wife. He further asserts that it would have been better if the ban had not been pronounced. See, however, *Encyclopedia Talmudit*, Vol. XVII, for other reasons.

ture of the medieval Ashkenazim and the scholiasts of the Church, as well as between the literature of the early Sephardim and that of the Muslims.[60]

We have already pointed out, in our discussion of the *Ba'alei Tosafot*, how their social milieu affected certain areas of the Halakhah. Attitudes towards general philosophy or secular poetry or the study of Biblical grammar, or even towards the respective non-Jewish religions — Christianity and Islam — can be attributed in large measure to environmental influences. Indeed, to control such influences the Rabbis from time to time found it necessary to raise their voices against the adoption by Jews of non-Jewish habits. Thus, for example, both Sephardi and Ashkenazi authorities warned against the introduction of non-Jewish music into synagogue services.[61] Nevertheless, one should not always assume — as is the tendency of some historians of Jewish life — that every halakhic decision or religious attitude is the result of such environmental influence. We must always bear in mind the unique sources as well as the unique development of Jewish law and life. And where such influence is apparent, we must recognize the peculiarly Jewish stamp which Jewish thinking imprinted upon it.

The Last of the Rishonim

Because of the frequent persecution and expulsions in France and Germany during the 13th Century, the period of the *Ba'alei Tosafot* was coming to an end. By this time, however, their works and mode of study were familiar to the Sephardi scholars in Christian Spain. The scholars of Provence, who were closer to Spain but maintained contact with their coreligionists in France, served as the intermediaries bridging the gap between the Torah of Sepharad and the Torah of Ashkenaz. Thus the Ramban, a Sephardi, accepted many a decision of the Tosafists and was more of a mystic than a rationalist.

The scholar who brought this merger to its climax, and who may be designated as the last great luminary of the Rishonim, was R. Asher b. Yeḥiel, the *Rosh*. Born in 1250 in the Rhine region, he was a

---

60   *Ibid.*, p. 27; S.W. Baron, *Social and Religious History*, Vol. VII, p. 6 ff.
61   Baron, *ibid.* p. 205.

disciple of the last of the Tosafists, the Maharam of Rothenburg, and indeed became his successor as leader of Ashkenazic Jewry. In 1303 he left the city of Cologne, where he had settled, and after over a year of wandering through Provence and Spain, he was invited to head the Yeshiva and Bet Din in Toledo. He brought with him not only the decisions of the Ashkenazic authorities but also their system of learning. Instead of the Sephardi greats, the Rif and the Rambam, serving as the basis of their studies, the Rosh insisted that the Tosafot be the basic text. The Rosh was very independent of mind, not hesitating to differ with the Geonim or the Rambam if his understanding of the Talmudic source differed from theirs. He also was opposed to the study of philosophy, and in his personal life followed the ascetic tendencies of Hasidei Ashkenaz. And yet he spoke out against those who would impose their stringencies upon others if they had no basis in the Talmud. He writes, "We maintain only that which we find in the Talmud. If a noble person, out of his great humility and piety does not wish to practice that which is permitted by the Talmud, he should practice such piety for himself and not write it down as instruction for future generations".[62] The Rosh also understood that a change in circumstances must bring a change in the law. Thus he rules that the change which had taken place since Talmudic times in the manner of Torah study changes the manner of fulfilling the Scriptural mitzvah which bids each Jew write a Sefer Torah for himself. He argues as follows: The purpose of the mitzvah is to promote the study of Torah, and since we no longer use the Torah scroll for purposes of study — which they did in Talmudic times — we fulfill the mitzvah nowadays by purchasing *ḥumashim* and *mishnayot* and the other texts currently in use.[63] His critical analysis of the Talmud also led him to assert that not everywhere is the statement therein that a certain law is *halakhah l'Moshe mi-Sinai* to be taken literally, and therefore to assume that the law is of Biblical force (*d'oraita*); the law can very well be of Rabbinic force (*d'rabbanan*), and the expression in question simply means that the law is as clear as if it were given from Sinai.[64]

The literary heritage of the Rosh is, first and foremost, his commentary to the Talmud known as *hilkhot* or *piskei ha-Rosh*, which follows tractates of the Talmud similar to the halakhot of the

62 Rosh to *Niddah*, chap. 10, Sec. 3.
63 Beginning of *Hilkhot Sefer Torah*.
64 Beginning of *Hilkhot Mikva'ot*.

Rif. It should be noted that many later teachers would advise their students to study the Talmud with Rashi and Tosafot and the Rosh.[65] The Rosh was also a responder to halakhic inquiries from all points, and his Responsa together with his Halakhot are a major authority for the rulings of the Shulhan Arukh. A collection of Responsa published a century after the Rosh entitled *Besamim Rosh* and purporting to include his Teshuvot has been found to be non-authentic.

The Halakhic Authority of the Rishonim

As we have seen, halakhic authorities are grouped together in their respective historic period: Tannaim, Amoraim, Geonim, and Rishonim. Theoretically, a later group is supposed to be bound by the opinions of an earlier group, especially post-Talmudic by Talmudic.[66] Actually, however, later authorities would examine the opinions of their predecessors and decide which of the earlier opinions are valid and still applicable, and which are not; and then the decisions of the later authorities would become binding upon their contemporaries and successors. The son of the Rosh formulated the process as follows: "The Ravad wrote that no one in our times is qualified to disagree with the opinion of a Gaon. However, my father the Rosh wrote that anyone who erred because he had not heard the opinion of the Geonim, but when he did hear it he found it right he reverses his own decision...and similarly with respect to the scholars of every generation...But if he does not find the opinion right and brings proof accepted by his contemporaries that his own opinion is right, he may disagree with them."[67]

In this pattern of the chain of halakhic authority a significant change took place as history moved from the period of the Geonim to that of the Rishonim. The Geonim had regarded themselves as the direct heirs of the Hakhmei ha-Talmud and exercised their authority for all Israel, even challenging the authorities residing in Eretz Yisrael. Their appointment as official heads of the Yeshivot

---

65   Cf. *Shakh* to *Sh. A. Yoreh De'ah*, 245:1.
66   See above, p. 48.
67   *Kitzur Piskei ha-Rosh* to *Sanhedrin*, Chap. 4, sec. 6.

was sanctioned by the Chiefs of the Diaspora (*resh galuta*), who in turn found sanction for their own hegemony in Scripture. *"The scepter shall not depart from Judah* (Gen. 49:10) refers to the Chiefs of the Diaspora in Babylonia who rule over Israel with the scepter."[68] But after the decline of Babylonia as the center of Jewish life, no religious authority received formal appointment to an office which could be construed as authoritative for all Israel. Thus religious authority in the Middle Ages was confined to a spiritual leader's own community; or spread beyond those confines only by virtue of his personal repute as a scholar of outstanding erudition.

Furthermore, since the authority of the halakhist was confined to his own community, in some areas he had to share it with the elders of the community. This was especially so with the many takkanot regulating the property and fiscal affairs of the members of the community, known as *takkanot ha-kahal*. Here the authority of the community was quite absolute. In the words of the Rashba, "The majority in each city with respect to its members has the same power which the Bet Din ha-Gadol (i.e. the Sanhedrin) had with respect to all Israel."[69] Often, leaders of a region would convene and adopt takkanot for their entire region. Typical of these are *takkanot Sh'U'M'*, regulations for the three cities of Speyers, Worms, and Mainz. One of them, for example, specified that if a woman died without child within the first year of her marriage, the husband has to return to his wife's family all the dowry he had received; and if she died within the second year, half the dowry has to be returned.[70]

The Jewish communities, which enjoyed autonomy in their internal affairs, also exercised penal authority, even to the extreme of capital punishment. This power was more taken for granted in Spanish communities, for when the Rosh came from Germany to Spain he was quite taken aback when apprised of it.[71] In the matter of marriages, however, the Rishonim were reluctant to exercise the authority which the Rabbis of the Talmud had exercised. The Talmud rules that if a man compels a woman to accept his offer of

---

68   *Sanhedrin* 5a.
69   See M. Elon, *op. cit.*, Chaps. 19 and 20.
70   Rabbinical interpretation of Biblical law affirmed that a husband inherited his wife regardless of the duration of their marriage; cf. *Bava Batra* 111b and Rambam *Hilkhot Nahalot* 1:8.
71   A.A. Neuman, *The Jews in Spain* (J.P.S. Phila. 5705), Vol. I, p. 141.

marriage, the marriage is invalid; "he acted improperly, so the Rabbis acted improperly with him (i.e. against the general rule that a contract entered into under duress is binding), and nullified his marriage."[72] In the Middle Ages it had become necessary for many communities, in order to eliminate certain abuses, to institute certain conditions for the marriage ceremony. The question then arose, could a marriage be declared annulled *ab initio* if those conditions were not complied with? Though theoretically the Rishonim felt that such power was not restricted to the Rabbis of the Talmud and could be exercised by any communally-appointed rabbi, they were loathe to declare so without reservation.[73] As a result, such powers were eventually abandoned by succeeding religious authorities.

In addition to the many Codes and Commentaries composed during this period, scholars were constantly adding to the Teshuvot (Responsa) literature, as individuals and communities turned to them from near and far for religious guidance. Menahem Elon, in his comprehensive survey of Jewish Law, points out the special weight that should be given to the Responsa, as compared to the other main branches of the halakhic literature, in that they deal with actual cases and therefore are presumed to be more reliable.[74] He goes so far as to assert that "these responders (of the post-Geonic period) were a sort of unofficial supreme court of Jewish Law.[75] The question however arises, How far beyond their own country and era are the *piskei Halakhah* of the renowned responders binding upon subsequent halakhists? It is reasonable to conclude that the latter are bound to take into account the Responsa of their predecessors before issuing a pesak Halakhah.[76] They nevertheless have the right, either to decide that the question before them

---

72   *Bava Batra* 48b.
73   A.H. Freiman, *Seder Kiddushin ve-Nissuin* (Jer. 5725). pp. 67ff.; *Encyclopedia Talmudit*, Vol. X, p. 106.
74   M. Elon, *Ha-Mishpat ha-Ivri* (Jer. 5733), Vol. III, pp. 1215 ff. See also B. Lifschitz, *The Judicial Status of the Responsa Literature* (Hebrew article in *Ha-Mishpat ha-Ivri* Annual, Vol. 9–10, pp. 290 ff.). It should be pointed out that not all Responsa, especially those of the later authorities, the Aharonim, deal with actual cases; some are discussions about theoretical cases posed by the author himself, or a response to a question concerning the clarification of a Talmudic statement.
75   M. Elon, *ibid.*, p. 1219.
76   This is not to say that they have to take into account all the extant teshuvot on

differs in some essential feature from the supposed precedent, or to muster a contrary opinion of another responder and to say, "This opinion I find more persuasive than the other."[77]

The Arba'ah Turim

Halakhic literature was now becoming so bulky that the time had come to make some compendium that would collect the opinions of the Rishonim in an organized fashion. This task was accomplished by the son of the Rosh, R. Yaakov b. Asher (1270–1343), the author of the *Arba'ah Turim* or Four Rows. In place of the Six Orders of the Mishnah, which included laws in effect only when the Bet ha-Mikdash stood in Jerusalem, R. Yaakov divided Jewish Law into four major divisions, as follows:

1. *Orah Hayyim*[78] or Way of Life, comprising the laws of prayer, Shabbat, and Festivals.

2. *Yoreh De'ah*[79] or Instructor of Knowledge, comprising the dietary laws, the mensturant woman and her purification (*niddah* and *mikvaot*), sundry mitzvot, and the laws of mourning.

3. *Even ha-Ezer*[80] or Stone of Help, comprising the laws of marriage, divorce and *halitzah*.

4. *Hoshen Mishpat*[81] or Breastplate of Judgment, laws concerning the processes of judgment (courts, judges, witnesses), and all

matters concerning property (contracts, loans, damages, etc.).

In his Introduction the author states, "My purpose is to gather halakhic decisions, and where there are differing opinions I shall cite them, but then I shall cite the conclusions of my father, the Rosh," The Arba'ah Turim (*Tur*, for short) soon became very popular, particularly among the Ashkenazim; the Sephardim still preferred to follow the Rambam as their halakhic guide. Also

the particular question before him, an almost impossible task. Fortunately, today there are digests and indices; and even a computer, which make the task of the modern halakhist easier; see below, p. 194.

77 Cf. *Bava Batra* 130b–131a.
78 Cf. Psalms 16:11.
79 Cf. Isaiah 28:9.
80 Cf. Gen. 2:18.
81 Cf. Exod. 28:15.

popular are R. Yaakov's notes to the Pentateuch called *Ba'al ha-Turim*, a collection of *gimatriyot* and *notarikon*.[82]

As we move from the 12th and 13th to the 14th and 15th Centuries, we find the map of Jewish settlements considerably changed. Sephardic Jewry was now dispersed in Italy, Turkey, Greece, North Africa (the *Maghreb* and Egypt). and Eretz Yisrael; while Ashkenazim had traveled eastward to Bohemia and Poland.[83] The need for religious instruction became intense as new communities sought to transplant the traditional practices to their new surroundings. Rabbis were constantly being asked the proper minhag, and the Responsa literature grew apace. Simultaneously. halakhic authorities were composing digests of the Halakhah, codifying laws and customs. Differences between Sephardim and Ashkenazim were becoming more pronounced as each branch of the Diaspora maintained its respective traditions and halakhic scholars referred more and more to their respective predecessors.

Among the many Ashkenazic responders who enriched the Halakhah in this period of transition, the following stand out: R. Yaakov b. Moshe ha-Levi Moellin (*Maharil*, c. 1360–1427) of Mainz, best known for his *Sefer Minhagei Maharil*; his disciple R. Yaakov b. Yehudah Weil (d. c. 1455); R. Yisrael b. Petaḥiah Isserlein (1390–1460) of Neustadt near Vienna, author of *T'rumat ha-Deshen*; R. Yosef Kolon *(Maharik* d. 1480), who studied under the Maharil and taught in many of the new settlements in Northern Italy. What characterized these poskim was their temerity and self-deprecation[84] which had its repercussions in the stringent decisions of their successors in Poland.(see below p. 00)

---

82 See above, p. 138.

83 This was the period of the "Black Plague", when much Jewish blood was shed and many Jewish communities were wiped out. For a brief description, see Margolis and Marx, *A History of the Jewish People* (JPS, Phila. 1938), pp. 404–409. In a recent volume, *Hakhmei Ashkenaz etc.* (Mossad Bialik, Jer. 1984), Y.A. Dinari takes issue with the view of the historians that — to quote Margolis and Marx — "On the intellectual side it was an orphaned generation, etc." The Halakhic literature produced by this generation suffices to correct this negative view.

84 See statement of Maharil, (quoted by Dinari, *op. cit.* Intro.), "Now this orphaned generation, in which no one knows between his right and his left; and the incidental discussions of the Rishonim are superior to the substantial Torah of the Aharonim." Though already in the Talmud we find the statement "If the Rishonim are like the sons of angels, we are like the sons of mortals, etc."

Outstanding Sephardi responders include: R. Yom Tov b. Avraham Ishbili (*Ritva* c. 1280–1340), disciple of Rashba and Ra'ah, whose commentaries to the Talmud have now been published in critical editions by the Institute for the Publication of Rishonim and Mossad Harav Kook; R. Yitzhak b. Sheshet Barfat (*Rivash* 1326–1407), who settled in Algier; R. Shimon b. Zemaḥ Duran (*Rashbaz* 1361–1444), who succeeded the Rivash in Algier and whose Teshuvot are known as *Tashbatz*. In the Balkans, to which many Spanish expelees migrated, Yosef b. Shlomo Taitatzk of Salonika was recognized as an outstanding halakhic authority.

One of the most unusual scholars of this period, a Sephardi who studied for a time under the Rosh, was Estori b. Moshe ha-Parḥi (c. 1285–1360), whose work on the geography of Eretz Yisrael both from its halakhic and historical aspects, *Kaftor ve-Pherah* (Knop and Flower: on Palestine and its Antiquities) is a classic. In addition to his broad knowledge of Talmudic literature, he was fluent in several languages besides Hebrew and studied all the sciences of his day. After arriving in Palestine — he was among the expelees from France under Philip IV (1306) — he lived for a time in Jerusalem, whence he undertook a scientific study of the holy places in Eretz Yisrael, traveling through the length and breadth of the land. To commit to writing the results of his research, he settled in Bet She'an (Beisan), to demonstrate that that city, contrary to popular opinion, is within the sacred boundaries of the Holy Land.[85] Two centuries passed before his work was published, and immediately it was recognized by the outstanding scholars as an authoritative volume on a subject which had long been neglected but which became more and more important as Jews streamed from the four corners of the Diaspora to the ancient Homeland.

The period of the Rishonim comes to a close at the close of the 15th Century. It is interesting to note that halakhic periods discussed up to this point in our history extend over approximately five centuries! Talmudic, 1–500 C.E.; Geonim, 500–1000 C.E.; Rishonim, 1000–1500 C.E. The challenges posed by the persecu-

---

(*Shabbat* 112b), this did not preclude the authorities from asserting that the Halakhah is according to the later authorities, on the grounds that "we are like dwarfs of the shoulders of giants;" i.e. we can see further than they, for we have examined their views but they have not examined ours.

85   See *Religious Foundations* etc. *op. cit.* pp. 43–44, for a brief discussion of the sacred boundaries of Eretz Yisrael.

tions and expulsions of both Christians and Muslims and by the constant migrations were met and overcome by the uninterrupted study of Torah and the determined leadership of the halakhic authorities. The abundant literature produced by the Rishonim has been brought to light largely in this century, as the tools of modern scholarship have been refined and ancient manuscripts have been transformed into printed texts. As we move along in history we shall see in what way post-medieval authorities met the challenges of their times, culminating in the challenge to their very authority.

9

The *Shulḥan Arukh: The Set Table*

ואלה המשפטים אשר תשים לפניהם (שמות כא, א):
ערכם לפניהם כשלחן ערוך

And these are the ordinances which you shall set before them (Exod.
21:1): Arrange them before them like a set table.*

The Bet Yosef

The *Arba'ah Turim*[1] soon "suffered" the fate common to most
Codes of Jewish Law; before two hundred years went by it was
already subjected to the critical analysis of a cluster of commentaries. Most significant among them is the *Bet Yosef* of R. Yosef b.
Ephraim Karo. Yosef Karo was born in Spain in 1488, but soon had
to take up the wanderer's staff with his family till they arrived in
Constantinople, where he received his first instruction in Torah.
From there he moved to Andrianopolis, where he came under the
influence of the noted kabbalist Shlomo Molkho. There he began
his famous commentary to the *Tur*, citing first Talmudic sources,
then elaborating upon the opinions of the Rishonim, especially of
the Sephardim, and finally drawing his own conclusions. Before
publishing this comprehensive work, which occupied him for
twenty years, Karo decided to settle in Safed, (*Tz'fat*) of the Galilee,
which by the middle of the 16th Century was a "city full of ḥakhamim and soferim," actually full with halakhic scholars and mystical
kabbalists, the latter being predominant. Karo combined in himself
the attributes of both; in his personal life he adopted the esoteric

---

*   *Mekhilta ad loc.*
1   See above, p. 146.

ways of the Kabbalah and steeped himslef in its lore, at the same time preserving his intellectual integrity in his study of the Halakhah.

Foremost among the halakhists then in Safed was Yaakov Berab, known for his abortive attempt to reconstitute the Sanhedrin.[2] Karo, who was the youngest of the four scholars originally selected by Berab to receive the traditional Semikhah, decided to produce a work, based upon his Bet Yosef, that would in perhaps a limited way serve as a central and unifying force in the absence of a Sanhedrin. This is the *Shulḥan Arukh*, which became in a relatively short time — with the reservations we shall soon discuss — the basis for all subsequent halakhic decision. Karo patterned his Shulhan Arukh after the four divisions of the *Tur*, but he did not cite any conflicting opinions. He rather followed the example of the Rambam's Mishneh Torah and set down the law in terse and decisive statements. He was guided primarily by the opinions of the Rif, the Rambam, and the Rosh, but also took into consideration the opinions of more recent Responsa. A moot question is the extent to which the Kabbalah influenced some of his decisions. One modern scholar sums it up as follows: "Not only did the author of the Shulhan Arukh *not* guard himself against the influence of the Kabbalah; he listened to it willingly as far as a great halakhic scholar like him could reconcile his views with it."[3]

One cannot understand Karo's decision to write the Shulhan Arukh without describing his ambience; mid-16th Century Safed. Here was a prototypical *kibbutz galuyot*, an ingathering of the Exiles from Spain, a gathering in one community of the outstanding *ḥakhmei Sefarad* of the time together with the outstanding proponents of the kabbalah, R. Yitzḥak Luria — the *Ari ha-Kadosh* — and his disciple R. Ḥayyim Vital. Here lived the great preacher R. Moshe Alshikh, and here lived the great poets, Yisrael Najara, composer of the hymn *Yah Ribbon Alam*, and Shlomo Alkabetz, composer of the liturgical poem *Lekhah Dodi*. Such an abundance of religious culture could not fail to have implications for all centers of the Jewish Diaspora.

---

2   See *Religious Foundations etc., op. cit.*, pp. 110–111.

3   Y. Katz, *op. cit.*, pp. 67

    For further discussion of relationship between Kabbalah and Halakhah, see R. Margaliot, *Sefer Sha'arei Zohar* and Yaakov Ḥayyim, *Kaf ha-Ḥayyim*.

Karo is also the author of the *Kesef Mishnah*, a commentary to Rambam's Mishneh Torah giving the sources to the Rambam's rulings and defending him against the strictures of the Ravad. Karo, like all other distinguished halakhic scholars, was the recipient of *sheilot* from many quarters, and his *teshuvot* are collected in his *Avkat Rokhel*. Other halakhic scholars who received their Torah training in Safed and left their mark in the history of the Halakhah with their Responsa include the following: R. Moshe mi-Trani (*Ha-Mabit*, 1500–1580), one of the ḥakhamim selected by Yaakov Berav for semikhah. R. David b. Shlomo ibn Zimra (*Radbaz*, 1480–1574) was Chief Rabbi of Cairo for forty years, and his halakhic decisions are quoted to this day. It is his decision that the Falashas of Ethiopia are full-fledged Jews that has prompted the State of Israel in our time to bring them to their ancient Homeland and reunite them with their fellow-Jews. Radbaz brought many Sephardi Jews into line with their Ashkenazi coreligionists as far as the calendar is concerned. In his day Jews in Egypt were still using the *minyan ha-shtarot*, reckoning the years from the time of Alexander's conquest of Palestine, in all their documents. Radbaz instituted that they use the *minyan ha-yetzirah*, reckoning the years from the Creation, a system of dating which had already been instituted in France and Germany by the Tosafists and which is employed by all of Jewry today. Radbaz, incidentally, did not give his approval to Berab's attempt to revive the traditional Semikhah. His disciple and successor in Egypt was R. Bezalel b. Avraham Ashkenazi (d. 1592), known for his collection of the opinions of the Rishonim entitled *Shitah Mekubetzet*, a standard text in Yeshivot to this day. The Ari ha-Kadosh was one of his disciples.

In preparing the Shulhan Arukh it had been Karo's intention, as it was that of previous codifiers, to provide a handy, yet comprehensive, digest of Jewish Law which could serve even the layman, who had to apply the manifold injunctions of his faith to his daily life. However, the Shulhan Arukh of a Sephardi could not serve the Ashkenazi Jew very well, for he was obliged to follow the decisions and customs of his own authorities. Before we can describe how this deficiency was overcome, we have to describe the rise of a new center of Torah learning for Ashkenazic Jewry.

Ḥakhmei Polin (Poland)

Though Jews had settled in Poland several centuries earlier,[4] it was only towards the end of the 15th Century that Torah scholars migrated from Germany to Poland and established Yeshiⱴot. R. Moshe Mintz was perhaps the earliest, coming from Mainz in 1474 to become head of the Jewish community in Posen (Poznan). The real founder of Torah learning in Poland was R. Yaakov Polack (1460–1530), who as a youth had studied in Germany but went back to Cracow to head a Yeshiva which attracted many native sons.

He accentuated in his teaching the analytic system of learning taught by the Tosafists by introducing the *pilpul ha-ḥilukim*, casuistic argument by means of which scholars could display their intellectual prowess in constructing speculative systems of interpretation and hair-splitting distinctions without reaching a *pesak halakhah*, a practical decision. And though many decried this system of learning, it persisted in the halls of Polish *batei midrashim*.

Yaakov Polack's foremost disciple was Shalom Shakhna of Lublin; and the latter's foremost disciple — and eventually his son-in-law — was R. Moshe b. Yisrael Isserlis (1530–1572), better known by his acronym, the *Rema*.[5] One of the basic texts in the Polish schools was the *Tur*, and the Rema decided to write to it a commentary to clarify its sources and bring it up-to-date. However, when Karo's Bet Yosef reached Poland, he was dismayed; the work had already been done, and in exemplary fashion, by Karo. Upon second thought, however, Rema decided to publish his commentary, which he called *Darkhei Moshe*, since Bet Yosef ignored many of the teachings and minhagim of the Ashkenazim. Once Karo published his summary of the Bet Yosef as the Shulḥan Arukh, Rema decided to add to it his *hagahot*, his notes, to set down the Ashkenazic practice. He called these notes a *mapah*, a tablecloth covering the "set table" of Karo. Together they constitute the authoritative Code of Jewish Practice; the Sephardim following the decisions of Karo, called the *meḥaber* or "composer" of the Shulḥan Arukh, and the Ashkenazim following the decisions of Rema.

---

4   See Margolis and Marx, *History of the Jewish People,* pp. 527 ff.
5   A good biography covering all aspects of Rema's life is that of A. Siev (Hebrew, Yeshiva Univ., New York, 1972).

153

An examination of the differences between Karo's decisions and those of the Rema will reveal some of the basic differences between Ashkenazi approach to halakhic decision and that of the Sephardim. Because of the system of pilpul which dominated in the Ashkenazic schools, there was great hesitancy among them in making clear cut decisions where earlier authorities had expressed contradictory opinions and the rule adopted was always to follow the more stringent opinion. This hesitancy, for example, reflected itself in declaring as forbidden slaughtered animals whose kashrut could be ascertained only after an examination of its organs, because of a categorical assumption that we lack today the competence to make such examination.[6] Force of law was given to many minhagim which added restrictions in marital relations or to those in mourning, and a dire warning was issued that "anyone who breaches the fence in such matters where the custom is to be strict will be bitten by a serpent."[7] Some restrictions due to stringent rulings were so severe that it became necessary to suggest that a lenient ruling may be adopted in case of "substantial loss" (*hefsed merubeh*) or "moment of urgency" (*she'at ha-dehak*).[8] In some of his Responsa Rema spoke out against those who would declare something forbidden where sanction could be found for permitting it, on the grounds that "the Torah had pity on Israel's wealth."[9] Well known is Rema's decision to permit a wedding ceremony on a Friday night, though forbidden by the Talmud, in order to spare embarrassment for the bride.[10] Rema also recognized the failings of the system of pilpul when, in the section dealing with the obligation to respect one's teacher, he says, "In these times, the chief quality of a rabbi is not in teaching the pilpul and the hilukim which are now customary, but in teaching the pesak halakhah and in setting before his pupil the truth."[11]

6   *Rema* to *Yoreh De'ah*, Sec. 30, par. 2.
7   *Ibid.*, Sec. 196, par. 13. See also *ibid.* par. 11, and sec. 391, par. 2–3, *inter alia*, for laws of mourning.
8   E.g., *ibid.* Sec. 69, par. 20.
9   Responsum 28. Cf. J.T. *Betzah* 3:4 (62a).
10   Responsum 125. Cf. Sh. A. *Orah Hayyim*, 339:4.
11   *Rema* to *Yoreh De'ah*, Sec. 242, par. 30.

Objections to Pilpul

Rema was not the only one of his generation who spoke out against the system of pilpul. R. Shlomo b. Yeḥiel Luria (the *Marharshal*, 1510–1584), a cousin of the Rema and his equal — if not his superior — in Talmudic erudition, found much to criticize in 16th Century Polish Jewry in addition to the faulty system of learning. He inveighed against the appointment of rabbis who were not *talmidei ḥakhamim* (scholars), and he derided those who were scrupulous in wearing a cap at all times — he argued that going bareheaded is at most a minor violation — while permitting themselves to eat food prepared by a Gentile. He also criticized the Rema for studying the Rambam's philosophical works, but staunchly defended the study of Kabbalah. In his time the first printed editions of the Talmud enjoyed wide distribution, and Luria appended to them many corrections of the text (*hagahot Rashal*). He is best known for his incisive Talmudic commentary *Yam shel Shlomo*, daring at times to dispute some of the conclusions of the Rishonim.

Another prominent contemporary of the Rema spared no words in castigating the system of learning current in his day.[12] He is R. Yehudah Loewy b. Bezalel (1520–1609), better known as the *Maharal mi-Prague* and famous as the creator of a "Golem" or Frankenstein monster. (Incidentally, the purpose of the Golem was to protect the Jewish community of Prague from the incessant and insidious propaganda of the Church which led to a series of expulsions). In Poland at that time children were introduced to the Talmud at a very early age, learning more by rote than by real understanding, skipping over the study of the Mishnah. The Maharal urged the inclusion of the Mishnah in the curriculum preliminary to the study of the Talmud as pedagogically sound and as recommended by the Mishnah itself.[13]

It was a disciple of the Maharal who wrote the *Tosafot Yom Tov*, a popular commentary to the Mishnah.[14] R. Yom Tov Lipman Heller (1579–1654) is also noted for his commentary to the Rosh, divided

---

12   A critique of the educational system of the time can be found in A.P. Kleinberger, *ḤaMaḥashavah ha-Pedagagiyut shel Hamaharal*, Jer. 5722, chap. 2. See also S. Assaf, *Mekorot le'Toldot ha-Ḥinukh*, Tel Aviv, 5685.

13   *Avot* 5:21.

14   For other commentaries, see above p. 82.

into two parts, *Ma'adanei Melekh* and *Lehem Hamudot*. Yet another contemporary of the Rema joined the ranks of objectors to pilpul; R. Mordekhai b. Avraham Yaffe, about whom we shall have more to say later. Despite this sharp criticism on the part of such noted scholars, this mode of study continued in all intensity in Central and Eastern Europe, surviving the appalling pogroms that took place in the 17th Century, when Cossack hordes under Chmielnicki devastated dozens of Polish communities. And this system of learning is still adhered to in many traditional Yeshivot of the 20th Century, in defiance of the principles of pedagogy.

Reactions to the Shulhan Arukh

The promulgation of the Shulhan Arukh was greeted at first with the same objections that greeted previous codes of Jewish Law. The foremost scholars in Poland at the time of the Rema argued that a digest of the Halakhah without specifying the sources was insufficient for arriving at a proper *pesak halakhah*. A Shulhan Arukh is an easy way out in place of the painstaking research required for a valid decision. Furthermore, it diverts students from the study of the Talmud and Rishonim, which is the only proper way of fulfilling the mitzvah of Talmud Torah. The most strenuous objector to the Shulhan Arukh was the Maharal of Prague. He wrote, "To decide halakhic questions from the Codes (Rambam, Tur, Shulhan Arukh) without knowing the source of the ruling was not the intent of these authors. Had they known that their works would lead to the abandonment of the Talmud, they would not have written them. It is better for one to decide on the basis of the Talmud even though he might err, for a scholar must depend solely upon his understanding. As such, he is beloved of God and preferable to the one who rules from a code but does not know the reason for the ruling; such a one walks like a blind person."[15]

Rabbi Mordekhai Yaffe, (1530–1612) a colleague of the Maharal, also objected to the Shulhan Arukh, though on somewhat different grounds. He was not satisfied with the Shulhan Arukh because of its brevity, but he was also not satisfied with the Bet

15   Quoted from the Maharal's *Netivot Olam* by A. Siev, *op. cit.*, p. 360, n. 2.

Yosef because of its prolixity, and therefore he decided to write a work that would be somewhat in between. His summation of the Halakhah, conceived as a commentary to the Tur, comprised five of the ten volumes published under the title *Levushim*. R. Mordekhai Yaffe was distinguished by his interest in secular sciences in addition to his Talmudic scholarship. Another work somewhat similar to the Levushim but more prolix, containing elements of Halakhah and *Mussar* (moral exhortation), Kabbalah and Homiletics, was written by R. Yeshayah Hurwitz (1560–1630). Entitled *shenei luhot ha-brit* (the two tablets of the covenant), it became known by its acrostic *Sh'L'aH'* with the honorific appendage *ha-kadosh* (the holy) because of its emphasis on the need for abstinence from worldly pleasures.

Another critic of the Shulhan Arukh, who also criticized the Levushim, was R. Yoel Shmuel Sirkis (d. 1640). He wrote an extensive commentary to the Tur similar to the Bet Yosef which he called *Bayit Hadash*, and he is therefore known by its acrostic as the *Ba'H'*. His critical notes, *hagahot ha-Bah*, are printed in most editions of the Talmud. One of his rulings created quite a stir; against the opinion of many authorities he permitted the use of *hadash*, i.e. grain grown after the 16th of Nisan, claiming that the prohibition did not apply to grain grown by non-Jews.[16] Bah was among the many who opposed the study of philosophy but defended the study of Tanakh and Dikduk (Hebrew grammar), and suggested that youngsters who are not good students of the Talmud should be given vocational training.

Yet another famous Polish Rosh Yeshiva found the Shulhan Arukh unsatisfactory. He was R. Meir b. Gedaliah (*Maharam mi-Lublin*, 1558–1616), who headed Yeshivot in the three largest Polish communities, Lublin, Cracow, and Lvov (Lemberg). His *hiddushim* to the Talmud, *Meir Einei Hakhamim*, is regarded as a significant contribution to the study of the Talmud, and it is included in many standard editions of the Talmud. Polish Torah also found its way to Italy through another *maharam*, R. Meir b. Yitzhak Katzenellenbogen (1482–1565), who studied under R. Yaakov Polack in Poland but headed the Yeshiva in Padua. Italy was a crossroads for the Spanish exiles, some remaining there, others moving on to Izmir and Kushta (Constantinople) and Salon-

16   See Tur, *Yoreh De'ah*, Sec. 293.

ica in Turkey, which was a great center of Torah at the time. One of its leading rabbis who did a great deal to assist these Exilees in their migrations was R. Eliyahu b. Avraham Mizrahi, (c. 1450–1525) Chief Rabbi of Constantinople. He is best known for his extensive commentary to Rashi, defending him from his critics. Mizrahi was also a respondent to many halakhic queries, and his Responsa have been published in two volumes. Following him as the outstanding rabbi in the Balkans (Salonica) was Shmuel b. Moshe di-Modena (*ha-Rashdam* 1506–1589), whose numerous Responsa were cited by most subsequent authorities. From Turkey many — Yosef Karo among them — moved on to Eretz Yisrael. Again we see that no amount of persecution and expulsion could weaken Jewish clinging to both the study and practice of Torah.

Commentaries to the Shulhan Arukh

Objections notwithstanding, the Shulhan Arukh in its combined form of the *mehaber* (Karo) with the Rema became firmly established as the standard text for every religious leader to consult before rendering a *pesak halakhah*. By this time, the number of halakhic authorities had become so numerous and halakhic opinions so varied that the average rabbi, pressed for answers to the many questions of his constituents and unsure of his own competence to decide between two great masters, had to have a ready authority upon whom he could rely without being challenged. However, Halakhah has a dynamic of its own, and the acceptance of the Shulhan Arukh by no means closed the door to continued analysis of all its sources and opinions. This is attested to by the not unexpected cluster of commentaries, which increased with each new edition of the Shulhan Arukh. We should not forget that by this time printing had long replaced the cumbersome copying of manuscripts, and more and more rabbis were anxious to see their *hiddushim* in print. In fact, the *Vaad Arba Aratzot* — the supreme constituent body of the Polish communities — tried to curb some of this activity by passing a regulation that authors must first obtain the approval (*haskamah*) of leading rabbis before publishing their works, a practice still observed by traditional scholars today.

Before we turn to the noteworthy commentators of the Shulhan Arukh who flourished in the 17th Century, we must record an

158

outstanding contributor to the study of the Talmud who preceded them. R. Shmuel Eliezer ha-Levi Idlish (*Maharsha*, 1555–1631)) was a Polish rabbi who despite his Talmudic erudition did not consider himself a *posek* and therefore did not publish any Responsa or commentary to the Shulhan Arukh. His efforts were devoted to a concise explanation of both halakhic and aggadic portions of the Talmud, especially a clarification of Rashi and Tosafot. His *hiddushei halakhot* and *hiddushei aggadot* have become standard works published in almost all editions of the Talmud. In his comments to the aggadic portions, which so often are cryptic and seemingly irrational, he gives a reasonable explanation, deliberately avoiding the mysticism of the Kabbalah.

The first to write an extensive commentary to the Shulhan Arukh was a Sephardi hakham from Turkey, R. Hayyim b. Yisrael Benvenisti (1603–1673). He is author of *Knesset ha-Gedolah*, whose major purpose was to bring the Shulhan Arukh up-to-date by citing the Responsa published after its appearance. His own Responsa, published in four volumes, reflect the conditions under which Jews of his time lived in Turkey. Another Sephardi, Hizkiah de Silva (1659–1698), who was born in Livorno but studied and lived most of his life in Jerusalem, wrote a critical analysis of the Shulhan Arukh "filling in its lacunae and adding his own conclusions" entitled *P'ri Hadash*. His independent thinking is displayed in his analysis of which liquids prepared by a non-Jew may or may not be consumed by a Jew. On the one hand, he would forbid drinking liquor made from grain in the house of a non-Jew — the Shulhan Arukh permits it — but permits drinking of non-Jewish coffee and chocolate.[17] He also agrees with the Radbaz that the milk of a non-Jew not supervised by a Jew though forbidden by the Talmud, may be consumed if there is no non-kosher animal in the non-Jew's herd, and he himself while in Amsterdam drank such milk.[18]

We return now to Poland, actually that part of Poland or Russia called Lithuania,[19] and especially to the city of Vilna. (Beginning with the 17th Century and culminating in the 20th, the system of learning in Lithuania diverged from the type of pilpul which characterized Polish learning, and we shall have more to say about that later.) The following native sons of Vilna wrote commentaries to

17 *Yoreh De'ah*, Sec. 114.
18 See Responsa *Hatam Sofer, Yoreh De'ah* no. 107.
19 Lithuania had a *Vaad* of its own and was not included in the *Vaad Arba Aratzot*.

the Shulhan Arukh which became standard in all subsequent editions: R. Shabbatai b. Meir ha-Cohen (*Shakh*, 1621–1663), to *Yoreh De'ah* and *Hoshen Mishpat*. R. Moshe b. Yitzhak Lima (1610–1666) wrote the *Helkat Mehokek* to *Even ha-Ezer*. R. Moshe Ravkash (d. 1672) wrote *Be'er ha-Golah*, mainly citing the sources. Going back to Poland, one of the first commentators was R. Yehoshua Falk (d. 1614), who studied under Rema and Maharshal. He first wrote a commentary to the Tur called *D'rishah U'P'rishah* and then to Shulhan Arukh *Hoshen Mishpat* called *Sefer Me'irat Einayyim (S'M'A')*. Another standard commentary to all four divisions was written by R. David ha-Levi (d. 1667), son-in-law of the Bah, and is entitled *Turei Zahav (Ta'Z')*. R. Shmuel of Fiorda (d. 1666) wrote the *Bet Shmuel* to *Even ha-Ezer*. The standard commentary to *Orah Hayyim* is the *Magen Avraham*, written by R. Avraham Abli Gumbiner (1637–1683). It received wide acclaim and authority, especially by the Polish hasidim, because of the author's positive attitude towards the Kabbalah and his insistence upon the sanctity of local minhag.

The Shulhan Arukh also spread to Western Europe, where Torah had declined in the 14th century because of the many persecutions and expulsions. It now, in the 17th and 18th centuries, experienced a resurgence of Torah learning, and we find distinguished talmidei hakhamim in Amsterdam, where there was a large Spanish-Portuguese community, in Frankfurt, Metz and the tri-cities of Altona-Hamburg-Wandsbek (*A'H'U'*). In the ancient city of Worms lived and taught Yair Hayyim Bachrach (1638–1701), best known for his Responsa *Havot Yair*. At this time there were two main centers for the printing of the many hiddushim and teshuvot being published; Livorno, mainly for Sephardi scholars, and Amsterdam for both Sephardim and Ashkenazim. We should also remember that it was from Amsterdam at this time, mainly through the efforts of Menasheh b. Yisrael, that the doors to Jewish settlement in England which had been closed for centuries were open once again to become a haven for Torah learning and scholarship.

With the Shulhan Arukh firmly established one would assume that controversies in Jewish life would be confined to the disputations of scholars concerning things prohibited and things permitted,[20] with all Jews living happily under the dominion of the Hala-

---

20 An example of such controversy, which arrayed scholar against scholar in

khah. This, however, was not to be. As the 17th Century came to a close the unity in Jewish life in Europe[21] was threatened by two major schisms, one egalitarian in character and the other anti-halakhic. The origins of these movements and the reactions to them by the masters of the Halakhah will be discussed in the next chapter.

fierce argument, was the question of the validity of a bill of divorcement (*get*) written in Cleves, Germany in 1766.

21 Sephardi communities in the Balkans, the Middle East and North Africa were not affected by these movements until much later.

10

Challenge and Response I: Hasidism

חסידים הראשונים היו שוהין
שעה אחת ומתפללין כדי שיכוונו לבם לאביהם שבשמים
The Hasidim of old would wait an hour and then pray,
so that they may direct their heart
to their Father in Heaven*

Revolts against the Halakhah

In the course of our discussion of the history of the Halakhah we
have made some passing reference to revolts against the basic
premise of the Halakhah; namely, the authenticity of the *Torah-she-
b'al-Peh*. They were antinomian in character; i.e. they challenged
the rule of ritual law in Judaism as taught by the Sages. The first of
these, at the very beginning of the systematic promulgation of the
Oral Law, was initiated by the Sadducees.[1] Then came Christianity,
with its mocking of Rabbinic or Pharisaic legislation. In the early
Middle Ages, in the period of the Geonim, the Rabbis had to
contend with the Karaites, who disputed the Rabbinic interpretation of Scriptural law.[2] These revolts, though they led to much
bitter polemic, and in the case of Christianity to much bitter persecution, dit not affect to any appreciable extent the course of halakhic activity, which proceeded according to its own dynamic. In the
middle of the 17th Century, however, when it seemed that the
Halakhah as defined in the Shulhan Arukh and its commentaries
would hold full sway over all segments of Jewry, there arose
another movement which developed into antinomianism which

---

*   Mishnah *Berakhot* 5:1
1   See above, p. 69.
2   See above, p. 118.

162

posed a most serious challenge to the Halakhah and to Rabbinic leadership.

Shabbatai Zvi

The messianic fervor which had been aroused by the kabbalistic teachings of Isaac Luria (the Ari ha-Kadosh) and Ḥayyim Vital in the middle of the 16th Century was sparked a century later by Shabbatai Zvi and his prophet Nathan of Gaza into a frenzy of messianic expectations which spread like wildfire through the entire Diaspora. In Europe these messianic hopes were reinforced by the great suffering brought about by the Chmielnicki persecutions, and indeed led to the appearance of another pseudo-Messiah, Jacob Frank. At first, most Rabbis did not pay too much attention to Shabbatai Zvi — in fact, a few were swept along by his pronouncements — but when he began to flout certain rulings of the Halakhah[3] they opposed him vigorously and the movement lost most of its adherents, especially after he embraced Islam. Nevertheless, the repercussions of this antinomian movement continued to create upheavals in Jewish life, leading — albeit indirectly[4] — to two other revolts against the Halakhah and Rabbinic leadership which left their mark upon Judaism to this day.

Before we turn to these revolts, we must record the contributions to halakhic literature of scholars who became embroiled in violent controversy over the vestiges of Shabbataiism which lingered in Europe during the 18th Century. Zvi b. Yaakov Ashkenazi (1660–1718), known as *Ḥakham Zvi*,[5] spent most of his years as

---

3   It had been hinted in Talmudic literature that certain laws of the Torah would be abolished in the Messianic era, and Shabbatai Zvi deliberately violated some halakhic prohibitions in order to demonstrate his Messiahship. See *Niddah*, 61b, statement of R. Yosef; *Berakhot* 12b and Rashba *ibid.* (quoted by M. Kasher, *Haggadah Shelemah*, p. 119), and J.T. *Megillah* 1:7 (70d) and Rambam, end of *Hilkhot Megillah* and *Hilkhot Yesodei ha-Torah* 9:1. See also *Yalkut Shimoni* to Proverbs, n. 944 that "all Festivals will be abolished etc.," and *Vayikra Rabbah* 13:3, "A new Torah will be issued."

4   See G. Scholem, *Major Trends in Jewish Mysticism* (Schoken Publishing House) on origins of Hasidism, and A. Rubenstein, *Bein Hasidut l'Shabtaut* in Bar-Ilan Annual 5727, pp. 324–339.

5   He received the title Ḥakham, customary among the Sephardim, when he studied among them in Salonica.

Rosh Yeshiva in Altona and Amsterdam. He fought fearlessly against the followers of Shabbatai Zvi, as a consequence of which he lost his position as Chief Ashkenazi Rabbi of Amsterdam. His Responsa cover a wide range of halakhic problems as well as discussions of the rulings of post-Shulhan Arukh authorities, displaying his thorough approach and keen mind. One interesting teshuvah is a reply to a query from London, written in English but translated for him into Hebrew, about his having stated that God is Nature (*teva*) and Nature is God.[6] He explains that he meant that God is the power and the will that produces all the manifestations of Nature, such as the clouds and the rain.

It was the Ḥakham Zvi's son Yaakov Emden (1698–1776), known by the acronym *Ya'B'Z'*, who even intensified his father's opposition to Shabbataiism and led him to his famous controversy with R. Yonatan Eibeschutz. He lived most of his life in the city of his birth, Altona, where he combined Torah learning with business. He wrote against some aspects of the Kabbalah — quite daring in his time — even questioning whether the entire Zohar is a product of the Tanna R. Shimon b. Yoḥai. Among his best known works are his Responsa and his *Siddur* with all the laws and customs of prayer. His adversary Yonatan Eibeschutz (1690–1764) was not only a keen Talmudist; he was an ardent student of the Kabbalah and interested in philosophy and the natural sciences, a rare combination in those days. He was Rosh Yeshiva in Prague, but concerned himself with all communal affairs. From Prague he went to Metz for a time and then was appointed to the prestigious position of Rabbi of the tri-cities A'H'U'. He had a reputation as an *ish mofet*, a miracle worker — a central feature of incipient Hasidism — and wrote *k'mayyot*, amulets, for the prevention of sickness and death.[7] This aroused the opposition of Yaakov Emden, who was living in Altona at the time, and he accused Eibeschutz of being a follower of Shabbatai Zvi. This led to a bitter controversy that gripped all of European Jewry, with distinguished rabbis called upon to either support or refute the accusation. A large majority supported Eibeschutz, whose important works include *Sefer K'reiti U'Pleiti* (a

6 Spinoza's pantheism could easily arouse suspicion if one ventured to identify God with Nature.

7 For the ambivalent attitude of the Halakhah to amulets, see Sh. A. *Yoreh De'ah* 179:12.

commentary to the Tur) and *Ya'arot D'vash*, a very popular book of sermons.

A contemporary of Emden and Eibeschutz who took sides in their dispute — he favored Emden and also fought against the vestiges of Shabbataiism — was Yaakov Yehoshua b. Zvi Falk (1680–1756), famous for his popular commentary to the Talmud entitled *P'nei Yehoshua*. This work is so cogent in its analysis of the Talmudic text that it became a standard text in Ashkenazi Yeshivot and was popular even among Sephardi scholars. One of the latter, who visited the *P'nei Yehoshua* and praised him highly, was Ḥayyim Yosef David Azulai (1724–1806), known by the acronym *H'I'D'A'*. Born in Jerusalem, he traveled throughout Europe soliciting support for the Hebron Yeshiva[8] and finally settled in Livorno. The *Ḥida* is distinguished for his intellectual curiosity and his prolific pen.[9] Numerous volumes of great halakhic scholars are known to us only through his interest in bibliography, recorded in his *Shem ha-Gedolim*. His major halakhic work is a commentary to the Shulhan Arukh entitled Birkei Yosef. One of his teachers was another Sephardi whose works became very popular among Ashkenazim. Ḥayyim b. Moshe ibn Attar (1696–1743) was born in Morocco, became a *darshan* (preacher) in Livorno,[10] and finally was appointed Rosh Yeshiva in Jerusalem. His most famous work, *Or ha-Ḥayyim*, is a commentary to the Pentateuch with both rational and mystical interpretations. Its profound inspirational character endowed the author with the honorary title *Ha-Kadosh*, "The Holy One". His halakhic work, entitled *P'ri To'ar*, is a commentary to the Shulhan Arukh highly regarded by the 18th Century Ashkenazic authorities.

This mutual popularity of Ashkenazic and Sephardic works was rather exceptional. Generally, each group based their halakhic rulings upon their respective authorities. By this time, the scope of halakhic decisions religious authorities were called upon to make

8   A tradition dating from Talmudic times was the despatch of scholars to the Diaspora communities for the support of schools of learning; see, e.g. J.T. *Horayot* 3:4 (48a), "R. Eliezer, R. Yehoshua and R. Akiva went up to Holat Antioch to make a collection for scholars." Also, A. Yaari, *Sh'luḥei Eretz Yisrael*, Jer. 5711.

9   A good biography is that of M. Benayahu (Mossad Harav Kook, Jer. 1959, Hebrew).

10   See above, p. 160.

differed in the two communities. In the Oriental countries, Jews continued to bring their disputes in all domestic and financial as well as ritual matters to the rabbinic courts, which enjoyed complete jurisdiction over the Jewish inhabitants; whereas in Europe many Jews became more involved in general business affairs and had recourse to the civil courts to resolve their financial disputes. Thus the rabbis there were primarily concerned with problems of ritual observance.[11]

The 18th Century continued to produce outstanding Ashkenazic scholars whose works became standard texts in the Yeshivot and whose halakhic decisions, as recorded in their Responsa and commentaries to the Shulhan Arukh, became authoritative for the poskim of the 19th and 20th Centuries. Two commentators to the Shulhan Arukh worthy of mention who flourished in this century — actually they wrote commentaries to the Shulhan Arukh's standard commentaries — were Yosef b. Meir Te'omim (1727–1792) and Arye Leib b. Yosef ha-Kohen Heller (1745–1813). The former is the author of *P'ri Megadim*, an elaboration of the opinions expressed by the Taz and the Shakh.[12] The latter is the author of *Ketzot ha-Hoshen* on Shulhan Arukh Hoshen Mishpat, and *Avnei Miluim* on Even ha-Ezer. He is also the author of the popular pilpulistic treatment of some of the major principles of Jewish Law entitled *Shev She'mattata*. However, before we record further contributions to the development of the Halakhah we must turn our attention to a movement which, though not overtly challenging the principles and practices of the Halakhah, was regarded by many authorities of the day as a threat to its hegemony in Jewish life.

Roots of Hasidism

To fully appreciate the social origins of the movement called *Hasidism*,[13] one must bear in mind the special position in Jewish life

---

11 See Y. Katz, *Goy shel Shabbat* (Jer. 5744), chaps. 6 and 8 for the increased economic enterprise which led to questions of Sabbath observance. See also M. Elon, *Ha-Mishpat Ha-Ivri* (Jer. 5733), Vol. III, p. 1246. Also, H.J. Zimmels, *Ashkenazim and Sephardim* (London 1976).

12 See above, p. 160.

13 The term *hasid* or "pious one" is Biblical in origin. In the Talmud it is applied to certain individuals distinguished by their piety, as well as to a group — *Hasidim*

enjoyed by the *talmid ḥakham* or scholar ever since Talmudic times. "How stupid are some people," exclaims the Talmud, "who rise in the presence of the Sefer Torah but do not rise in the presence of a great scholar."[14] The Talmud's primary understanding of the injunction *Rise before the aged* (Lev. 19:32) was a command to honor the scholar, interpreting the work *zaken* (old person) by the acrostic *Zeh Kanah ḥokhmah*, "this person acquired wisodm,"[15] and so has it been codified by Rambam[16] and Shulhan Arukh.[17]

The honors accorded a scholar were many. In Talmudic times a very distinguished scholar would be called up to the reading of the Torah even before the Kohen or Levi.[18] In post-Talmudic times, when rabbinic humility precluded scholars from arrogating to themselves such privilege,[19] the talmid hakham would be called up third (*shlishi*), right after the Kohen and Levi. This practice was so entrenched by medieval times that Rabbenu Tam rose up to *shlishi* on Shabbat during the week in which he was in mourning after his sister.[20] The privileges due a Kohen to speak first and bless first were also accorded the talmid hakham who also had the privilege of sitting up front in the synagogue or bet ha-midrash.[21] The Halakhah ruled that scholars are exempt from municipal taxes levied for the protection of the city on the grounds that they, and not the gendarmes, are the true *neturei karta*, "guardians of the city".[22] Even a young scholar's honor was safeguarded; anyone who dared disrespect him was placed under a social ban.[23]

ha-Rishonim — who were especially scrupulous in their observance (e.g. Mishnah *Berakhot* 5:1). (For other references, see Encyclopedia Judaica, Vol. 7, p. 1383). An abundant literature has developed on modern Hasidism. See, for example, H.M. Rabinowicz, *The World of Hasidism* (Hartford, 1970) or the chapter in G. Scholem's *Major Trends in Jewish Mysticism*.

14 *Makkot* 22b.
15 *Kiddushin* 32b.
16 *Hilkhot Talmud Torah* 6:1.
17 *Yoreh De'ah* 244:1.
18 *Gittin* 59b; *Megillah* 22a.
19 See discussion in *Bet Yosef* to *Tur Orah Ḥayyim* 135; and references in *Pithei Teshuvah* to *Yoreh De'ah* 243:2, sec. 3.
20 *Tur Yoreh De'ah* 400.
21 Cf.*Bava Batra* 120a; *Horayot* 13b.
22 *Bava Batra* 22a; J.T. *Hagigah* 1:7 (76c).
23 *Mo'ed Kattan* 17a.

Special honor and reverence had to be given to one's master who taught him Torah; fear of his teacher was equated to the fear of God.[24] One had to rescue his teacher from peril before rescuing his father,[25] and restore his teacher's lost article before that of his father, "for his father brought him into this world, but his teacher brought him into the (eternal) world-to-come."[26] All this, and much more, was codified by the codifiers[27] and became standard practice in all Jewish communities.

Hasidism

In post-Medieval Polish Jewry the emoluments and encomiums of the scholar were securely upheld, and were an added incentive for the study of Torah and the achievement of scholarship. *Torah iz di beste sechorah*, "Torah is the best merchandise," was a common refrain sung in a lullaby. Thus the chief goal now was excellence in Talmudic studies, and this could best be demonstrated by one's ability to engage in pilpulistic discourse and write *hiddushim* which had little relation to the practical significance of the text.[28] The sermons infrequently delivered by the rabbi of the community — his chief responsibility was not preaching, but heading the Yeshiva and answering questions of Jewish Law — usually dealt with abstract Talmudic interpretations, scarcely understood by the untutored in the congregation. Thus a gap was created between the talmid hakham and the unlearned, referred to disparagingly as an *am ha-aretz*.[29] Already in the days of the Talmud Rabbi Akiva reported on the hostility between the scholar and the ignoramus. "When I was an *am ha-aretz* I would say, 'Would that someone give me a talmid hakham and I will bite him like a donkey.' "[30] On the other hand, the exalted position of the scholar would, among the less sensitive talmid hakham, lead him to look with disdain, if not

24   *Avot* 4:12, *Pesaḥim* 22b.
25   *Horayot* 13a.
26   Mishnah *Bava Metzia* 2:11.
27   Rambam *Hilkhot Talmud Torah* 5:1; Sh.A. *Yoreh De'ah* 242:1.
28   Cf. *Rema, Yoreh De'ah* 242:30.
29   For the different meanings of this term, see Encyclopedia Judaica, Vol. I, pp. 834–5.
30   *Pesaḥim* 49b.

indifference, upon the unlettered. In such a milieu, the masses of Jewry, whose knowledge was confined to the pages of the Siddur and the weekly portion of the Humash, felt deprived of a sense of importance and relevance to the sacred tomes of the Talmud. Furthermore, the preoccupation on the part of the scholar with the minutiae of Jewish Law tended to obscure the underlying spirit of Judaism, the "service of the heart" and the love and joy which one should experience in living in accord with Jewish tradition. Thus Judaism became for the untutored Jew a religion of despair, a gloomy burden instead of a joyous inspiration; a despair deepened by the impoverishment following the Chmielnicki pogroms and the disappointment following the pseudo-messianic hopes aroused by Shabbatai Zvi and Jacob Frank and which turned out to be ephemeral illusions.

To correct this unhappy situation was the goal of the founder of modern Hasidism, Israel b. Eliezer, best known as the *Ba'al Shem Tov*, or "Master of the Good Name" (c. 1700–1760). He preached the importance of the unlettered Jew who observed the precepts of the Torah in a spirit of comradeship and joy. A hasidic melody or *nigun*, and an homiletic observation of the *rebbi* or *zaddik*, were endowed with as much significance as an halakhic discourse. An anecdote or parable spoken by Hasidic mentor became part of sacred lore, almost on a par with the sacred literature based on the Talmud. To inspire the average Jew with a closer feeling of the Divine Presence, the Shekhinah, selections from the mystical writings of the Kabbalists were introduced into the prayer-book, and the *Zohar* — the Bible, as it were, of the Kabbalists — became the oft-quoted source of instruction. Indeed, the Hasidim adopted *nusah Sepharad* for their version of the daily prayers in place of the long-accustomed *nusah Ashkenaz* in order to follow the practice of the sephardi Kabbalist Isaac Luria, better known as the *Ari ha-Kadosh*.[31]

Already for the medieval Hasidim[32] the thrice-daily statutory prayer required by the Halakhah embedded in the text many mystical references.[33] The charismatic number of words in a prescribed prayer would determine for them the exact wording, and thus we

31 See above, p. 151.
32 See above, p. 126.
33 See G. Scholem, *Major Trends etc.*, pp. 100 ff.

find variations from the established *nusaḥ* in the Shemoneh Esreh and Sabbath Kiddush recited by the Hasidim of today.[34] The insistence that more important in prayer is the *kavanah*, the intention of the heart, rather than the routine recitation of the text, led to a relaxation of some of the rigid requirements set by the Halakhah. Thus, Hasidic rabbis would begin their morning devotions long after the time prescribed by the Shulhan Arukh. Mystical kavanah was also attributed to the performance of the mitzvot. Thus introduced into the liturgy were certain prayers to be recited prior to the performance of a mitzvah in order to verbalize these esoteric intentions. Typical of these is the one recited before the blessing over the *arba'a minnim*, the four species held aloft and waved on Sukkot during the recitation of Hallel. The opening sentence reads, "May it be Thy will...that with the fruit of the goodly tree (the etrog), branches of the palm trees, (the lulav), boughs of thick trees (the myrtle) and willows of the brook, the letters of Your singular name (the tetragrammaton) will approach each other and become as one in my hand."[35] Since it is the Zaddik who is privy to these mystical meanings — and with some he is even privy to what is going on in Heaven — the reverence and adulation which traditionally was reserved for the talmid hakham was transferred to the Hasidic Rebbi, distinguished more by his esoteric insight than by his halakhic acumen.

These deviations from the accepted norms and attitudes of the tradition alarmed the leaders of rabbinic Judaism, who by nature were conservative and wary of any change or innovation in Jewish life. Furthermore, they were painfully mindful of the extravagances and ultimate defection from Judaism of the followers of Shabbatai Zvi and Jacob Frank. They therefore pronounced a ban against this "new religion." For over a century the rift between the Hasidim and the Talmudists — designated by the new movement as *mitnagdim* or "opponents" — remained fierce. In practically every Jewish community in eastern Europe — Jewry in western Europe, as we shall see, was confronted by a different and more serious challenge —

---

34   *Tur Oraḥ Ḥayyim* 113. See Siddur of Yaakov Emden for enumeration of the words of the Kiddush.

35   This prayer has become a standard text in practically all editions of the Siddur today, including nusaḥ Ashkenaz. See, however, the condensed version in the Hertz Siddur, where this kabbalistic notion is eliminated.

there were two distinct communities, each with its spiritual leader, the *Rav* of the mitnagdim and the *Rebbi* of the Hasidim, each maintaining their separate synagogues and houses of study.

Leading Opponents of Hasidism

From the score or more of Talmudic scholars who flourished in the 18th Century and published their halakhic works, two may be singled out because of their great influence upon their own and subsequent generations. Yeḥezkel b. Yehudah ha-Levi Landau (1713–1793), Rosh Yeshiva in the distinguished community of Prague, is known as the *Nodah Bi-Yehudah* after the title of his Responsa.[36] Though opposed to the Shabbataians and their use of *kemayot* or amulets, he nevertheless defended Eibeschutz in the latter's controversy with Yaakov Emden. He was more outspoken — even to the point of derision — against the Hasidim, especially condemning their innovations in the liturgy.[37] His Responsa display his broad command of all Rabbinic literature, as well as his keen understanding of its principles and its application to all sorts of issues at hand. In them we begin to see the development of modern science and how it impinged upon halakhic rulings. Quoted to this day is the Nodah Bi-Yehudah's responsum concerning post-mortem examinations (autopsies) for the purpose of medical instruction, a violation of the law prohibiting the disgracing of a corpse.[38] Rabbi Landau also wrote ḥiddushim to the Talmud (*Tsiyyun l'Nefesh Ḥayah* or *Ts'laḥ*) and glosses to the Shulhan Arukh (*Dagul me-Revavah*).

The other leading opponent of Hasidism was Eliyahu b. Shlomo Zalman (1720–1797), better known as the Vilna Gaon and by the acronym *Hagra* (Hagaon Rabbi Eliyahu). His contemporaries also conferred upon him the honorary title *ha-Ḥasid* because of his

---

36 Published in two editions: *Mahadura Kamma* and *Mahadura Tinyana*, with over a dozen commentaries (Vilna, 1899).

37 *Yoreh De'ah, mahadura Kamma* no. 93.

38 Nodah Bi-Yehudah forbids post-mortems categorically on the grounds that no *immediate* benefit would be derived from them. One may speculate if his decision would be otherwise were he aware of the immediate communication possible today to physicians all over the world of advances in medical practice that can save lives; see below, p. 214.

exemplary saintliness. In order to pursue his studies of Rabbinic literature with utmost intensity and concentration, he secluded himself in his study and did not engage in public or communal affairs, allowing himself but two or three hours of sleep a night. Probably for the same reason he did not head a Yeshiva, and the number of his disciples was very limited.[39] Nevertheless, his influence upon the Jewry of Lithuania and the adjacent provinces in Russia and Poland was felt for generations.[40] Lithuanian Jewry, down to the humblest shopkeeper and artisan, became infused with a reinvigorated enthusiasm for the study of the Torah, and many a business man could be found whose familiarity with the Talmud equalled that of the rabbi of his community. The most distinguished disciple of the Gaon, Hayyim of Volozhin (1749–1821) founded at the suggestion of his master the renowned Yeshiva of Volozhin which for a century produced the spiritual leaders and halakhic masters of Eastern Europe, who in turn founded a dozen or more other centers of learning which flourished until they were swept away by the Nazi hordes four decades ago. The heads of these Yeshivot developed a characteristic method of study which we will have occasion to discuss as we pass from the 18th to the 19th and 20th Centuries. It should also be noted that it was a small group of the Gaon's disciples who, at his suggestion, laid the foundation for a new Jewish settlement in the Old City of Jerusalem. They were known as *Perushim* and their descendants today still adhere to *minhagei ha-Gra* which has spread to many Ashkenazic synagogues in Israel.

The Vilna Gaon's major contribution to Halakhah were his critical analyses — known as *Haga'ot Hagra* — of its primary sources, including in addition to the Talmud itself the halakhic Midrashim and the Tosefta, sources which had long been neglected by scholars addicted to pilpul. Though he did not have before him the many manuscripts available today, his encompassing knowledge of all the sources — even including the aggadic Midrashim (particularly Midrash Rabbah) and the Kabbalah (particualrly the Zohar) — and his prodigious memory enabled him to establish the

---

39 In their Introduction to the Gaon's commentary to *Orah Hayyim*, his sons enumerate seven disciples.

40 A folkloristic treatment of the Gaon's influence can be found in Y.L. Maimon, *Sarei ha-Me'ah* (Mossad Harav Kook, Jer. 5710), Vol. I.

proper text of these classics. This was not for him an academic exercise; he wanted to establish the authenticity of the rulings of the poskim, as we see in his *Bi'ur Hagra* to the Shulhan Arukh. His inclination to go back to primary sources led him to an intensive study of the *Tanakh* (the three divisions of the Hebrew Bible), especially to that of the Pentateuch, in which he found hidden allusions to countless Talmudic statements.

The Gaon understood that in order to explain certain obscurities in *Seder Zeraim* or agricultural laws, it was necessary to study mathematics, and he instructed one of his disciples, Barukh of Shklov, to translate Euclid's Geometry into Hebrew. In his Introduction, Barukh quotes his master as saying, "As one lacks knowledge of the sciences one correspondingly lacks hundredfold a knowledge of Torah." This intellectual approach to secular knowledge is in sharp contrast to the Gaon's attitude towards philosophy. Commenting upon Maimonides' contention that amulets and whispering verses to heal a scorpion's bite are of no effect,[41] the Gaon writes, "All later authorities disagreed, since many incantations are mentioned in the Talmud. He (Maimonides) followed philosophy and therefore he said that witchcraft and holy names and incantations and demons and amulets are all false. But philosophy[42] led him astray in most of its teachings to explain the statements in the Talmud as allegory and uproot their simple meaning. God forbid I should believe in them (the teachings of philosophy); rather all (Talmudic) statements are to be understood literally, though they also have a hidden meaning; not of the masters of philosophy which are external (to the faith), but of the masters of the truth (i.e. the Kabbalah)."[43] This negative attitude towards philosophy — no doubt because of its non-Jewish origins — has led the heads of the traditional Yeshivot today, the spiritual heirs of the Gaon, to oppose all secular studies except those required for professional careers.

41   *Hilkhot Avodat Kokhavim* 11:11–16.
42   The original statement said, "the accursed philosophy," but the adjective has been expunged in the printed edition. See S.K. Mirsky, *Bein Sh'ki'ah Lizriḥah* (Jer.-N.Y. 5711) p. 347, n. 24.
43   *Bi'ur Hagra, Yoreh De'ah* 179:13.

Hasidism's Loyalty to the Halakhah

The irony of history can be seen in that it is precisely the Hasidic movement, so forcefully opposed by the Gaon of Vilna, which cherishes the teachings of the Kabbalah which he embraced so uncritically. Furthermore, Hasidism kept masses of East European Jews who otherwise might have been lost to Judaism, securely within the camp of traditional Jewry and even strengthened their allegiance to Torah and its halakhic interpretation. Hasidism, unlike the Sadduceeism and Karaism of earlier generations, was not a rebellion against the Halakhah, nor even an attempt to reform it; it was a revivalist movement infusing a fresh spirit into a faith which had been losing sight of its meta-halakhic goals. Hasidim adhered to the major requirements of Jewish Law, and were distinguished from their fellow Jews primarily by such externals as a peculiar garb and an adoration of their Rebbi as being possessed of miraculous powers. Their underlying unity with rabbinic Judaism, which forestalled their breaking away from the main stream of Jewish life, can be attributed to the fact that the major emphases of their movement have their roots in the halakhic tradition of the Talmud. Not all Talmudic Sages disparaged mundane pleasures; on the contrary, they looked askance at those who would deny themselves legitimate pleasures.[44] Furthermore, joy in performing religious duties is ranked high in importance. "The Divine Presence," avers the Talmud, "abounds not in gloom but in gladness, in *Simhah shel Mitzvah*."[45] Sincerity in the service of God, and not the number of *halakhot* studied, is paramount, for "the Almighty seeks (the good intention of) the heart."[46]

The adherence of Hasidim to the Halakhah is evidenced by the important contributions to halakhic literature made by Hasidic spiritual leaders of the 18th and 19th Centuries. The list — though by no means all inclusive — of those whose works have been accepted and studied by non-Hasidic scholars is impressive.[47] Shmuel Shmelke Hurvitz of Nickolsburg (1726–1778); his brother

---

44 J.T. *Kiddushin* 4:12 (66b); *Nedarim* 10a.
45 *Pesaḥim* 117a.
46 *Sanhedrin* 106b.
47 A brief biography of each of these scholars can be found in Yitzhak Rafael, *Sefer ha-Ḥasidut* (Tel Aviv, 5715).

Pinḥas ha-Levi of Frankfurt am Main (1730–1805), author of *Sefer Hafla'ah* and *ha'Makneh*; Moshe Teitelbaum of Uhel (1759–1841), *Yismaḥ Moshe*; Menaḥem Mendel of Lubavitch (1789–1860), *Zemaḥ Zedek; Ḥayyim Halbershtam of Zanz (1793–*1877), *Divrei Ḥayyim*; Yehudah Aryeh Leib of Gur (1847–1905), *Sfat Emet*; Avraham Bornstein of Sochatshov (1840–1910), *Avnei Nezer* and *Eglei Tal*. Special mention must be made of the two distinguished rabbis who though they were not Hasidic Rebbis lived in the city of Brody, a great center of Hasidic Jewry, Ephraim Zalman Margaliot (1760–1828) and Shlomo Kluger (1785–1869). All of the above enriched the Halakhah with their numerous Responsa, responsive to the peculiar needs of their age and their distinctive followers.

One branch of Hasidism — *Habad*[48] or Lubavitch[49] — laid special emphasis upon the study of Torah; and its founder, Schneur Zalman of Liady, composed a Code of Jewish Law known as *Shulhan Arukh Harav*. Nevertheless, even for him and his followers the Halakhah does not represent the totality of Jewish wisdom and teaching. For the Hasidim, the Halakhah is *nigleh*, the revealed Torah, revealed at Sinai to all Israel; whereas there existed from time immemorial and continues to exist a corpus of esoteric lore known as *nistar*, the hidden Torah, hidden from Israel as a whole and revealed to only a chosen few in each generation since the days of Adam. Only in the generation of the Baal Shem Tov, for reasons known to his devotees, was it decreed in Heaven that this esoteric lore be revealed to all Jews. Thus, side by side with the *Shulhan Arukh Harav*, R. Schneur Zalman composed the *Sefer ha-Tanya*, the Shulhan Arukh, as it were, of this esoteric tradition. It has become — at least as far as Ḥabad is concerned — a primary text of Jewish studies, equal in importance to the study of the Talmud.[50]

Though the author of the standard Shulhan Arukh, Joseph Karo, had lived in a community steeped in the lore of the Kabbalah,

---

48 So called because the three Hebrew letters are an acrostic of the three words which play an important role in the thinking of this sect: *Ḥokhmah* (wisdom), *Binah* (understanding), and *Da'at* (knowledge).

49 After the city in which its spiritual leaders lived. The headquarters of the Lubavitcher movement today and the seat of its present leader are in Brooklyn, N.Y. but their branches and activities are world-wide.

50 Cf. Shulhan Arukh ha-Rav, Hilkhot Talmud Torah 4: "The scholars of the *Emet* (i.e. the Kabbalah) said that everyone has to study *Pardes* (i.e. mystical interpretations) for his salvation."

he did not permit its teachings to determine his halakhic decisions to any noticeable extent.[51] Not so with many Hasidic teachers, who would place upon their Kabbalistic tradition the stamp of normative Judaism. A comparison, for example, of the first page of Karo's Shulhan Arukh with that of R. Schneur Zalman is indicative of this difference. Both mention the need to mourn the destruction of the Temple; but the former only tersely. The latter, however, dwells upon it and quotes the Zohar's injunction to rise at midnight to recite the special prayers for the *Ḥurban* known as *tikkun ḥatzot*. Hasidic authorities base many of their customs and their particular version of familiar prayers upon the mysteries (*sod*) of Yitzhak Luria. In general, one may say that Hasidic Halakhah lays greater stress upon *minhag* because of its imputed mystical, i.e. divine origin, and resists more adamantly any change of the environment.[52] From the evidence we can gather in the modern State of Israel, this can be said not only of the Hasidim but of the non-Hasidic community of Torah scholars whose origins lie in Eastern Europe, particularly Lithuania.

Lithuanian Yeshivot and the Mussar Movement

The renewed concentration on Torah study in Lithuania and environs, prompted by the Gaon of Vilna and his disciple Ḥayyim of Volozhin, led to the same excesses which had given rise to Hasidism; namely, a concentration on the dialectical and ritualistic aspects of the Halakhah, and the overbearing desire to achieve distinction as a Talmid Hakham. Again Jewry was confronted by the perennial problem of the overshadowing of the mitzvot that deal with social relationships and ethical conduct (*bein adam la-haveiro*), and the preponderance of intellectualism estranging the masses. In Lithuania, where Hasidism had made little inroads, the attempt to correct this imbalance came from a deeply perceptive and sensitive individual, the founder of the *Mussar* movement,[53]

---

51 See above, p. 151.

52 For a study of Hasidic law and custom, see A. Wertheim, *Halakhot ve-Halikhot Be-Ḥasidut* (Jer., 5720).

53 For a history of the Mussar movement, see D. Katz, *Tenuat ha-Mussar*, Tel Aviv 5714.

Israel Lipkin (1810–1883), better known as Yisrael Salanter, i.e. from the town of Salant. The term Mussar as found in the Bible is apposite to both *Hokhmah* (wisdom) and Torah,[54] and means both moral instruction and discipline, and that is how it was understood by Salanter. He emphasized the importance of self-discipline, which can be achieved through introspection and self-analysis. He strove to focus the Torah student's attention on the development of his personal character and on the consideration of the needs and sensitivities of one's fellowman. He recommended the introduction into the curriculum of the Yeshivot the study of the so-called "Mussar literature"; primarily the *Hovat ha-Levavot* ("Duties of the Heart") of Bahya ibn Pekuda, the *Kuzari* of Yehudah Halevi, and the *Mesilat Yesharim* ("Path of the Righteous") of Moshe Hayyim Luzzatto. To take charge of this new program of studies, a new member was added to the faculty of the Yeshiva, the *mashgiah* i.e. the person who would supervise the ethical development of each student and lead discussions dealing with related subjects. The most prominent among these adjuncts to the Rosh Yeshiva was Nosson (Nathan) Nata Finkel of the Slabodka Yeshiva.

Yisrael Salanter was also founder of a new institution in the Yeshiva world, the *Kollel*, which has now become a most prominent feature of Torah study. Until his time, Yeshiva students remained in the Yeshiva until they married; after marriage they would leave the Yeshiva. Many would continue their Torah studies, but privately in their own homes or in the homes of their parents-in-law — who would support the young couple for a number of years — or in the town's Bet ha-Midrash. Salanter, however, organized a group of married students to study together, and he went about to raise support for this new institution, comparable to the graduate department of a university.

The Halakhic Personality

Not all Roshei Yeshiva welcomed Salanter's Mussar program; indeed, some opposed it vigorously. Their contention was that the Halakhah contains within itself its own checks and balances. A sincere pursuit of Talmudic studies — *Torah lishmah* or Torah for

54   Cf. Proverbs 1:2,8.

its own sake — will develop in the student the qualities of humility and sensitivity to one's fellowman so essential for proper spiritual leadership. This can be seen in the personalities of the great masters of the Halakhah through the ages. A combination of the highest scholarship, with attention to the minutiae of religious duty, together with the deepest moral sensitivities characterized the lives of Rabbi Akiva of Talmudic times, of Maimonides of the Middle Ages, and of the *Ḥafets Ḥayyim* (Israel Meir ha-Cohen of Radun) of modern times. These exemplary personalities and countless others in each generation were fashioned by singular and unquestioned devotion to the Halakhah, which they regarded as the *summum bonum* in human experience.

True, the Sages of the Talmud recognized that this is not always the case. Occasionally a Talmid Ḥakham may conduct himself in an unprincipled and repugnant manner. Such reprobate conduct was severely condemned; it causes *Ḥillul ha-Shem*, the profanation of God's Name. "One who studied Scripture and Mishnah and further studies under great masters but his dealings are not trustworthy and he does not speak gently to people, what do people say about him? 'Woe to him who studied Torah...see how corrupt and loathsome are his ways.' " Such students, however, are exceptional; the real Talmid Ḥakham is quite different. Of him the Talmud says, "One who studies Torah and deals honestly and speaks gently, of him people say, 'See this one who studied Torah, how pleasant and proper are his ways.' "[55]

Everyone who reads the biographies of the noteworthy halakhic masters of all ages and climes will bear this out; and those of the 19th Century with whom we are presently concerned are excellent examples. Rabbi Joseph B. Soloveitchik, a contemporary scion of the House of Volozhin,[56] in a classic thesis entitled *Ish ha-Halakhah* (The Halakhic Man)[57] describes how the personality of the halakhist was fashioned by his concept of the Halakhah. Like the pure mathematician, who conceives *a priori* propositions which later are applied to the concrete objects of the physical world, so the hala-

---

55 *Yoma* 86a.
56 His father's father was Ḥayyim Soloveitchik, who married a granddaughter of the Netziv, who was married to the granddaughter of Ḥayyim of Volozhin.
57 First published in 1944 in the Journal of the Yeshiva University, *Talpiot*, and since republished and also rendered in English.

khist sees the Halakhah as consisting of ideal propositions revealed in the Torah which have to be applied to the real world. In other words, the halakhist proceeds from an ideal abstract world to the pragmatic world of human society. And even where the circumstances of life are such that these ideal propositions can no longer be applied — for example, the offering of sacrifices in the Bet ha-Mikdash today — the laws concerning these offerings are studied with equal intensity. The eschatology of the halakhist is not to be found in some supernatural existence or mystical union with the Divine, but in the subjection of the real world to the yoke of the Halakhah. Hence, the Ish ha-Halakhah has neither the rapturous ecstasy of the religious mystic, nor the amoral and detached approach of the scientist. He is not overly humble; rather he recognizes his individual worth as a teacher of the truth as it is imbedded in the Halakhah. Thus he is rarely a man of compromise; he is steadfast and adamant in his views, for they reflect a divine order. He is fearless in championing the rights of the poor in face of the indifference to their plight on the part of the rich. To sum it up, the Halakhic Man's inspiration is the establishment in this world of the ideals of the Halakhah, which essentially are justice and righteousness.[58]

The Yeshiva of Volozhin

What are the particular contributions of the House of Volozhin to the Halakhah? Whereas in most Yeshivot the study of the Talmud was confined to the "practical" tractates — i.e. *Berakhot, Seder Mo'ed, Seder Nashim and Seder Nezikin*[59] — the founder of the Volozhin Yeshiva introduced a comprehensive curriculum covering all tractates of the Talmud from beginning to end. For R. Hayyim of Volozhin, the intensive study of Torah for its own sake was to be the exclusive and overpowering motivation of the Yeshiva student.[60] Succeeding R. Hayyim as head of the Yeshiva was his

58 See *ibid.* p. 698 for the reason given by Rabbi Hayyim for opposing the introduction of Mussar in the Yeshiva.
59 See above, p. 79–81; cf. *Berakhot* 20a, "In the time of Rav Yehudah all learning was (only) in Nezikin etc."
60 See N. Lamm, *Study...of R. Hayyim of Volozhin*, N.Y. 1966.

grandson Naftali Zvi Yehudah Berlin (1817–1893), known by the acronym *N'Tz'I'V'* His outstanding contribution is his thoroughgoing commentary to the She'iltot of Aḥai Gaon[61] entitled *Ha'amek She'eilah*. The Netziv concentrated his studies upon such primary sources as the halakhic midrashim and the works of the Geonim, thus enabling him to resolve many difficulties in the Talmud by establishing the correct reading of the text. He was also a prolific respondent; his Responsa are collected under the title *Meishiv Davar*.

His grandson through marriage Ḥayyim Soloveitchik (1853–1918), who became rabbi in Brisk (Brest-Litovsk) after the Volozhin Yeshiva was closed in 1892[62] and is therefore known as Reb Ḥayyim Brisker, introduced a new method in the analysis of Talmudic law, a method copied and somewhat exaggerated in the European Yeshivot which flourished after the closing of Volozhin. Basing himself upon a distinction mentioned in the Talmud[63] between vows (*nedarim*), where one imposes the ban upon the object (*ḥeftza*), and oaths (*sh'vuot*), where one imposes the ban upon himself, i.e. upon the person (*gavra*), Ḥayyim of Brisk says that in every halakhic ruling one must determine whether it is a result of the nature of the subject itself; i.e. the *ḥeftza* of the ruling, or a result of the person's or *gavra*'s involvement with the subject. Through these distinctions R. Ḥayyim explains many halakhic rulings which seem to be inconsistent with other rulings, especially rulings of the Rambam which the Brisker would subject to a special scrutiny because of their importance. This dialectical approach to Jewish Law inhibited R. Ḥayyim from serving as a responder and *posek* rendering definite practical decisions.[64] In Lithuania at this time (second half of the 19th Century) the chief responder was the rabbi of Kovno, Yitzḥak Elḥanan Spector (1817–1896), whose Responsa are collected under the title *Be'er Yitzḥak*. Incidentally, the institution which subsequently developed into the Yeshiva University of today was originally named after this great halakhist.

---

61 See above, p. 117.
62 See below, p. 188.
63 *Nedarim* 2b.
64 For a fuller treatment of the works of the Netziv and Ḥayyim of Brisk, see S.Y. Zevin, *Ishim ve-Shitot* (Tel Aviv 5712).

Before we proceed into the 20th Century and record the Challenge and Response of the Halakhah to the technological advances which are characteristic of that century, we have to go back to the 18th Century and describe the manner in which the Halakhah was confronted by a challenge to its hegemony in Jewish life more threatening than that of Hasidism.

11

Challenge and Response II: Haskalah (Enlightenment) and Reform

כי דבר ה' בזה, זה המגלה פנים בתורה שלא כהלכה
Because he has despised the word of the Lord
(Num. 15:31); This is the one who interprets
the Torah not in accord with the Halakhah*

Reform Judasim

The seeds of Reform Judaism, whose founders declared their absolute rejection of the Talmud and the authority of Rabbinic
Judaism,[1] were first sown in Berlin in the middle of the 18th
Century. Members of upper-class families were desirous of entering
the society of their non-Jewish neighbors, and felt that to do so they
would have to discard some of the religious practices which made
Jews so peculiar, and hence so despised, in the eyes of the Christian
community. Strangely enough, they found justification for their
desire to mingle with their neighbors at the expense of their Judaism
in the ideas of a strictly observant Jew, Moses Mendelssohn
(1729–1786). Though he wrote[2] that the mitzvot of the Torah have
to be obeyed, even as the Rabbis understood them, he nevertheless
argued that Jews should participate in the culture of the majority;
and in Germany this meant the cultivation of the German language
and literature. To advance this goal Mendelssohn wrote a translation of the Pentateuch into modern German called *Bi'ur* or
"clarification."

---

* *Sanhedrin* 99a.
1   At a conference of liberal rabbis in Brunswick, Germany, June 1844.
2   In a work entitled "Jerusalem" or "Upon Ecclesiastical Power and Judaism,"
     published in 1783.

The seeds of German culture which Mendelssohn assisted in sowing sprouted roots of assimilation and reform which he failed to foresee. German culture at the time was dominated by a circle of humanists who denigrated religion in general. The Age of Reason had already dawned in Western Europe with the scientific discoveries of Descartes and Newton, enthroning Science and Human Reason as the new objects of worship in cultural and literary circles.

Coincident with this social striving was the movement for political Emancipation; i.e. the granting to Jews of civil rights equal to those enjoyed by the non-Jewish population, rights which had been denied Jews over the centuries.[3] The first official resolution granting equal citizenship to Jews was passed — against strong opposition by the Catholic Church and an assortment of AntiSemites — in 1791 by the French National Assembly, swayed by the slogans of *liberté* and *egalité* proclaimed by the French Revolution. The spread of Emancipation for Jewish inhabitants to other parts of Western Europe came with the conquests of Napolean's armies, who brought with them these revolutionary concepts of freedom and equality for all peoples. However, the invitation to the Jewish people to full citizenship carried with it a price; the abandonment of much of their distinctive religious ritual. It beckoned to Jews to leave not only the physical confines of the Ghetto but also the spiritual confines of their religious traditions. Many Jews, particularly in Germany, were ready and willing to pay the price of admission to Christian society; some by complete repudiation of the religion of their fathers,[4] and many more by repudiation of the Halakhah. They asserted that not only was halakhic Judaism a barrier to participation in the general culture; it even constituted an antithesis to the noble ethical ideals of the Hebrew Prophets. These ideals, being universal in character, implied — so said the Reform thinkers of the time — that Israel's mission was to preach them to the Gentiles, and when eventually the Gentiles would accept them Israel would no longer need to preserve its identity as a Chosen People. Consequently, they abandoned the traditional faith and

3 For a brief discussion of the historical background to the problem of Emancipation and its effect upon Jewish identity, see M. Lewittes *Light of Redemption*, *op. cit.* pp. 25–27.
4 Prominent among those who embraced Christianity were the daughters of Moses Mendelssohn.

hope in the ingathering of the Exiles and the restoration of Jewish national sovereignty in Eretz Yisrael. For them, Germany was their Homeland, and their primary allegiance was to the German state.

Reform Judaism manifested itself mainly in two areas, in synagogue worship and in the education of the young. Radical changes were introduced in the liturgy of their "Temples,"[5] expunging references to Israel's Redemption, introducing prayers recited in German, and the accompaniment of organ music to the prayers, a practice borrowed from their Protestant neighbors. Some even went so far as to change the Sabbath day from Saturday to Sunday. As for the education of Jewish children, new schools were opened in which , in addition to Jewish studies of Bible and the Hebrew language, general subjects were taught by Christian teachers. As a result, the number of students in the traditional schools — the elementary ones called *ḥadarim* (plural of *ḥeder*, literally, "a room") and the secondary and higher ones, Yeshivot — declined. (In the traditional schools Talmud was the main subject, and no secular subjects were taught.)

With the large migration of German Jews to the United States in the middle of the 19th Century, the center of Reform Judaism was transferred to America. Its leaders may have disputed the extent to which Reform Judaism should adapt itself to its new environment, but they persisted in maintaining most of the radical reforms instituted in Germany,.so that the religious services and the preaching in the Reform Temples in America were not very different from those in the Protestant Church. Reform Judaism became for many, especially for those who had become quite affluent, a temporary way station on the way to complete assimilation.[6] Despite recent tendencies on the part of some Reform rabbis to introduce into their synagogues traditional rituals, such as the Bar Mitzvah or the Tallit, Reform Judaism still retains its ideological severance from the Halakhah. An example of this is its recent resolution to recognize a child born from a Jewish father and a non-Jewish mother as Jewish, a deliberate departure from Talmudic law.[7] Thus Reform Judaism remains to all intents and purposes outside the limits of Halakhic Judaism.

5   See above, p. 170, re the Hasidim and the liturgy.
6   See *Our Crowd* by Stephen Birmingham, N.Y. 1977.
7   Mishnah *Kiddushin* 3:12.

Rabbinic Opposition to Reform

The reaction of the traditional rabbis — who would later be designated "Orthodox" — to these non-conformist practices and the
heretical ideas upon which they were based, was unambiguous and
uncompromising. The serious consequences to such radical changes
were already manifest in assimilation and apostasy. The rabbis
would concede no concessions that would open the door to a freer
association with the general community and its culture. Even the
slightest change in custom or tradition was condemned outright,
and Reform Temples were placed under the ban of the *herem*. Even
Moses Mendelssohn's translation, the *Bi'ur*, was put into herem, it
being the opening wedge to modern culture.

Among the many Rabbis who expressed their absolute opposition to Reform from its beginning, three stand out, both because of
their great influence upon the Jewish community and because of
their great stature as masters of the Halakhah. We have already
mentioned the first among them, Yehezkel Landau of Prague.[8] The
other two were Akiva Eger of Posen (1761–1837) and his son-in-
law[9] Moshe Sofer of Pressburg (1762–1839), better known as the
Hatam Sofer, the title of his Responsa. Though both were equally
opposed to the slightest deviation from halakhically sanctioned
custom, they differed in the manner in which they expressed their
opposition. Akiva Eger was a saintly personality, extremely modest
and completely absorbed in the world of the Talmud, and therefore
was less aggressive and strident, satisfied to join his colleagues and
attach his name to the manifestoes condemning Reform. The
Hatam Sofer, on the other hand, issued scathing pronouncements
against the reformers, campaigning against them with the slogan
hadash assur min ha-Torah, "anything new is forbidden by the
Torah."[10] Sofer's zealousness left a great imprint on Hungarian

---

8   See above, p. 171.
9   By his second marriage.
10   A reference to Lev. 23:14 prohibiting the consuming of the new (*hadash*) grain
     before the bringing of the *Omer* offering on the 16th of Nisan. See Responsa
     Orah Hayyim n. 28, where the discussion concerns the proposed removal of a
     bimah (platform in the synagogue for the Torah reading) from the center.
     Following Rambam *Hilkhot Tefilah* 11:3 and Tur sec. 150, the Orthodox insist
     upon having the bimah separate from the platform upon which the Holy Ark
     (*Aron Kodesh*) is placed, though many synagogues today officially Orthodox do
     not comply with this provision.

Jewry, reaching its climax in the Orthodox separating themselves from the general Jewish community and constituting an Autonomous Orthodox Confession.[11]

Akiva Eger is especially renowned in halakhic circles for his glosses to the Talmud (*Gilyon ha-Shas*)[12] and Shulhan Arukh (*Hiddushei R. Akiva Eger*). His keen mind and phenomenal memory are also evident in his Hiddushim to the Talmud and his Responsa. Moshe Sofer is the *posek par excellence*; his Responsa, numbering well over a thousand, soon acquired an almost universal recognition as authoritative Halakhah. His independent approach to halakhic problems can be seen, for example, in a responsum[13] dealing with a woman with a vaginal discharge and presumed to be a *niddah*. After quoting statements of Rashi and Tosafot, he writes, "All this was said only according to their understanding (of the process of menstruation). However, begging their pardon, they are not correct in what they say, for the truth is...according to the scholars and the surgical books...and I have in front of me other books from expert physicians who are not Jewish."

Notwithstanding this seemingly modern approach, Hatam Sofer would brook no deviation from the custom of his country that women cover their heads so that not even a single strand of hair be visible, a custom based upon a teaching of the Zohar.[14] Elsewhere he reaffirms this by stating, "I am accustomed to say that anyone who questions our habits and customs is to be suspected of heresy."[15] The contemporary halakhist, in considering the opinions of the Hatam Sofer, may well ask himself — as one may ask of all the noteworthy poskim[16] — how far beyond his own country and era are his decisions to be regarded as binding?

To refute the contention of the reformers that the Talmud is alien to Biblical teaching, the opponents of Reform wrote works designed to demonstrate how the teachings of the Talmud flow

---

11 For a resume of the Hatom Sofer's Yeshiva in Pressburg and its influence upon other Yeshivot, see A. Fuchs, *Yeshivot Hungaria* etc. (Jer. 5739).

12 See H.D. Chavel, *Mishnato shel ha-Gaon R. Akiva Eger* (Jer.-N.Y. 5732).

13 *Yoreh De'ah* no. 167.

14 *Orah Hayyim* no. 36. Cf., however, *ibid.* no. 51, where he states that "anyone who mixes the words of the Kabbalah with halakhic decisions is guilty of sowing diverse seeds (*kil'ayim*)."

15 *Ibid.* no. 51.

16 See above, p. 145–146.

from the text of the Torah. First among these was Yaakov Zvi Mecklemburg of Koenigsberg (1785–1865) who wrote *Ha-ketav ve-ha-Kabbalah*; i.e. the Written Torah and the Tradition of the Sages. Second was Naftali Zvi Yehudah Berlin, the Netziv,[17] whose commentary to the Pentateuch is entitled *Ha'amek Davar*. Third, whose work is the most comprehensive since it covers all of Tanakh, was Meir Leibush Malbim of Bucharest (1898–1879). He called his commentary *Ha-Torah ve-ha-Mitzvah*.

The Modern Orthodox

There were two notable exceptions to the absolute opposition to secular studies as the defense against Reform. Samson Raphael Hirsch of Frankfort-on-Main (1808–1888), without conceding one iota of the obligations imposed by the Halakhah, did maintain that secular knowledge and the religious tradition — or as he phrased it, *Torah im Derekh Eretz* — were compatible, and he organized schools which included general studies in their curriculum. In his writings,[18] Hirsch stressed the absolute commitment to the Sinaitic revelation of the Torah and the duty to observe the mitzvot; but at the same time he underscored their ethical and universal implications. Azriel Hildesheimer (1820–1898) held a similar point of view, and founded, first in Eisenstadt and then in Berlin, a rabbinical seminary where the students not only received the traditional instruction in Talmud and Poskim but also studied philosophy and the sciences in the university. His foremost disciple and eventual successor as head of the seminary, David Hoffman (1843–1921), himself both a Talmid Hakham of the first order and a graduate of the university, made an important contribution to halakhic literature in his Responsa *Melamed l'Ho'il*, demonstrating how one can even utilize the results of scientific investigation to clarify questions of Jewish Law.[19] It should be noted that when one compares the

17   See above, p. 180.
18   "The Nineteen letters of Ben Uzziel", "Horeb", "Commentary to the Humash". These have now been translated into English.
19   See e.g. nos. 30 and 88. Hoffman also wrote a commentary to Leviticus and Deuteronomy, in which he not only demonstrated the inherent connection between the Pentateuch and the Talmud, but also refuted the vicious criticisms of the Wellhausen school which was then flourishing in Germany.

halakhic decisions of these Modern Orthodox rabbis with those of the strict traditionalists one cannot help but perceive the readiness of the former to recognize the peculiar needs of Jews living in a modern open society and thus lean towards a more lenient perception of the Halakhah.[20]

Meanwhile, the ideas of the Haskalah travelled eastward from Germany to Lithuania and Poland. There the battle against Enlightenment and Reform had to be waged not only against the *maskilim* but also against the Czarist government, which attempted to "Russify" its Jewish subjects by decreeing, among other things, that the Russian language be taught in the Yeshivot. The rabbis resisted this attempt, whose real purpose was to have the Jews completely assimilated, and rather than yield to this *gezerah*, they decided to close the Yeshiva in Volozhin. By this time, however, (1872) many other Yeshivot were flourishing in Europe, the major ones being Mir in Poland, and Slabodka in Lithuania.[21]

The Roshei Yeshiva in those countries were also opposed to other manifestations of the Haskalah movement. This movement had revived a long dormant interest in the study of Bible and the Hebrew language. One of the results of this revival was the *magnum opus* of Shmuel David Luzatto (1800–1865) of the "Instituto Rabinico" in Padua. His commentary to the Pentateuch and several books of the Prophets examined the text from a critical literary point of view, rather than the traditional interpretations. Hence the study of Tanakh in the traditional Yeshivot — except for the weekly review of the Sidrah with Rashi's commentary — was frowned upon.[22] The Gaon of Vilna had already condemned the Rambam's philosophy, a subject taken up by the maskilim, and so the study of the *Moreh Nevukhim* and even of the *Kuzari* was also frowned upon.

20 See, e.g. Responsa *Melamed l'Ho'il* of David Hoffman, no. 23 re desecrators of the Sabbath (*meḥallelei Shabbat*) in our times.

21 Slabodka Yeshiva was transferred to Hebron in 1924 under the leadership of Moshe Mordekhai Epstein (1866–1933). After the 1929 massacre in Hebron, the Yeshiva was transferred to Jerusalem. The Yeshiva of Mir was transferred to Jerusalem after World war II.

22 Cf. *Shulḥan Arukh ha-Rav, Hilkhot Talmud Torah* 6: "Therefore it is not customary now to teach children all the Tanakh as in previous days, for then there were no written (i.e. printed) Bibles and the teaching was oral. Nevertheless one has to teach and review with the pupils many times all the *parshiyot* of the Torah, for in them are the mitzvot and mishpatim."

THE CHALLENGE OF REFORM

Though the rabbis who graduated from the Orthodox Rabbinical seminary in Berlin were learned and strictly observant, the heads of the traditional Yeshivot strongly condemned the establishment of rabbinical seminaries. This saying "no" to any and all innovations in Yeshiva instruction was carried over into the 20th Century to the large Jewish community in America. It was only due to the courageous foresight of Dr. Bernard Revel (1885–1940) that Yeshiva College — later Yeshiva University — became a reality despite the tremendous opposition of the European rabbis.[23]

The Historical School: Conservative Judaism

Not all those who sought reforms in Jewish life were willing to sever in one fell swoop their connection to Talmudic-Rabbinic Judaism. They knew that the radical cutting off of their roots by the leaders of the Reform movement was in large part due to a distortion of the Talmudic tradition. They therefore embarked upon a critical study of the tradition, to show on the one hand its development through the ages but at the same time to bring to light the positive values enshrined in it. Change, they argued, should not be in conflict with the spirit of historical Judaism, but in consonance with its logical development. Surprisingly enough, this historical approach was first advanced by two Jews from Galicia, that part of Poland which had been absorbed by the Austro-Hungarian Empire, who were deeply impressed with the ideas of Moses Mendelssohn.

Nahman Krochmal of Tarnopol (1785–1840), known primarily for his *Moreh Nevukhei ha-Z'man*, and Solomon Yehudah Rapoport of Lemberg (1790–1867), who became chief rabbi of Prague, examined the sources of the Jewish tradition, tracing the development of its major ideas and demonstrating its vitality and enduring worth. They stimulated other young scholars to pursue such studies in the so-called "scientific" method. Leopold Zunz (1794–1886), who made a pioneer study of synagogal homiletics and liturgy, was one of the founders of the *Verein feur Kultur und Wissenschaft der Juden*. Another scholar was Zecharias Frankel (1801–1875), whose *Darkhei ha-Mishnah* and *Mavo l'Yerushalmi* are pioneer studies of the early development of the Halakhah. Another classical work was

---

23 See A. Rothkopf, *Bernard Revel* (J.P.S. Phila. 1972), chap. 7.

produced by Isaac Hirsch Weiss (1815–1905), his *Dor Dor ve-Dorshav* being a blend of profound Talmudic study and the critical method tracing the development of the Talmudic and post-Talmudic literature.[24]

Zecharias Frankel founded a rabbinical seminary in Breslau to train rabbis who would combine Talmudic training with academic training. It might seem that his seminary and the one founded by Hildesheimer in Berlin, having the same basic educational philosophy, were little different from each other. However, this is not so. Hildesheimer may have seen development in the past, but he did not seek any further development — read "change" — for the present. On the contrary, his students kept to the strict observance of every traditional custom and law of the Shulhan Arukh. Whereas in the Breslau seminary, the sloughing off of certain customs not vital to the preservation of Judaism — for example, wearing a head-covering at all times — was acceptable.

Towards the end of the century, another scholar of academic bent, this time hailing from England, made a lasting contribution to the scientific study of Judaism when he unearthed the *Genizah*, thousands of documents related to Jewish life in the Middle Ages which had been stored in the Ezra synagogue in Cairo. Academician though he was, Solomon Schechter (1850–1915), was deeply concerned about Jewish life, and therefore he accepted in 1902 the call to head the Jewish Theological Seminary in New York, where he laid the foundation of the Conservative Movement in America. Members of the Seminary's faculty made significant contributions to halakhic literature; though it must be emphasized, not to the Halakhah itsef, i.e. the actual practice of Judaism by Orthodox Jews.[25] Louis Ginzberg (1873–1953) published a commentary to

24 A criticism of this work, presenting a more traditional point of view, is the *Dorot ha-Rishonim* of Isaac Halevy. A criticism of Graetz's History of the Jews, which is critical of the Rabbis, is the *Toldot Yisrael* of Zev Yavetz.

25 E.g. they did not publish any commentaries to the Shulhan Arukh or extensive Responsa. A graduate of the seminary, Isaac Klein, wrote a Digest of Jewish Law, a sort of Kitzur Shulhan Arukh, but it does not follow the pattern of the Shulhan Arukh. These "scientific" contributions to halakhic literature are classified as *ḥokhmat Yisrael*, in contradistinction to the halakhic works produced by the traditional rabbinic authorities of the Yeshivah world. The former approach to studies of the rabbinic literature is the salient feature of the "Jewish Studies" programs now conducted in many universities throughout the world. The question has been raised as to the value of these studies in the

the Jerusalem Talmud and a collection of *aggadot* entitled "Legends of the Jews". Saul Lieberman (1904–1984) made a monumental study of the Tosefta, as well as commentaries to several tractates of the Jerusalem Talmud.

A basic tenet of Conservative Judaism is loyalty to the Halakhah. However, combined with this is a concept which Schechter called "Catholic Israel", viewing Judaism from a broad aspect of the totality of Jewish life. This idea led in the course of time to the allowing of an accommodation to what were considered to be the exigencies of modernism, thus compromising Conservative Judaism's loyalty to the Halakhah. An early expression of this was the introduction of mixed pews in congregational worship.[26] Much latitude was countenanced in other aspects of synagogue life, some Conservative rabbis permitting the playing of instrumental music at Sabbath services, others permitting riding to synagogue on Shabbat.[27] Furthermore, added to the faculty of the Seminary in the

strengthening and continuity of the halakhic tradition. Prof. Eliezer Schweid of the Hebrew University has made the following observation: "The clear superiority of the Orthodox (i.e. Yeshivah) education in the passing on of the tradition lies in the fact that it is faithful — albeit in a dogmatic, rigid and exclusive manner — to the methodology of the tradition being transmitted. It not only maintains the authority of the sources, it also retains the style in which their contents have been passed on."

26   Though there is no explicit ban in the Talmud against mixed pews in the synagogue this was taken for granted; cf. *Kiddushin* 52b. "How come there is a woman in the *azarah* (Temple Court)?" See however *Tosafot ad. loc. s.v. Vekhi Ishah.* The Rabbis saw to it that there should be segregation of the sexes at wedding ceremonies and lectures; *Kiddushin* 81a and Rashi *ad loc.* Orthodox practice requires not only the separation of the sexes in separate sections; it also insists upon a *mehitzah* or barrier between the sections. Contemporary poskim argue as to the required height of the mehitzah; some requiring one high enough to hide the women from the view of the men from the bottom up to their shoulders. See B. Litvin, *The Sanctity of the Sages* (N.Y. 1962), the teshuvah of R.Moshe Feinstein. (I don't know whether the five and a half ft. mentioned there is a misprint or not but it should read four and a half. ft.) Extremists demand they be completely covered from view; In Ashkenazi synagogues the custom was to build a women's gallery on an upper story, following the example of the balcony built in the *Ezrat Nashim* of the Temple during the festivities of the *Simhat Bet ha-Sho'evah*, see *Sukkah* 51b. (I don't understand why the poskim equate a gathering for festivities with assembling in a synagogue for prayer).

27   See S. Siegel (ed.), Conservatve Judasim and Jewish Law (N.Y. 1977).

twenties was the late Mordecai Kaplan (1884–1984), whose theology was decidedly unorthodox. (Eventually his followers broke away from the Conservative movement to form the Reconstructionist movement, sanctioning many radical departures from tradition.) These deviations led the Orthodox leadership to condemn Conservative Judaism as being beyond the limits of Orthodoxy and a threat to the continuation of traditional Judaism in America. Some Orthodox leaders went so far as to declare prayer in Conservative synagogues as null and void, and a ban was pronounced against Orthodox rabbis joining rabbinical associations in which Conservative and Reform rabbis are also members.[28]

Digests of the Shulhan Arukh

The most effective antidote to the spread of Reform Judaism in Central and Eastern Europe was the continued intensive study of Torah both in the Yeshivot and in local groups of *Ba'alei Batim* (laymen). Concurrently came an expansion of halakhic literature, as rabbis published their writings with increased frequency. The many commentaries which were being added to the Shulhan Arukh created the need for new Digests of Jewish Law, so that even the layman could have some handy reference to the requirements of the Halakhah in his daily conduct. Yehudah b. Shimon Ashkenazi (Poland, first half of 18th Century) composed a concise summary of the main rulings of the Shulhan Arukh called *Ba'er Heitev*. The *Ḥayyei Adam* and the *Ḥokhmat Adam* are the respective digests of the *Oraḥ Ḥayyim* and *Yoreh De'ah* written by Avraham b. Yeḥiel Michal Danzig of Vilna (1748–1820). About a century and a half ago Shlomo b. Yosef Ganzfried of Hungary (1804–1886) composed for the layman a handbook of Jewish Law which he called *Kitzur* (abridgement) *Shulhan Arukh* and which became extremely popular. It has been published in many editions, with commentaries to bring it up-to-date,[29] and it is now translated into English under the

---

28 See, e.g., M. Feinstein, *Iggerot Moshe, Oraḥ Ḥayyim* IV no. 91/6.
29 E.g. S.Z. Braun, *She'arim Metzuyanim B'Halakhah* (N.Y. 5711). An interesting edition is the *Sha'ar ha'Mizraḥ* of Yizḥak Bar-Da (Ramat Gan 1983) giving the customs followed by the Oriental Jews.

title "Code of Jewish Law". The latter can hardly be considered an adequate exposition of Jewish Law in view, on the one hand, of its provincial nature, and on the other, its lack of dealing with the numerous problems which have arisen since its first publication.

A more elaborate review of the Shulhan Arukh, citing the sources for the latter's decisions and not infrequently disagreeing with them, was composed by Yehiel Michal b. Aharon ha-Levi Epstein of Novaradokh (Lithuania, 1829–1908), and called *Arukh ha-Shulhan*. This is a work designed more for the rabbinic posek than for the layman. An up-to-date — that is, up-to-date 75 years ago — clarification and resolution of the decisions recorded in Shulhan Arukh Orah Hayyim that has gained wide acceptance by halakhic authorities today is the *Mishnah B'rurah* of Yisrael Meir ha-Cohen Kagan of Radun, Poland (1839–1938), better known as the *Hafetz Hayyim* after his ethical treatise on "the guarding of one's tongue from speaking evil." He writes in his Introduction, "Where I have seen two opinions among the *Aharonim*, I was not lazy and searched in all the works of other Aharonim especially in *Bi'ur Hagra*,[30] to see which opinion is decisive." The Hafetz Hayyim's contribution to the development of the Halakhah leads us from the 19th Century into the 20th. Before we record the contributions of the halakhic masters of this century, we must record how the continued increase in halakhic works led to some new trends in the halakhic literature.

Collections of Teshuvot

The number of Teshuvot written after the publication of the Shulhan Arukh grew apace, as the masters of the Halakhah responded to the many inquiries coming from far and near. The time soon came when no posek, who had to take into account the many opinions expressed in writing by the post-Shulhan Arukh authorities, had access to them. Thus the need arose for collections of Responsa in condensed form, arranged according to the pertinent sections of the Shulhan Arukh. Two brothers, Hayyim Mordechai and Ephraim Zalman Margaliot (Brody, end of 18th Century), published a collection called *Sha'arei Teshuva* containing responsa

---

30   See above, p. 173.

to the first of the four volumes of the Shulhan Arukh. Their work was completed for the other three volumes by Avraham Zvi b. Yaakov Eisenstadt (1813–1876) in his *Pithei Teshuvah*. An elaboration of this work to *Yoreh De'ah*, adding Responsa of the late 19th Century, was composed by Zvi Hirsch Shapiro of Munkacs, Hungary in *Darkhei Teshuvah*. Currently, a monumental collection of teshuvot is being processed by a group of scholars in Jerusalem in a project named *Otzar ha-Poskim*.[31] At the same time, the Maharshal Institute of Jerusalem is compiling a collection of teshuvot pertaining to Shulhan Arukh *Orah Hayyim*. Modern technology is being utilized in Bar-Ilan University in Israel to store in a computer's memory many thousands of such halakhic answers. Simultaneously, the Institute of Research in Jewish Law at the Hebrew University in Jerusalem is preparing indices of the Responsa of the Spanish and North African scholars of the 11th to 15th centuries. The completion of such projects, which may yet take many years, will provide the future posek with a digest of the numerous opinions that have been made on a particular question of Jewish Law during the entire course of the history of the Halakhah.

Studies in Methodology of the Talmud

The beginnings of the Halakhah are in the Talmud. Thus a branch of halakhic literature, which has some bearing upon halakhic decision-making, is that of "Introductions to the Talmud", i.e. examinations of the Talmud's *kellalim*, its basic rules and methodology. Best known among these works, since it is published in most standard editions of the Talmud after tractate *Berakhot*,[32] is the *Mevo ha-Talmud* of Samuel b. Joseph ibn Nagrela of Granada (d. 1056)[33] better known as Shmuel ha-Nagid. An even earlier *Mevo ha-Talmud* was written in Arabic by Shmuel b. Hofni Gaon of the 10th Century, but it is no longer extant. An Italian scholar of the

---

31   To date (summer 1986) 16 volumes, covering secs. 1 to 71 in *Even ha-Ezer*, have been published. In their files, they have references to over one million responsa, to which new responsa are constantly being added.

32   Since only fragments of the original are extant, supplementary comments have been added.

33   References to biographies can be found in S.W. Baron, *Social and Religious History*, Vol. III, p. 306, n. 41. See also *ibid*. Vol. VI, p. 335, n. 35.

18th Century, Malachi b. Yehudah ha-Cohen, is the author of a similar work on the principles of the Talmud entitled *Yad Malachi*, the topics arranged according to the letters of the alphabet. A Lithuanian scholar of the 19th Century, Zvi Hirsch Chajes, known for his glosses to the Talmud, also published a *Mevo ha-Talmud*, including the principles of halakhic ruling.[34] A work of this nature has also been published in English, the *Introduction to the Talmud* of A.L. Strack.[35] A pioneer work in studies of the Talmud is the *Dikdukei Soferim* of R.N. Rabinowitz (1835–1888), who examined numerous manuscripts and recorded the many various readings of the text.[36] The 20th Century has been enriched with new studies, examinations of the Talmud's structure and development. Prominent among these are the works of Y.N. Epstein,[37] H. Albeck,[38] and Avraham Weiss.[39] And the Institute of the Israeli Talmud based in Jerusalem is continuing its monumental work of publishing the entire Talmud with all variant readings.[40] Another significant project, collecting the opinions of the many commentators to the Talmud in condensed form,[41] is the *Otzar Meforshei ha-Talmud* being prepared by the Makhon Yerushalayim.

Encyclopedias of the Halakhah

The ever-increasing bulk of Rabbinic literature created the need for another aid for both student and scholar in understanding and arriving at halakhic decisions. This took the form of the arrangement of subjects according to the sequence of the letters of the alphabet, each subject containing a survey of the halakhic literature pertaining to it. The first such encyclopedia of the Halakhah was

---

34 Included in *Kol Sifrei Maharatz Hayyut*, Jer. 5718.
35 J.P.S. Phila. 1931.
36 He covered tractates *Berakhot, Seder Mo'ed, Seder Nezikin, Zevahim, Menahot* and *Hullin*. S. Feldblum (N.Y. 5726) published *Dikdukei Soferim* for *Gittin*.
37 *Mevo'ot l'Sifrut ha-Tannaim, Mevo'ot l'Sifrut ha-Amoraim*, published by Magnes Press.
38 *Mavo l'Talmudim*, Dvir-Tel Aviv 5729.
39 *Hithavut ha-Talmud Bishleimuto*, N.Y. 5703 and *Mehkarim B'Talmud*, Jer. 5735.
40 To date (fall 1986) Mishnah *Zera'im* and tractates *Ketubot, Sotah, Yevamot* and *Nedarim* have been published.
41 Similar to the *Shitah Mekubetzet*, see above, p. 152.

composed in the early 18th Century by Yitzhak Hizkiah b. Shmuel Lampronti of Ferrara (1679–1756) under the title *Pahad Yitzhak*. A century and a half later, a bulkier though somewhat less systematic work, the *S'dei Hemed*, was published by Hayyim Hizkiah b. Raphael Eliyah Medini (1832–1904), born in Jerusalem but for many years rabbi in Ismir.

A much more systematic and comprehensive encyclopedia of the Talmud, *Entziklopedia Talmudit*, is currently being prepared in Jerusalem by a group of scholars who began their work under the general editorship of the late Shlomo Yosef Zevin. Covering halakhic opinion from its very inception to the present day, seventeen volumes have already appeared covering the letters *alef* through *het*. The scientific nature of this work can be seen by the thorough research done, the use of numerous manuscripts, and the photographs accompanying the text where additional clarification is required.[42] Since this work will no doubt serve as the standard reference to any halakhic opinion for many years to come, as is already the case, it is to be hoped that — as is done with major encyclopedias — new editions will be published in the future to include the latest opinions of contemporary scholars concerning the problems which are now confronting us as as a result of the technological advances of our age. These are the problems which are the subject matter of our next chapter.

Sephardi Hakhamim in the 18th and 19th Centuries

The winds of Enlightenment and Reform did not reach Oriental Jewry with any measurable impact until the late 19th century. Among this Jewry there was no popular movement for political Emancipation, nor was there any desire to enter into the social and cultural life of the majority; namely, their Muslim neighbors. The latter were adherents of an Islamic faith which had little in common either with the liberal ideas of Western culture or with the rich philosophic heritage of early medieval Arabic culture, and therefore it had little attraction for the Jews. The latter were proud of

---

42   Special supplements with the results of recent research have been published; e.g. concerning the boundaries of Eretz Yisrael and *Herem D'Rabbenu Gershom*.

and content with their traditional culture, which was based — as elsewhere in Jewish life — upon the twin cornerstones of the Halakhah and local custom. Jews in the Orient continued to regulate their internal affairs and communal institutions under the autonomous rule of their spiritual leaders, who constituted their courts of law (*batei-din*) and who based their halakhic decisions upon the rulings of *Maran* ("our Master"), as they called Yosef Karo. They also instituted many *takkanot* to improve the spiritual life of their flock, as well as to regulate their domestic and fraternal arrangements.

One of the major problems that the Oriental ḥakhamim had to deal with was the reconciliation between the customs brought to their countries by the *megorashim*, the expellees from Spain and Portugal, and the older customs of the indigenous population. The practice was for a group of Jews immigrating from the same city to establish themselves as a *kehillah* in their new locale and maintain for themselves the customs of their place of origin.[43] The influence of the megorashim was greatest in the Balkan countries, where Ladino soon became the *lingua franca* of the Jews, though it was pretty strong in Morocco as well. A related problem dealt with in Oriental communities was the rapid spread of the Kabbalah, bringing with it changes in the *nusaḥ* of the prayers and in the curriculum of studies in the Yeshivot. In many communities, the study of the Zohar became as important as the study of the Talmud, and several Yeshivot where the Kabbalah was the main subject were established in Eretz Yisrael. Many hakhamim wrote as many commentaries to the Zohar as to the Talmud, and selections from the Zohar were introduced into the daily prayers.

A picturesque community of Jews who had been isolated from world Jewry for centuries was that of Yemen (*Teiman* in Hebrew), where Jews lived scattered throughout North and South Yemen in small communities. The outstanding Yemenite ḥakham of the period now under discussion was Yiḥya Zalaḥ, chief rabbi of Sana'a for almost fifty years (second half of the 18th Century). Author of Responsa *Pe'ulat Zaddik*, he wanted to maintain the traditional customs of Yemenite Jewry based upon the teachings of the Rambam, who was recognized during his lifetime as their spiritual guide.

---

43   See M. Elon, *Ha-Mishpat ha-Ivri*, p. 701, n. 301, and *Toldot ha-Yehudim B'Artzot ha-Islam* (Merkaz Zalman Shazar, Jer. 5741), pp. 251–252.

However, he could not stem the tide of the spread of Yosef Karo's Shulhan Arukh and the Kabbalah, though the custom to study regularly the Mishneh Torah of the Rambam has endured to modern times. Despite the increase in international commerce and contacts with isolated Jewries that took place in the 19th Century, Yemenite Jewry managed to maintain its traditional way of life. Even before, however, as is seen from an interesting teshuvah of Yihya Zalah, attempts were made to persuade them to adopt practices which were widespread in other parts of the world. It appears that a certain rabbi from overseas (probably Egypt) had convinced a previous Yemenite leader that it is a most serious offense to have a haircut during the period of Sefirat ha-Omer, something unknown in Yemen heretofore.[44] From recent testimony it is apparent that Yemenite Jews did not accept this and other forms of mourning during this period.[45]

Iraqi Hakhamim

Iraq, ancient Babylonia, cradle of Talmud Bavli and fortress of the Geonim, lost its glory as the center of halakhic authority shortly after the year 1000 C.E. It experienced a revival as a *makom Torah* in the 18th Century with the arrival of Zedakah b. Saadia Huzin (1699–1773) from Syria to Baghdad to become its chief rabbi. Among his many halakhic writings is his collection of Responsa entitled *Zedakah U'Mishpat*. He established several Yeshivot — called *hesger* or "closed circle"[46] — sponsored by philanthropic Jews where small groups would study Talmud together. He also instituted many takkanot, supplanting some of the indigenous customs with those practiced in Syria and Eretz Yisrael. One takkanah worthy of mention is that pregnant and nursing women should not fast on Tisha B'Av.[47] In addition to his Responsa he wrote a commentary to the Tur entitled *Me'il Zedakah*.

Zedakah Huzin's disciple and successor as chief rabbi of Baghdad for fifty years was Moshe Hayyim (d. 1839), most revered for his

---

44   See *ibid.*, p. 209.
45   See Y. Kapah, *Halikhot Teiman* (Jer. 5728), p. 28.
46   Compare the institution of the *kloyz* in Eastern Europe.
47   Cf. Sh.A. *Orah Hayyim*, *Rema* to sec. 550:1 and sec. 554:5.

saintliness and widely acknowledged as an eminent Talmudic scholar. He did not leave many writings, but his influence endured
because of his disciples and his takkanot. One of the latter stipu-
lated that Iraqian Jewry should follow the rulings of the Ḥida.[48]
Moshe Ḥayyim's disciple and successor as leader of Iraqian Jewry
was Abdullah Somekh (1813–1889) whose *Bet Midrash l'Rabbanim*
(Rabbinical seminary) attracted many students who subsequently
became spiritual leaders in many Oriental communities. His major
halakhic work is entitled *Zivḥei Zedek*. The chain of Iraqian leadership was passed on from him to Yosef Ḥayyim (1835–1909), grandson of Moshe Ḥayyim and the most striking personality of all. He
composed over sixty books, including one in colloquial Arabic
especially for women.[49] He was an outstanding preacher and exe-
gete, and many of his sermons are now being published under the
title *Ben Ish Ḥayyil*. His *Sefer Ben Ish Ḥai* is the Shulhan Arukh for
Iraqian Jews, who in the past century have largely left Iraq for
India, the Far East, the Americas and Eretz Yisrael. His many
Responsa, directed to inquirers from all Middle Eastern communities, are collected in *Sefer Rav Pa'alim*. He brings to a climax the
illustrious chain of ḥakhamim who restored — albeit in provincial
boundaries — some of the ancient glory of Babylonian Jewry.

North African Ḥakhamim

Jews had been living all across North Africa, from Egypt in the East
to Morocco in the West, for centuries, with thriving communities
and distinguished Talmidei Ḥakhamim. These communities became,
in the 16th and 17th Centuries, havens of refuge and resettlement
for many of the megorashim, who brought with them their cultural
and spiritual baggage, breathing fresh spirit into the indigenous
communities. Here also the teachings of the Kabbalah penetrated
and assumed a significant aspect of religious life. This penetration
was so profound that the scholar Moshe ibn Mussa (18th Century),
traveling through North Africa, denounced the priority that the
rabbis gave to the study of the Kabbalah over that of the Halakhah.
Morocco had the largest concentration of North African Jewry,

48   See above, p. 165.
49   See Yosef b. Nayyim, *Malkhei Rabbanan* (Jer. 5691).

199

and the list of its distinguished cholars is legion. We have already mentioned the well-known author of the *Or ha-Ḥayyim* commentary to the Torah.[50] His earlier contemporary was Yehudah ibn Attar (1655–1733) of Fez, renowned for his Talmudic erudition and to whom all Moroccan Jewry addressed their halakhic questions. Even more prominent was Yaakov b. Reuven ibn Zur (1673–1752), author of *Mishpat U'Zedakah b'Yaakov*, which became a standard reference work for subsequent rabbis. He edited a *Sefer ha-Takkanot* listing the many regulations and halakhic decisions handed down by Moroccan spiritual leaders. Following him in compiling these takkanot — including those of the *megorashim rabbanei Castillia* — was Avraham b. Mordekhai Ankawa (b. 1810) in his *Kerem Hemer*.[51] A glace at the index will indicate the wide range of social, economic and religious matters with which Moroccan spiritual leaders were concerned.[52] Another distinguished Moroccan halakhist was Raphael b. Mordekhai Birdugo (1747–1822) of Meknes, who was called *Ha-Mal'akh (the Angel) Raphael* because of his saintliness. His main halakhic works are *Torot Emet, Mishpatim Yesharim*, and *Sharvit ha-Zahav* (ḥiddushim). His *kitzur ha-Takkanot* and some Responsa are included in Kerem Hemer mentioned above.[53] A great Talmudic scholar and kabbalist was Yaakov Abuhaziera (1807–1880) founder of a dynasty of mystical spiritual leaders, the present generation now living in Israel. He was the subject of many legends recorded in a book entitled *Ma'aseh Nissim* (Tales of Miracles) and he was revered by Moroccan Jewry as a miracle worker.[54] Head of a Yeshiva, he was also very active as a communal leader.

The outstanding hakham in Algiers in the 18th century was Yehudah Ayash (1700–1760), Rosh Yeshiva and author of *Bet Yehudah and Mateh Yehudah*. The Hida writes of his visit to Tunis in

---

50 See above, p. 165.
51 Recently published by Mercaz Zalman Shazar (Jer. 5737) with an Introduction by Shalom Bar-Asher of the Hebrew University.
52 See, for example, A.H. Freiman, *Seder Kiddushin ve-Nissuin* (Jer. 5725), pp. 102–105, 265–269, on marriage procedures.
53 For an interesting legend concerning him, see *Toldot ha-Yehudim b'Artzot ha-Islam, op. cit.*, p. 316.
54 Thousands of Moroccan Jews now living in Israel go to Morocco on his *yahrzeit* to visit his grave.

1773 and of the outstanding scholar Avraham Tayyib, author of *Birkat ha-Zevah* on the laws of shehitah.[55] Some decades later, the distinguished scholar in Tunis was Uzziel Al-Ḥayyakh, author of *Mishkenot ha-Ro'im*, where the halakhic subjects are arranged in alphabetic order. A contemporary halakhist of the same region was Yitzhak Tayyib, whose major work *Erekh ha-Shulḥan* is arranged according to the sections of Karo's Shulhan Arukh. An important volume of Responsa entitled *Ginat Veradim* (Garden of Roses) was written by Avraham Halevi of Cairo (early 18th Century). A century later, Eliyahu Bekhor b. Avraham Ḥazzan (d. 1908), author of Responsa *Ta'alumot Lev*, served as rabbi in Alexandria.[56]

Enlightenment in the form of Western culture came to North African Jewry with the colonial expansion of European countries — especially France — in that region in the 19th Century. Isaac Adolphe Cremieux (1796–1880), who had fought so much for the civil rights of French Jewry, thought that by bringing French culture into North African Jewish communities he would be able to alleviate their oppressive condition. In 1840 he established in Cairo the first of a chain of schools throughout the Middle East under the aegis of the Alliance Israelite Universelle, in which, in addition to the traditional Hebrew subjects (*limudei kodesh* or "sacred studies"), the French language and mathematics were taught. In Morocco, the first such school was established in Tetuan in 1860. The establishment of these schools did not meet on the part of the local rabbinate with the same uncompromising opposition that haskalah schools were met with in Eastern Europe. However, the Oriental rabbis did insist that the *limudei kodesh* should not in any way be affected by the new curriculum. Nevertheless, the Alliance schools did lead many to assimilation, especially in Algeria where Jews were granted French citizenship. To counteract the influence of these schools, an organization called *Otzar ha-Torah* was founded in order to establish and support a chain of Jewish schools with a definitely traditional atmosphere.

---

55 See *Toldot ha-Yehudim* etc., *op. cit.* p. 314.
56 An analysis of several of his Teshuvot by Z. Zohar can be found in *Studies in Contemporary Jewry II* (Indiana Univ. Press, 1986), pp. 18–51.

Ḥakhamim in the Ottoman Empire

In the period under discussion, the main centers of Jewish life in the Balkans were in the three cities of Kushta (Constantinople, ancient Byzantium, modern Istanbul), Salonica and Izmir. With the settlement in this area of so many megorashim,[57] one of the major halakhic problems confronting the ḥakhamim of the area was the status of the *anusim*, the Marranos who were returning to an open avowal of Judaism. Did they require an act of conversion, or not? What about their marriages, which had been performed in the Church? There already existed a large corpus of teshuvot dealing with these questions by Sephardi ḥakhamim of the 15th and 16th Centuries; including such outstanding local men as Eliyahu Mizraḥi of Kushta and Shmuel di Modena of Salonica,[58] in addition to hakhamim of Eretz Yisrael and North Africa. In the 17th century, the Responsa of Yosef b. Moshe of Trani (the *Maharit*) of Kushta, Ḥayyim b. Yisrael Benvenisti[59] and Yosef Escapa of Izmir and Ḥayyim Shabbatai of Salonica, also served as precedents.

The 18th century marked a decline in halakhic scholarship in the Balkans, more energy being devoted to homiletics and the translation of the Torah classics into Ladino. A most popular book was the *Me'am Lo'ez* of Yaakov Kuli of Kushta (1685–1732), a collection of comments to Genesis and Exodus written in Ladino.[61] Another popular non-halakhic work of this period is *Shevet Mussar*, a tract of moral exhortation written by Eliyahu ha-Cohen of Izmir (d. 1729). However, a most significant contribution to halakhic literature came from the pen of Yehudah b. Shmuel Rosanes (1657–1727), chief rabbi in Kushta.[61] His *Mishneh l'Melekh* is a penetrating analysis of the Rambam's Mishneh Torah and is published with most standard editions of the Rambam. Another penetrating commentary to parts of the Mishneh Torah entitled *Sha'ar ha-Melekh* was written a century later by Yitzhak Belmonte of Izmir. The 19th Century brought to the fore one of the most

---

57   See above, p. 197.
58   See above, p. 158.
59   See above, p. 159.
60   Published in many editions, also translated into Hebrew.
61   Because of the many kehillot there, there were three chief rabbis who served simultaneously.

prominent latter-day Sephardi poskim, Ḥayyim Pallagi of Izmir (1788–1869). His halakhic work, mostly Codes in the manner of the Shulhan Arukh, are entitled *Lev Ḥayyim, Kaf ha-Ḥayyim*[62] and *Nishmat Kol Ḥai*.

What happened in North Africa also came to pass in the Balkans; namely the founding of modern Jewish schools where European languages and culture were taught. The rabbis were opposed to this innovation in Jewish education, and they pronounced a ban (*herem*) against them. While Oriental communities by and large maintained their traditional way of life and the observance of the mitzvot — thus, for example, until the 20th century the port of Salonica was closed on Shabbat since most of its workers were Jewish — the level of Torah learning declined. (The spread of the Kabbalah had a part in this trend.)

We bring this section to a close with the mention of the halakhic scholars in Eretz Yisrael during this period. (Syria, with its major Jewish centers in Damascus and Allepo, was a close adjunct of Eretz Yisrael.) After the decline of 16th Century Safed as the illustrious Torah center, the main center moved to Jerusalem, though until the aliyah of Hasidim in the later 18th Century the community there — almost all Sephardim — was relatively small. Nevertheless, the number of ḥakhamim in 17th Century Jerusalem increased, attracted to the Bet Yaakov Yeshiva. The outstanding talmid ḥakham there was Moshe b. Yehonatan Galanti (1620–1689), who had left Safed to settle in Jerusalem. He is the author of Responsa *Magen ha-Elef*. His grandson, Moshe b. Yaakov Ḥagiz (1672–c. 1760), left Jerusalem for Hamburg, Germany, where he became one of the most outspoken opponents of the Shabbatai Zvi movement. Eventually he returned to Eretz Yisrael, and is primarily known for his *Leket ha-Kemaḥ*, Responsa arranged according to the sections of the Shulhan Arukh. A half-century later, the outstanding scholar in Jerusalem was Yom Tov b. Yisrael Yaakov Algazi (1727–1802), whose responsa are entitled *Simḥat Yom Tov* and *Kedushat Yom Tov*.

---

62   Not to be confused with the *Kaf ha-Ḥayyim* of R. Yaakov Ḥayyim Sofer (beg. 20th Century), a popular Sephardi commentary to the Shulhan Arukh.

Interestingly enough, the thriving communities in the Balkans were the major support of the small impoverished communities in Eretz Yisrael. In Kushta there were the *P'kidei* (officials of) *Eretz Yisrael*, who collected and distributed funds for the Holy Land. In 1740, Ḥayyim Abulafia left Izmir to establish a Jewish community in Tiberias, and shortly thereafter a small community was estab lished in Hebron, the fourth of the "Four Holy Lands" (*Aratzot*) of the Holy Land. In the 19th Century, Eliyahu b. Suleiman Mani (1818–1899) founded a Yeshiva in Hebron which attracted many scholars. In this period, the Turkish authorities would appoint a *Ḥakham Bashi* (Chief Rabbi) who was also called *Rishon l'Tziyon*. One of the first appointees was Yosef Rafael b. Ḥayyim Ḥazzan (1741–1820), whose commentary to the Shulhan Arukh is called *Ḥikrei Lev*. His grandson Ḥayyim David Ḥazzan (1790–1869) author of *Torat ha-Zevaḥ* on the laws of Sheḥitah and Responsa *Nediv Lev*, also served as Rishon l'Tziyyon.

The late 18th Century aliyah to Eretz Yisrael from Eastern Europe; i.e. of Ashkenazim, was made up of two streams, Hasidic followers of the Ba'al Shem Tov and Mitnagdic followers of the Gaon of Vilna. They set up their own respective kehillot, unwilling to merge with the indigenous Sephardim, and refusing to recognize the Ḥakham Bashi as their spiritual leader. One of the settlers was Yisrael of Shklov who wrote *Pe'at ha-Shulḥan* dealing with the laws of agricultural products, laws which obtain only in Eretz Yisrael. In the 19th Century, the Ashkenazim did not have a single chief rabbi in Jerusalem. The outstanding talmid ḥakham was Shmuel Salant (1816–1909), whose piskei halakhah, published in several Torah periodicals of the time, were accepted as authoritative . He helped establish in 1841 that most important educational institution, the Etz Ḥayyim Yeshiva on the higher level, which produced the most important leaders of the *Yishuv* (the settlers), and which functions to this very day. The ranks of Ashkenazi scholars were augmented by the arrival in 1877 of Yehoshua Leib Diskin of Brisk (1817–1898), who brought with him the fierce opposition of the Lithuanian rabbis to any innovation in the traditional educational system. From the contemporary records it would seem that his main activity was to pronounce bans against any project that smacked of Haskalah, such as the founding of modern schools or the publication of journals in Hebrew. Even before his arrival, a ban had been pronounced against the proposal of Moses Montefiore, the great benefactor of the Yishuv, to establish a school for girls, something unheard of in traditional circles. Incidentally, the Sephardi rabbi Ḥayyim Nissim Abulafia did not oppose the opening of the school.

The Ashkenazi settlers also set up committees in Europe for their maintenance. These were called *kollelim*, and the monies they distributed to the settlers were called *ḥalukah*, or "distribution."[63] As a result, monies which originally went for the maintenance of Sephardim was being diverted to Ashkenazim, resulting in conflicting claims between the two communities. Leading European rabbis were called upon to deal with this problem, and they worked out certain compromises as to the distribution of the funds. The seriousness of this problem can be understood when we realize that about eighty-five percent of the settlers depended upon these funds for their meagre sustenance. Its religious importance can be seen in the statement made by Ḥatam Sofer that "Upon us falls the duty to support the settlers in Eretz Yisrael not merely in order to help them fulfil the mitzvah of dwelling in Eretz Yisrael, but for our own duty to keep the Torah alive, *for if not for the settlers in Eretz Yisrael the Torah, God forbid, may evaporate.*"[64]

The differences between the Ashkenazim and the Sepharadim in Eretz Yisrael persist into the 20th Century, but of this in another chapter.

63 For a review of the activities of the Ashkenazi Kollelim and the establishment by them of new neighborhoods (*shekhunot*) in Jerusalem, see *Mossad ha-Yesod*, Jer. 5718.
64 *Oraḥ Ḥayyim* no. 203.

12

Challenge and Response III: Modern Technology and Medical Practice

א״ר אמי, גדולה דעה שניתנה בין שתי אותיות, שנאמר כי אל דעות ה׳
(שמואל א ב, ג)

Rabbi Ami said, "Great is knowledge, for it is
placed between two names of God, as it is said, *A God
of knowledge is the Lord* (I Sam. 2:3)*

In the course of our survey of traditional Jewish Law, we have seen
on occasion how the masters of the Halakhah have responded to
novel situations and the exigencies of economic circumstances.[1]
Fully cognizant that the Torah is a *Torat Hayyim*, a Law of Life,
they have been able to preserve the continuity of the halakhic
tradition while at the same time acknowledging the special
requirements of their contemporary society. Some have been more
sensitive to these needs and bolder in decision, tending to incline
law to life; others were less so, emphasizing the duty to incline life to
law. It has been pointed out that the tendency in later generations,
particularly in Ashkenazic Europe, has been more to hesitancy than
to boldness; more to declare things in doubt and therefore to adopt
the more stringent attitude. This became more pronounced in the
19th Century, when the Machine Age dawned and the rabbis were
confronted with novel devices as well as with novel — indeed,
heretical — ideas.[2] Hesitant or not, rabbis were called upon to

---

* *Berakhot* 33a
1   See, e.g., Reconciling law with life, above, p. 125.
2   M. Elon, *Ha-Mishpat Ha-Ivri*, p. 1248.

respond to these confrontations, and the sheer volume of Responsa multiplied, adding grist to the mills of the 20th Century responders.

No matter how novel and unprecedented were the devices of the 19th Century, those of the 20th were infinitely more so. More and more legal ingenuity and acumen were required in order to find some basis in the existing Halakhah for the rulings now being demanded. Necessity being the mother of invention, a more profound and critical analysis of the halakhah did develop in the latter half of the previous century, as we have recorded above.[3] And we do find in most recent Responsa literature less hesitancey to deal with a problem and state an unambiguous opinion than heretofore. Before we record the names of the prominent halakhic authorities of this century, let us examine the nature of the problems to which they were called upon to respond.

Electricity and the Halakhah

From the moment man, as a result of scientific discovery, found the method whereby to harness electrical energy and produce both light and power, the Halakhah-abiding Jew was confronted with a host of problems. What is the nature of the light kindled in an electric bulb; is it *eish* (fire) and thus to press the button and turn on the light on Shabbat would constitute a violation of the commandment *Do not burn* eish *on the Sabbath day* (Exod. 35:3); or can one argue that this is not the burning which the Torah proscribed?[4] Is the electric bulb considered a *ner*, a candle, and consequently a woman can fulfil the mitzvah of *hadlakat ha-ner* for Shabbat and Yom Tov by turning on electric lights; or must it be wax candles?[5] Further-

---

3   P. 119.

4   See *Ha-Ḥashmal B'Halakhah - Makhon Mada'ei Technologie* (Jer. 5738), Vol. II, pp. 28–65.

5   Re the use of wax candles for the Sabbath lights, see *Tosafot Shabbat* 20b. *s.v. ad kan* and the *Rosh ad loc.* for the objection of the Geonim and the men of Narbonne. Today, there is a further halakhic problem with the custom to pronounce the benediction over the wax candles. The mitzvah of *hadlakat ha-ner* was instituted so that we should not have to eat our Friday night *se'udah* in the dark; see Rashi *Shabbat* 25b, *s.v. ḥovah*. What mitzvah, then, is there in the lighting of the candles when we have the light of the electric bulbs illuminating our table.? We may resolve this problem in that for the woman the kindling of the candles serves another purpose, the acceptance upon herself the sanctity

more, in the *havdalah* service on Saturday night may one pronounce the benediction *borei me'orei ha-eish* (Creator of the lights of the fire) over the light in an electric bulb; or must one use the special candle of intertwined wicks (*avukah*)? Is there any difference as far as these questions are concerned between a fluorescent neon bulb and a translucent bulb? And is there any halakhic distinction between *hadlakat ner* for Shabbat and the *hadlakat ner* for Ḥanukkah?[6]

A special problem was raised by the poskim with regard to the turning on of an electric light on Yom Tov. On Yom Tov, the kindling of fire is permissible, but the Sages restricted this to kindling with a flame that had already been kindled before Yom Tov, thus proscribing the producing on Yom Tov of a flame *de novo* (*nolad*) by rubbing together inflammable material.[7] The question then is as follows: When pushing the button or turning the switch are we creating fire *de novo* (assuming, of course, that electric light is "fire"); or are we simply connecting two wires to allow the flow of electrical energy which was already produced by the generator in the electric power station? Generally speaking, Sephardi rabbis were inclined to permit turning on the electric light on Yom Tov, whereas the Ashkenazim would forbid it.[8]

A particular use of fire on Yom Tov which was a matter of controversy among poskim for several centuries has now been questioned by a recent commentator on halakhic decisions.[9] The Sages permitted the use of fire on Yom Tov only if it is for a common wide-spread use, but not if only a few people use it for that purpose.[10] When tobacco smoking was introduced into Europe

---

of the Sabbath. Thus nowadays the kindling is a ceremonial act, regardless of our non-dependence upon it for illumination. To keep its ceremonial feature, one should wherever possible use wax candles and not the ubiquitous electric bulb.

6 Other related questions can be found in *Ha-Ḥashmal B'Halakhah (op. cit.)*, Vol. I, Part 1.

7 Mishnah *Betzah* 4:7.

8 Almost all poskim agree that it is forbidden to strike a match on Yom Tov in order to produce a flame. All agree that it is forbidden to extinguish a fire directly, but some would permit an indirect extinguishing (*geram kibbui*). The question remains whether extinguishing the electric light is *geram kibbui* or not.

9 Rabbi J.D. Bleich in *Tradition*, Vol. 21, No. 2 (Summer 1983).

10 *Ketubot* 7a; cf. *Betzah* 22b, where the Sages forbid *mugmar*; i.e. the placing of incense on glowing coals since it is not a common practice.

many rabbis permitted it on Yom Tov, primarily on the grounds that smoking is healthy. Now that medical research has demonstrated that smoking is not only not healthy but even injurious to health, and statistics show that less than half of the population are smokers, there is no warrant for permitting smoking on Yom Tov. (Some halakhists would forbid smoking at all times because of its harm to one's health).[11]

Machine-baked Matzah

Another series of problems arose when machines could be activated by the turning of a switch connecting an electrical circuit. There are two fundamental questions confronting halakhic authorities here. First of all, what *melakhah*; i.e. category of labor prohibited on Shabbat is involved here where there is no visible light or flame? Assuming that such a labor is involved,[12] would increasing or diminishing the amount of current already flowing in a closed circuit be comparable to adding or subtracting fuel from a burning lamp, which is respectively considered by the Talmud as "burning" and "extinguishing"?[13] How these questions affect the use of certain electrical devices we shall discuss later.

A second halakhic question is this: If the turning of a switch by a human hand sets into motion a series of automatic operations, do we regard these operations as having been done by the person himself and consequently he is directly responsible for them; or is he merely a *gorem*, an indirect causative factor, and the consequences of his intial turning of the switch cannot be attributed to him directly?[14] A question of this sort became actual even before the harnessing of electrical energy; when the activating of machines became possible through steam propulsion. Already in 1838, when the first machine for the baking of matzot for Passover was put into operation, the kashrut of machine matzot became the subject of a most heated controversy among the 19th century poskim, some of

---

11 R. Moshe Feinstein, though he advises against smoking, does not find any halakhic basis for forbidding it; *Iggerot Moshe, Yore De'ah*, part II, no. 76.
12 See *Ha-Ḥashmal B'Halakhah, op. cit.*, Vol. II, chap. 2.
13 *Betzah* 22a; see *Tosafot ad loc. s.v. ve-hamistapek*.
14 See *Encyclopedia Talmudit*, Vol. VI, *s.v. gerama b'nizakin*.

whom have been mentioned in the previous chapter. One basis of the controversy revolved around a question of fact; are such matzot actually free from the possibility of having become *ḥametz* (leavened) in the course of their being processed from dough into the baked product, or not? Here, the vast majority of poskim, especially as the machines became more sophisticated, agreed that there is no suspicion of *ḥametz*. Indeed, they are more free of such suspicion than the "hand matzah" baked in the traditional manner. But there is another element involved in the baking of matzah for Passover. The Talmud rules that such matzah has to be baked *lishmah*; i.e. with deliberate intent that they are being prepared for the fulfilment of the mitzvah.[15] Some poskim contended that in setting the machine in motion the person is only a *gorem*, and his *lishmah* does not devolve upon the automatic operations. This lack of *lishmah* renders the matzah invalid for the fulfilment of the mitzvah to eat matzah on the first night of Pesaḥ. Others, on the other hand, contend that the automatic operations are a direct result of the person's intent, and since his turning of the switch was *lishmah* the entire process is deemed *lishmah*.[16] It should be noted that some poskim, particularly Hasidic rabbis, proscribe machine matzah on the grounds that in its early stages it was declared forbidden because of its innovative character, and we should abide by such decisions. This will account for the fact that Hasidim today still prefer the hand-baked to the machine-baked matzah, and not only for the Seder meal but for the entire Passover.

Problems Involving Electrical Appliances and Telecommunication

The question mentioned above of the extent of liability in matters of *gerama* or indirect activation affects the use of many common electrical appliances on Shabbat. When mechanical refrigerators

---

15   *Pesaḥim* 38b.

16   Cf. *Me'ilah* 21a, where accomplishing something through a non-intelligent person (a minor or an idiot) is equivalent to placing it upon an animal to carry it to a certain destination, where the act is attributed to the person who activated the animal. See also *Ha-Ḥashmal B-Halakhah*, Vol. I, p. 69, for another instance of *lishmah*. For a list of the poskim involved and a summary of their arguments, see *ibid.* pp. 90 ff.

first appeared on the market, many rabbis were inclined to forbid their use on Shabbat on the grounds of gerama. When you open the refrigerator door you are admitting warm air which activates the electric motor; ostensibly there is a direct cause and effect relationship between your opening the door and the creation of an electric current. However, it is now widely accepted that this is less than gerama, since the warm air admitted by your action does not activate the motor instantaneously. Nevertheless, there are some poskim who would permit the opening of the refrigerator door only while the motor is running. A related problem with which Sabbath-observing Jews are now confronted is the increasingly widespread use of doors that are opened automatically, either by treading on a step or passing through an electric eye. Rabbinic opinion would caution us to avoid such entrances on Shabbat.

Modern instruments of communication present halakhic problems on weekdays as well as on the Sabbath. Does one fulfil the mitzvah of listening to the sound of the Shofar on Rosh Hashanah or the reading of Megillat Esther on Purim by hearing it broadcast over the radio or TV? May one erase a tape recording on which the name of God has been recorded?[17] for the writing of a *get*, the document for a religious divorce, it is an absolute requirement that the scribe and witnesses hear the husband order them to write and deliver the *get*;[18] can such an order be given over the phone?

All poskim today agree that it is forbidden to use the telephone on Shabbat, even with automatic dialing, for in addition to the activating of an electric current there is the *gezerah* of the Sages against producing sound (*hashma'at kol*), as in the playing of a musical instrument.[19] However, since these "labors" are achieved by speaking — in itself permissible — and not by actual manipulation, the activity is only a gerama and not a Biblical infraction, and in such case permission may be granted in extenuating circumstances, such as calling a doctor even though no question of life or death (*piku'ah nefesh*) is involved. Much controversy still surrounds the use of a microphone on Shabbat even if the electrical circuit to which it is attached was opened before Shabbat. The objectors — and they have won the day in Orthodox circles — base their

17   Cf. *Makkot* 22a.
18   Sh. A. *Even ha-Ezer*, sec. 120.
19   J.T. *Betzah* 5:2 (63a); Mishnah *ad loc.*

objection largely on the prohibition against hashma'at kol. (One authority distinguishes between the ordinary electric microphone and the transistor type, the latter being permissible.)

An ancient controversy between Bet Shammai and Bet Hillel revolved around the setting into motion on Erev Shabbat a process which continues by itself on Shabbat,[20] Bet Shammai prohibiting and Bet Hillel permitting. Since the halakhic principle affirms that we follow the opinion of Bet Hillel, it is consequently permitted to set a time-clock before the onset of Shabbat that will automatically turn on the lights during Shabbat. Ostensibly, this applies as well to the setting of a clock for other operations to commence automatically on Shabbat. Following this principle, it has been possible to solve many halakhic problems. According to the Talmud[21] it is forbidden to milk a cow on Shabbat. This prohibition created a very serious problem for religious kibbutzim, whose economic survival depended upon the daily milking of their dairy herd, and rabbis were hard put to find a way out of this halakhic dilemma. Now, fortunately, there are milking machines which can be set before Shabbat to begin operating on Shabbat. Jews who lived in high-rise apartment buildings or who had to spend Shabbat in a hotel had to make sure that they were on a lower floor in order to avoid the use of an elevator. Now we have the Shabbat-elevator which stops and starts without any pushing of buttons, a boon for Sabbath-observing Jews. (Some strict interpreters of the law would forbid the use of such an auatomatic elevator on the grounds that by stepping into it one augments the electric currency necessary for its operation, a case of adding fuel to a burning lamp.) There are currently in Israel two Institutes concerned with these techno-halakhic problems, searching for ways to solve them by means of special devices. Applying the principle of gerama in the lenient way, the Tzomet Institute has invented various devices incorporating constantly operating electronic scanners which determine through some non-prohibited signal when an electric circuit should be connected automatically. These devices have been especially helpful in hospitals in Israel that are conducted according to the Halakhah.

---

20   Mishnah *Shabbat* 1:5–8. There are exceptions; see Mishnah *ibid.* 1:10.
21   *Shabbat* 95a. Rishonim are divided as to whether milking is forbidden *d'oraita* or *d'rabbanan*.

Which brings us to the problem of modern medical practice and the Halakhah.

Medical Practice and the Halakhah[22]

There is a long-standing affinity between Medicine and the Halakhah. The Talmud not only discusses the halakhic aspects of medical practice, which contain significant and fairly accurate anatomical information;[23] it offers a great deal of therapeutic advice as well.[24] Its basic statement that "permission (*reshut*) is granted the physician to heal"[25] has been expanded by the Halakhah that it is a *mitzvah* for the physician to heal; and correspondingly there is a mitzvah for the sick person to seek medical treatment,[26] even though he must pray and put his trust in the Divine *Rofeh Holim* (Healer of the Sick). The Halakhah also discusses the fees a physician may demand, and his responsibility in case of malpractice.[27] Thus it is not surprising that many masters of the Halakhah were outstanding physicians; and even those among them who were not practicing physicians responded to the manifold questions involving medical treatment with a great deal of expertise. As in the case of technological advancement, so with the recent tremendous advances in medical research and practice there has been a corresponding increase in the Responsa literature dealing with medical problems, as well as the establishment of special institutes dealing with Medicine and the Halakhah.[28]

---

22   Two comprehensive reviews of these problems have been published in English; Immanuel Jakobovits, *Jewish Medical Ethics* (N.Y. 1979), and F. Rosner and J.D. Bleich (editors), *Jewish Bioethics* (N.Y. 1979). An excellent digest in Hebrew is entitled *Hilkhot Rof'im U'Refuah*, (Mossad Harav Kook, Jer. 5738).

23   Cf. Mishnah *Oholot* 1:8, the human bone structure; Mishnah *Niddah* 2:5, the female reproductive organs.

24   See, e.g. *Gittin* 68b–70a. Rishonim have already indicated that the cures mentioned in the Talmud are no longer applicable. The Sages did forbid many cures based upon superstition, calling them *darkhei ha-Emori* (ancient Canaanite practices); Mishnah *Shabbat* 6:10.

25   *Bava Kamma* 85a.

26   Based on the command *You shall be most careful for yourselves* (Deut. 4:15).

27   Sh. A. *Yoreh De'ah*, sec. 336.

28   *Makhon al yad Bet ha-Holim Shaare Zedek; Makhon l'Heker ha'Refuah B'Halakhah*, both situated in Jerusalem.

Autopsies and Transplants[29]

We have already mentioned (above, p. 171) the teshuvah of R. Yeḥeskel Landau that generally speaking post-mortem dissection for purposes of medical instruction is not permissible. The Talmudic basis for such a ban is not too conclusive, and many responders have disagreed with Landau's conclusion, especially in recent times with the results of medical research being communicated far and wide and speedily. However, latter-day poskim would restrict the permissibility of autopsies to where there is a suspicion of a criminal act, or a suspicion of a disease which may affect the surviving relatives. In any event, the autopsy has to be performed with due regard to the dignity of the corpse and any dismembered parts of the body have to be brought to a decent burial.

A related problem is that of transplanting organs for therapeutic purposes, either from a cadaver or from a living person. In the former case, there is an additional — and much more serious — problem; when is the fact of death established. The Talmudic precedent establishes the cessation of breathing as the criterion.[30] However, in view of the fact that modern methods of resuscitation have revived persons whose breathing had apparently ceased, poskim today would require, in addition, complete cessation of the heartbeat, to be determined by means of the sophisticated instruments now available. As for the permissibility of transplants in general, halakhic authorities see one particular qualification in the case of a living donor; that there be no quantifiable risk to the donor, for one should not enter into a dangerous situation in order to save the life of another.

Abortion

The status of the unborn child (the foetus; Hebrew, *ubar*) is discussed in the Talmud in several contexts. Is the foetus a limb of its mother, or a separate entity?[31] Is it a person as far as the acquisition

---

29 For further discussion and references, see D.A. Frenkel in *Jewish Law and Current Legal Problems* (ed. N. Rakover, Jer. 1985), pp. 195 ff.

30 *Yoma* 85a.

31 *Nazir* 51a.

of goods or an inheritance is concerned?[32] Most crucial, however, is the question, If one kills a foetus, is he a murderer or not? The Talmudic sources are not absolutely conclusive.[33] Where the continuation of the pregnancy represents a clear danger to the life of the mother all agree that the foetus, even if full term but its head has not yet protruded, must be eliminated.[34] What has made the question of induced abortion so controversial nowadays in halakhic circles are the novel reasons being advanced for such procedure, some based on sociological attitudes and some on medical grounds. Economic grounds, as far as the Halakhah is concerned, are in no way regarded as sufficient. But what if dire economic circumstances of the family are liable to affect the mother's mental health if another baby is born; does the Halakhah take into account the presumed psychological damage? Furthermore, does the Halakhah take into consideration the presumed abnormalities of the potential child, and decide that rather than bring into the world a human being that will be an insufferable burden to both its parents and itself, we may preclude such a possibility by inducing abortion? Today, with ultra-sound and amniotic fluid tests, it is possible to predict the birth of a Tay-Sachs diseased or Down's Syndrome child; should such children be brought into the world notwithstanding, because the Halakhah permits abortion only if the mother, and not the child, is affected? It is difficult to lay down general principles that will cover all cases, except this: "The judge can judge only on the basis of what he sees;"[35] each case has to be decided on its own merits and on the understanding of the particular posek.

32 *Bava Batra* 141b; *Yevamot* 67a.
33 See *Hilkhot Rof'im U'Refuah, op. cit.*, pp. 33–46 for sources and argument pro and con. Incidentally, the Talmud asserts that a foetus is not formed till the forty-first day after the beginning of pregnancy, and therefore the poskim agree that a pregnancy may be terminated before that time, provided there is some sufficient reason.
34 Mishnah *Oholot* 7:6.
35 *Bava Batra* 131a.

Contraception and Sterilization[36]

There are two methods of contraception mentioned in the Talmud. One is the insertion in the vagina of a wad of cotton that will absorb the semen; though the commentators differ as to whether the insertion may be made before or only after intercourse. They also differ whether this is permissible only in the three instances mentioned in the Talmud, where pregnancy may cause harm either to the mother or the child; or all married couples may resort to this method.[37] With the recent development of the contraceptive pill, the poskim are inclined to permit its use in all cases,[38] with the following reservations. Before employing contraception, the husband must have already fulfilled the mitzvah of *pru u'revu*, "Be fruitful and multiply," i.e. procreate and bring children into the world. According to Bet Hillel, one has fulfilled the mitzvah if he has produced both a son and a daughter, though one is advised to continue to have children beyond the minimum requirement.[39] A second reservation is the effect that the pill might have on the woman's menstrual cycle and the incidence of bleeding between periods, raising problems of niddah.

A second method of contraception mentioned in the Talmud is *coitus interruptus*.[40] This method is condemned; it is "emitting seed in vain," a grievous sin. However, when a specimen of semen is

36 A comprehensive review of these laws published in English is David M. Feldman's *Birth Control in Jewish Law*, N.Y. 1968. A briefer treatment can be found in G. Ellinson, *Procreation in the Light of the Halakhah*, published by the Dept. for Torah Education of the World Zionist Organization.

37 *Ketubot* 39a, Rashi and *Tosafot ad loc.* Some commentators express surprise that the Rambam does not mention this ruling in his Code. However, the use of the cotton is recorded as the opinion of the Tanna Rabbi Meir only; the Hakhamim do not recommend it. Halakhically, there is no difference between the insertion of a wad of cotton or the insertion of a diaphragm.

38 A precedent is found in the case of Yehudit, wife of R. Hiyya, who drank a contraceptive potion because of the pain she experienced during childbirth (*Yevamot* 65b). A woman is permitted to do this because she is not obligated to the mitzvah of *pru u'revu* (Mishnah *ibid.* 6:6).

39 Mishnah *Yevamot* 6:6; Talmud *ibid.* 62b. There are also demographic considerations nowadays against the widespread practice of birth control by Jews. The number of Jews has diminished considerable due to the ravages of the Holocaust and assimilation and the low birth-rate.

40 *Yevamot* 34b.

required for examination in cases of infertility, it may be collected in this way, but not by means of masturbation. Contraception by use of a sheath on the male organ is equivalent to coitus interruptus, and similarly condemned. A recently developed method of contraception is sterilization through surgery, in the woman by sealing her fallopian tubes, in the male by severing the vas deferens. This is tantamount to castration, in the case of the male absolutely forbidden by the Torah (Lev. 22:24), and in the case of the female forbidden by the Sages.[41] However, where castration is a concomitant of therapeutic surgery, as in the case of prostatitis or a cancerous ovary, we apply the principle, "Nothing stands in the way of saving life."[42]

Artificial Insemination[43] — Surrogate Mothers

Modern medical research is constantly seeking cures for cases of infertility. One of the earliest remedies for a woman who cannot conceive by natural intercourse is artificial insemination. Halakhic authorities were quick to respond to the question if such a procedure is permissible. Where the donor of the semen is the husband, almost all the poskim agree that it is permissible, though some stipulate that the insemination should not be done while the woman is a niddah. Where the donor of the semen is not the husband, all poskim agree that it is forbidden, though they concede that if done it is not considered an act of adultery and the subsequent child is not a mamzer. However, the child is regarded as the offspring of the donor, which creates a serious problem if he is unknown. One rabbi suggested that this problem is solved when the donor is a non-Jew, for a child conceived from a union of a non-Jew with a Jewess is not considered the child of a non-Jew. Perhaps in a case like this — as in other cases created by modern medicine — we have to deal not only with the technical halakhic aspects but with the moral-ethical aspects as well.

---

41 *Shabbat* 110b–111a; Rambam *Hilkhot Issurei Biah* 16:11.
42 A surgeon in the U.S. has recently developed a surgical procedure which avoids castration in prostatectomy.
43 For the problem of adultery, see M. Drori, *Aritificial Insemination; Is it Adultery?* in Jewish Law and Current Legal Problems, *op. cit.*, pp. 200 ff.

A further development in the reproductive process, raising many more questions, is that of the test-tube baby. When both the ovum and the sperm come from a married couple and the fertilized ovum is deposited in the womb of the wife for gestation and birth, there is no problem. But where an ovum is removed from a woman and is fertilized in a test-tube with her husband's sperm, but is them deposited in the womb of another woman for gestation and birth, the question arises, Who is the mother of the child, the woman who provided the ovum, or the woman who carried it for nine months and through whose birth-canal it emerged? One rabbi concluded that though genetically the offspring is the child of the woman who produced the ovum she cannot be considered the mother from the point of view of the Halakhah, for neither conception nor birth occurred in her body.[44] As for the paternity of a test-tube baby, it depends solely upon the donor of the sperm, as in the case of artificial insemination.

Euthanasia

A basic principle of Judaism is the preservation of human life. *You shall not stand by the blood of your neighbor* (Lev. 19:16); i.e. Do not stand by indifferently when your neighbor is dying, but do everything in your power to keep him from dying. The Sages of the Talmud have already indicated some of the complexities of this commandment. To what extent am I called upon to sacrifice my wealth, or even my person, in order to save a life?[45] If two people are drowning and I can save only one, which one should I save?[46] The dilemmas facing us today, with instruments that can sustain almost indefinitely the life of a dying person, have increased a thousandfold; should we or should we not attach these instruments and keep the heart beating even though the patient is in an irreversible coma?

Here, as in every other novel problem, the halakhic authorities have searched for precedent in the Talmud and Rishonim, though

---

44   Rabbi Y.D. Berger of the London Bet Din, in the Journal of European Rabbis (*Seridim*, Vol. 4, Jer. 5743). Rabbi Shlomo Goren, former Israeli Chief Rabbi, disagrees. He maintains that the crucial factor is the genetic origin of the child.

45   Cf. *Bava Kamma* 60b–61a; 81b. See also above, p. 214, *transplan* .

46   Mishnah *Horayot* 3:7–8.

the drawing of analogies is in itself problematical considering the radical difference in the means of sustaining life between those days and ours. One ruling is clear; even though a person's death may seem to be imminent, anything done to hasten his death is tantamount to murder.[47] However, one medieval authority says that if the person is in great pain, one should pray for his death.[48] (Not all authorities have accepted this ruling). Another authority goes a step further and says that if there is some external factor that keeps the patient alive, one may remove that factor and thus indirectly hasten the person's death.[49] A recent authority rules that if a patient's breathing and heart beat have ceased while a respiratory machine is attached, the machine may be removed; but as long as the patient is breathing with the help of the machine, it may not be removed.[50] A moot question is the weight that should be given to the desires of the immediate family; is the decision up to them whether to prolong life or not? And to what extent are we to rely upon the opinion of the attending physician, in whose hands are the instruments? Here, even more than elsewhere, the spiritual authority and the physician must cooperate, for both of them are motivated by the same imperative to save the lives of our fellowmen.

Twentieth Century Responders

The foregoing has been a rather cursory and incomplete survey of the challenges to Halakhah posed by the scientific advancement of the 20th Century. We have passed over such diverse problems as the use of a dishwashing machine for both meat and dairy dishes, or the reciting of prayers for a person who underwent a colostomy, or the use of anesthesia in circumcision, or the status of a deaf-mute — declared by the Talmud as having no intelligence whatsoever — who can hear by means of a sophisticated hearing-aid, or the ritual preparation of frozen meats, or the use of a polygraph machine and fingerprints and voice recordings in a court of law. All these and

47   Mishnah *Shabbat* 23:5.
48   *Ran* to *Nedarim* 40a.
49   *Rema* to Sh. A. *Yoreh De'ah* 339:1.
50   *Hilkhot Rof'im U'Refuah, op. cit.*, p. 203.

more are subjects of many hundred of Responsa that have demonstrated the continued vitality of the Halakhah. Who are the outstanding halakhists who responded to these challenges?

We have to distinguish between the halakhists of the first half of the 20th Century and those of the second half, when the aftermath of World War II brought about a radical shift in the venue of halakhic activity. Furthermore, it is only in the post-War decades that the whole new field of both electronics and genetics developed. Foremost among European-Ashkenazic scholars because of his encyclopedic range of halakhic sources and his profound analysis of their basic principles was Yosef Rozen of Dvinsk (1858–1936), known as "the Rogachover" after his birthplace. Questions were addressed to him from all quarters, and he responded to each and every one tersely, citing sources but not elaborating upon them. His works, including a commentary to the Rambam, are entitled *Tzofnat Pa'ane'ah.*[51] His singularity can be seen in the fact that he does not refer to the opinions of the Aharonim at all, and only to a few of the Rishonim; his sources are the primary ones of the Babylonian and Jerusalem Talmuds.

His older contemporary and rabbi in the same city of Dvinsk was Meir Simha ha-Cohen (1843–1926), author of the very popular commentary to the Humash *Meshekh Hokhmah,* a harmonious blend of Halakhah and Aggadah. He is also known for his commentary to the Rambam entitled *Or Same'ah*. In the greatest center of Lithuanian Jewry, Vilna, called "the Jerusalem of Lithuania," the chief rabbi before World War II was Hayyim Ozer Grodzinsky (1863–1940). In contradistinction to Yosef Rozen and Hayyim Soloveitchik of Brisk, of whom he was a devoted follower, Hayyim Ozer, conscious of his position as a posek, would examine the opinions of the Aharonim — the commentators to the Shulhan Arukh — before submitting his own pesak halakhah. His numerous Responsa are collected in the three volumes entitled *Ahi'ezer*, and were recognized as authoritative by all Ashkenazi Jewry. Most interesting is his response to a question concerning the withdrawal of Orthodox Jews in Germany from the general Jewish community (*gemeinde*), which included Reform Jews, and setting up separate Orthodox communities, a policy fostered by Shimshon Rafael Hirsch. R. Hayyim Ozer writes, "This question cannot be decided

51   Cf. Gen. 41:45.

by Talmudic sources or the poskim; only by correct reasoning and a proper illuminating outlook. Not all places and times are alike in this matter; only the local authorities can decide on such a step in order to safeguard the Torah."[52] We must also take notice of the influence wielded by the heads of the European Yeshivot of the time: Moshe Mordekhai Epstein of Slabodka, Barukh Ber Levovitz of Kamenetz, Eliezer Gordon of Telz, Shimon Shkop of Grodno, Elhanan Wasserman of Baranovicz and others. Though they are known more for their ḥiddushim than for their Responsa, their disciples are the ones who rebuilt the Yeshiva world after the ravages of World War II, fostering the renaissance of Torah learning and halakhic guidance in Eretz Yisrael and America.

There are several important poskim who flourished in the first half of the 20th century whom we shall mention in the next chapter, since their major contribution to halakhic development was in response to modern Zionism and the State of Israel, the subject of our next chapter. However, we cannot leave this period before we mention a rather unique collection of Responsa created out of the ravages of the Holocaust. Ephraim Oshry published a collection of Responsa under the title *Mi-Ma'amakin* (from the Depths), "questions of moment in the days of slaying and destroying by the murderous hordes of Hitler during the years 1941–1945 in the Kovno Ghetto." In his Introduction, the author describes how even in "the valley of death" he continued the study of Torah and taught that "just as one is obliged to pronounce a blessing over the good things that befall him, so is one obliged to pronounce a blessing over the evil things."[53] Among the questions asked are: May one save his life by acquiring a certificate of apostasy to Christianity; Are parents required to say Kaddish after young children killed in the Holocaust; May a pregnant woman induce an abortion, since the Nazis decreed that they will kill every Jewess who becomes pregnant.[54] Appended to the volume is a list of Roshei Yeshiva and their students who perished in the Holocaust. Fortunately, Rabbi Oshry lived to tell the tale, and so did several Roshei Yeshiva,

---

52   Published in *Sefer ha-Zikaron l'Gaon Y.Y. Weinberg* (Jer. 5730).
53   Cf. Mishnah *Berakhot* 9:5.
54   See also R. Kirschner, *Rabbinic Responsa of the Holocaust Era* (N:Y. 1985).

"brands plucked from the fire," who survived the Holocaust and reestablished their Yeshivot in the United States.[55]

Another survivor of the Holocaust whose Responsa make a significant contribution to halakhic literature for modern times is the late Yeḥiel Yaakov Weinberg (d. 1966). Successor to David Zvi Hoffman as head of the Berlin Rabbinical Seminary, he combined the penetrating Lithuanian approach to Talmudic studies with a practical assessment of the conditions of modern life. Thus he favored the celebration of Bat-Mitzvah for girls and found no objection to a Jewish youth organization which engaged in mixed social activites. He also encouraged the attempt to find an halakhic solution to the problem of women whose husbands from whom they are separated and divorced in the civil courts refuse to give them a *get* as required by the Halakhah.[56] His Responsa are collected in the four volumes of *S'ridei Esh* (Remnants of Fire).

The foremost contemporary responder in the Diaspora is the recently departed Moshe b. David Feinstein (1895–1986), head of Yeshiva Tiferet Yerushalayim in New York City. Two generations of American rabbis have been turning to him for answers to every conceivable question which has some halakhic bearing. Anyone wishing to describe Orthodox Judaism in 20th century America would perforce have to look at these questions, the responses to which have been published in the ten volumes of *Iggerot Moshe*. His competence and authority as a posek have been recognized worldwide, and he has engaged in polemical discussion with the leading scholars in Eretz Yisrael. Rabbi Feinstein has taken an uncompromising stand against the Conservative and Reform movements in America, pronouncing a ban against Orthodox rabbis joining any organization which includes in its membership rabbis of non-Orthodox movements. He has also ruled that any wedding ceremony conducted by a Reform rabbi is invalid, to such an extent that even if the couple lived together for years as husband and wife they do not need a *get* upon separation.[57]

Another outstanding American responder — he subsequently moved to Israel — was the late Menaḥem Mendel Kasher (1895–1985), editor of that encyclopedic collection of Biblical

55   See W.B. Helmreich, *The World of the Yeshiva* (N.Y. 1982), chaps. 1 and 2.
56   See his Introduction to E. Berkowitz, *T'nai B'Nissuin U'B'Get* (Jer. 5727).
57   *Iggerot Moshe, Oraḥ Ḥayyim*, no. 91/6. See *Tradition*, Vol. 21, No. 3, pp. 7–39.

commentaries, the *Torah Shelemah*. Among other notable teshuvot, Rabbi Kasher has published a thoroughgoing analysis of the problem faced by a Jew upon upon crossing the international date-line; which day is Shabbat for him, according to the community he left or the community he arrives at?[58] Among his other published works are the *Haggadah Shelemah* citing all the various versions of the text, and *Ha-Rambam ve-ha-Mekhilta D'Rashbi*, based upon manuscripts from Yemen and the Cairo Genizah.

Another abundant and important source of teshuvot for the modern era are the several rabbinic journals in which rabbis from all quarters discuss the manifold problems confronting the Halakhah today. Prominent among these is the series of volumes now numbering twenty-five entitled *No'am*, begun in 1958 and published annually in Jerusalem by Makhon Torah Shelemah. To give an example of its coverage, the very first volume deals primarily with the problems raised by artificial insemination, and includes the opinions of such universally recognized scholars as Yeḥiel Yaakov Weinberg of Montreux, Yaakov Moshe Toledano of Tel Aviv, Yosef Eliyahu Henkin of New York, Menaḥem Mendel Kasher of New York, Ovadiah Hadaya and Shlomo Zalman Auerbach of Jerusalem.

In the United states, the most important rabbinic journal of this century is *Ha-Pardes*. Its first editor was Shmuel Aharon ha-Levi Pardes, who moved from Poland to Chicago, where he resumed publishing Ha-Pardes in 1926. Its current editor is Simḥah Elberg of New York. The vast majority of its contributors were European-trained members of the Agudat Ha-Rabbanim, decidedly non-Zionist in their orientation. The Rabbinical Council of America publishes its own rabbinic journal entitled Ha-Darom. Its editor for many years was the late Ḥayyim Dov Chavel, known for his edition of the works of the Ramban (Naḥmanides). The Rabbinical Coun-

---

58 This question became quite controversial during World War II, when Lithuanian Yeshiva students fled to Kobe, Japan, and were faced with the problem which day to observe as Yom Kippur. Rabbi Kasher ruled that the international date-line is the crucial factor, as did most of the rabbis in Eretz Yisrael at the time, with the exception of the Ḥazon Ish (see below), who ruled that 180 degrees east of Jerusalem is the crucial factor. The question was even more complicated for the Jewish personnel serving in the Pacific Islands or the Phillipines, where some rabbis felt that the deciding factor is the continent of Asia.

cil also publishes the English-language magazine *Tradition*, embracing both halakhic and philosophic topics.

Contemporary Scholars in Eretz Yisrael

The opening wide to Jews of the gates of Eretz Yisrael with the establishment of the State of Israel has brought with it a renaissance of traditional Torah study in the Holy Land. Roshe Yeshiva and their students who had survived the Holocaust replanted their institutions in Israel and resumed the intense mode of Torah learning which had prevailed in eastern Europe. Out of this renewed flourishing of Talmudic scholarship emerged the foremost living poskim of our time. The very creation of the State, with its formal recognition of the Chief Rabbinate and the Rabbinic courts, has focussed the attention of those halakhic masters who did not shut themselves off from contemporary society to the pressing demands of the hour. A prime example of one such pressing demand were the halakhic problems raised by the creation of the Israeli Defense Forces. The Talmud, in addition to codifying the rules of warfare as prescribed by the Torah[59] distinguishes between several types of war waged by the Jewish people, each type with its particular halakhic implications. It lays down this rule: "All (the Ḥakhamim and R. Yehudah) agree that the wars fought by Joshua to conquer (the land of Canaän) were obligatory; the wars of the House of David for expansion (of territory) all agree were optional: when do they disagree, wars fought to reduce the number of idolators that they should not rise up against them; the Ḥakhamim call them a mitzvah and R. Yehudah calls them optional."[60]

A category not mentioned specifically by the Talmud is spelled out by Maimonides; a war fought to save Israel from an enemy rising against them. This also is a *milḥmet mitzvah*, an obligatory war.[61] When war is a *milḥemet mitzvah* the Talmud rules, "All are obliged to join the war effort, even a groom from his chamber and a

---

59 Deut. 20; Mishnah *Sotah* chap. 8.
60 *Sotah* 44b. The reference is to a preemptive attack against a potential enemy.
61 *Hilkhot Melakhim* 5:1. Cf. J.T. *Sotah* 8:11 (23a) and S.Y. Zevin, *Milḥamah l'Or ha-Halakhah*, in Vol. XIII of Torah she-b'al-Peh of Mossad Harav Kook.

bride from her bridal-canopy.'"[62] Furthermore, in a milḥemet mitz-vah many of the labors prohibited on Shabbat may be performed if required for the waging of the battle.[63] Thus the first question to be resolved was the status of the wars fought by the Israel Defense Forces to repel the attacks of its enemies. Secondly, what is the status when there is no actual warfare, but the surrounding enemy is poised for battle and the Defense Forces have to be on battle alert. Thirdly, which functions performed by a regular army are indispensable and consequently permitted on Shabbat, and which are dispensable and should not be performed on Shabbat. These and countless other questions, many of them technical in nature, had to be answered. It was Shlomo Goren (b. 1917), the first Chief Chaplain of the Israel Defense Forces, who undertook this difficult task. He not only familiarized himself with the theoretical aspects as found in the Talmud and Rambam, but he actually joined the forces and became a paratrooper, thus becoming familiar with all the practical activities of an army engaged in warfare. He made his decisions with a most uncommon boldness, not having much precedent to affirm them.

Rabbi Goren subsequently became Israeli Ashkenazic Chief Rabbi, in which office he continued in his characteristic boldness to pronounce decisions which other rabbis disputed vigorously or hesitated to accept. Most noteworthy was his decision to declare the wives of the personnel that went down with the submarine Dakar free to remarry even though no bodies were recovered and no one was able to testify to their drowning.[64] Presently Rabbi Goren has no

---

62 A quotation from Joel 2:16. I have translated *yotz'im* "to join the war effort," since some Rishonim maintain that women do not enter the battlefield but are conscripted to assist in the supply services; cf. Mishnah *Sotah* 8:2 for such a category. The ultra-Orthodox do not permit their daughters to enter any sort of service connected with the military; just as they do not permit their sons, who presumably devote themselves to the higher duty of Torah-study, to be conscripted. The Zionist Orthodox have made an arrangement (*hesder*) with the army for their sons who study Torah to study part-time and serve part-time. Their daughters have the option of either joining the army, which does not impose any combatant duty for women, or serving the State (*sherut le'umi*) for a year in some social or educational capacity.

63 Cf. *Shabbat* 19a.

64 One of his most hotly disputed decisions was in a matter of children whose legitimacy was questionable because their mother had remarried without having received a *get* from her first husband. Rabbi Goren ruled that the children

official position in the rabbinate, but he continues to publish halakhic opinions on all problems concerning modern technology and medical practice. His remarkable familiarity with all the Rabbinic sources is displayed in these and in other published writings, especially in his thorough commentary to Tractate *Berakhot* of the Jerusalem Talmud.

Rabbi Goren's Sephardi colleague in the Chief Rabbinate was Ovadiah Yosef (b. 1920), a most prolific responder as seen in the many volumes of his Responsa entitled *Yabi'a Omer*. Rabbi Yosef is a champion of the Sephardi Halakhah, and decries the tendency among the Sephardim to adopt Ashkenazi practices.[65] He is also opposed to reciting the blessing over Hallel on Yom ha-Atzmaut, a practice favored by Rabbi Goren. Ovadia Yosef is also the author of *Ḥazon Ovadiah* dealing with the laws of Pesaḥ; in which connection mention should be made of the difference in practice between Sephardim and Ashkenazim with respect to the eating on Pesaḥ of rice and vegetables included in the category of *kitniyot* or legumes.[66] Another prolific responder whose published teshuvot entitled *Aseh Lekha Rav* grow from year to year is the Sephardi Chief Rabbi of Tel Aviv, Ḥayyim David Halevy. He is a more forthright champion of the religious significance of Medinat Yisrael.

A widely esteemed Ashkenazi posek today in Israel is the head of Yeshiva Kol Torah in Jerusalem, Shlomo Zalman Auerbach. In one of his teshuvot concerning artificial insemination — with the husband as donor, he rules, there is no problem — he raises a most interesting question which has implications for a procedure which has just begum to perturb all legal and medical minds. His question at the time was quite theoretical; If a husband died a day or two after his wife was artificially inseminated with his semen, the presumption being that conception, i.e. the fertilization of her ovum,

are not considered *mamzerim*, having determined that the first marriage had been invalid.

65   Thus he severely criticises the Sephardi women who recite a blessing over mitzvot, such as Lulav and Shofar, from which women are exempt *min ha-Torah*, for this is contrary to the ruling of the Sephardi codifiers Rambam (*Hilkhot Tzitzit* 3:9) and *Maran* (Yosef Karo in Sh. A. *Oraḥ Ḥayyim* 589:6) that they should not recite the blessing. Some Sephardi halakhists have ruled that they may recite the blessing; see E.G. Ellinson, *Ha-Ishah ve-ha-Mitzvot* (Jer. 5742), Vol. 1, p. 58.

66   See *Encyclopedia Talmudit*, Vol. 16, pp. 101–107.

occurred after his demise, was the mitzvah of *yibum* consummated. Very recently, however, with the development of sperm banks, the question is no longer theoretical; a woman can readily conceive from the sperm of a deceased donor. Would in such case the objections raised by the halakhists to impregnation with a donor other than the husband still apply? Another problem to which Rabbi Auerbach addressed himself in a lengthy article[67] concerns a woman who can conceive only during the period when she is a *niddah*. According to the Torah, this period extends only for seven days from the onset of the menstrual flow. However, it has been accepted from Talmudic times that the period be extended to twelve days.[68] Rabbi Auerbach suggested a method by means of which an infertile woman could technically obviate becoming a niddah, but his suggestion met with such strong opposition that he subsequently issued a statement that he did not intend to issue a decision *halakhah le'ma'aseh*, i.e. that it actually be put into practice.

The posek whose opinions in medical matters — and in other matters as well — are most highly regarded is Eliezer Yehudah Waldenberg, halakhic advisor to Shaare Zedek Hospital in Jerusalem. In more than a dozen volumes, in a series entitled *Tzitz Eliezer*, this prolific responder has rendered clear-cut decisions in all questions concerning modern methods of treatment. Taking issue with Moshe Feinstein, he permits an abortion where examination has disclosed that the foetus is afflicted with a debilitating disease such as Tay-Sachs. A phenomenon which for centuries was extremely rare but has recently become much less infrequent is the combination of halakhic with medical expertise. Physicians who are observant Jews and have had a Yeshiva training preparatory to their medical training are enabling poskim today to base their opinions not only on "book" knowledge but on a thorough understanding of all aspects of the problem. Here, as elsewhere, we have proof of the verity of the Vilna Gaon's statement that "as much as one lacks a knowledge of other wisdoms he will correspondingly lack a knowledge of Torah a hundredfold."

---

67 *Noam*, Vol. 7.
68 *Niddah* 66a; *Rema* to *Yoreh De'ah* 196:11. Orthodox feminists have called for the cancellation of this extension, but — as indicated in the article under discussion — no halakhist would be willing to entertain such a notion, even in case of hardship.

Feminism and the Halakhah

A custom dating from Talmudic times calls upon those present at a Brit-Milah to recite immediately after the circumcision the prayer, "Just as he (the infant) entered the Covenant, so may he enter into *Torah, Ḥuppah* (the wedding canopy) and *Ma'asim Tovim* (good deeds).[69] However, in the prayer recited at the naming of a baby girl, the word *Torah* is invariably omitted. It is told that a pious father in the Middle Ages inscribed the following prayer at the birth of his daughter, "May she sew, spin, weave, and be brought up to a life of good deeds."[70] The omission of *Torah* in the prayer for a girl is a consequence of the opinion of the Tanna Eliezer b. Hyrcanus that "He who teaches his daughter Torah is as if he teaches her lewdness."[71] This again is a reflection of his opinion that "A woman's wisdom is only in the spindle."[72] For centuries traditional Jewry followed this opinion and made no provision for the formal education of girls. All they knew of Jewish ritual and observance they learned from the practice of their parents and the customs of the community in which they lived.

In the early 20th Century, when secular public education became widespread and Jewish girls were sent to the public schools, religious leaders began to question this traditional practice of no formal Jewish education for girls. It was quite paradoxical, they argued, for girls to receive a secular but not a religious education, a phenomenon that could undermine their faith and commitment to Jewish observance. No less a strict halakhist than Meir Simḥa ha-Cohen of Radun, the Ḥafetz Ḥayyim, conceded that R. Eliezer's

---

69   *Shabbat* 137b. J.T. *Berakhot* 9:3(14a) reads, "Just as you (the father) brought him into the Covenant, so may you bring him into Torah and Ḥuppah," and omits *ma'asim tovim*.

70   Quoted by I. Epstein in *The Jewish Library* (ed. Leo Jung, N.Y. 1943), p. 123. A similar discrimination between the sexes is found in the ruling (*Berakhot* 59b; Sh.A. *Oraḥ Ḥayyim* 223:1) that a blessing of thanksgiving is recited upon the birth of a son, but not upon the birth of a daughter. *Mishnah B'rurah*, however, notes that the father should recite *she-heḥeyanu* the first time he sees his baby daughter.

71   Mishnah *Sotah* 3:4. The word "lewdness" is a translation of the original Hebrew *tiflut*. Others maintain that is means "nonsense"; see E.G. Ellinson, *op. cit.* p. 148, n. 25.

72   J.T. *Sotah* 3:4 (19a).

opinion was tenable only in previous ages, when children would not question the practices of their elders. Nowadays, he contended, when non-Orthodoxy is rampant, if girls are not taught the fundamentals of Judaism and its moral imperatives, their defection from tradition is an imminent possibility.[73] Thus the needs of the hour demanded the establishment of Jewish schools for girls; a demand first met in Poland with the founding of the network of Beit Yaakov schools, and soon adopted in other Jewish communities throughout the world. Thus by now in many synagogues, when the *mi-she'berakh* for the birth of a daughter is recited, one can hear *Torah* as well as *Ḥuppah* included in the blessing for a Jewish girl's future.

Though halakhic scholars were ready to sanction instruction for girls, they confined the studies to Torah she-bikhtav, the Ḥumash, and the mitzvot which women are obliged to observe; thus ruling out the study of Torah-she-b'al-Peh, such as Mishnah and Talmud.[74] However, as girls began to taste the fruits of knowledge, and especially as the teachers required for the girls' schools — invariably women — had to have broader knowledge than just Ḥumash and Kitzur Shulhan Arukh, the scope of instruction for girls became broader and deeper, until the number of Orthodox women studying Talmud and Jewish Philosophy in addition to the Sciences and Liberal Arts increased considerably.[75]

Coincident with this increase in Jewishly knowledgable women arose the general Feminist movement of recent times, with its strident demands for "the equality of the sexes." Orthodox women, no longer confined within the walls of a cultural ghetto, could not fail to be influenced by this movement. Having gained access to basic Jewish sources, they noticed some of the inequalities imbedded in Jewish Law which convey a sense of female inferiority.[76] They also began to feel more keenly their exclusion from some of the

---

73 *Likutei Halakhot* to *Sotah* 21a.

74 A distinction assumed by Maimonides, *Hilkhot Talmud Torah* 1:13 and recorded in Sh. A. *Yoreh De'ah* 246:6. *Rema ad loc.* adds the requirement that she learn the laws pertaining to women.

75 A glance at the courses in Jewish Studies offered by Stern College for Women of Yeshiva University, or of the Jerusalem College for Women (*Mikhlalah l'Banot*), will substantiate this.

76 E.g., the usual inclusion of women in the same category as deaf-mutes and minors; or the disqualificaiton of women as witnesses for most court procedures.

religious observances which the Halakhah imposes upon men exclusively.[77] Among the issues raised by Orthodox feminists are the halakhic restrictions against abortion for economic and social reasons;[78] the ruling that only men are empowered to issue a *get*; the exemption of women from certain mitzvot, such as tefillin; and most recently the disqualification of women to constitute a minyan and consequently being barred from conducting regular congregational prayers (*tefillah b'tzibbur*) among themselves.

The response to these demands upon the part of contemporary halakhists — some "modern Orthodox" among them — has been negative, and often unsympathetic. Basically they assert that Torah she-b'al-Peh (i.e. the Halakhah) is *min ha'shamayim*, and thus impervious to subjective emotional considerations. Thus the late Rabbi Moshe Feinstein, responding to a query concerning Orthodox Jewish feminists, stated: "At the outset, one has to know that a principle of our pure faith is that the entire Torah, both written and oral, was given by God Himself on Mt. Sinai through Moshe Rabbenu, and it is impossible to change even one iota (*kotz*)." He qualifies this by adding that the Sanhedrin and Torah scholars have the duty to institute new regulations (*takkanot*) and add prohibitions as hedges against possible violations of Torah laws. He explains the Torah's exemption of women from certain mitzvot because they are by nature occupied with the rearing of children. He reiterates that even though social and economic circumstances may have changed "there exists no power to change anything, even if the whole world may agree to do so; and these women (i.e. the feminists) who stubbornly fight for change are deniers of the Torah (*kofrot*)," He does concede that women may accept upon themselves mitzvot for which they are not obligated by the Torah — putting on tefillin excepted[79] — but this is so only if they want to observe them as mitzvot and not in order to impugn the Torah, an intention which he attributes to the Orthodox feminists.[80] Addi-

77   A fervent expression of these feelings, though occasionally based upon a misunderstanding of a text, can be found in Blu Greenberg, *On Women and Judaism; A View from Tradition* (JPS Phila. 5742).

78   See above, p. 214–215.

79   For an explanation of this exception, see E.G. Ellinson, *op. cit.*, p. 61.

80   *Iggerot Moshe, Orah Hayyim*, Vol. 4, no. 49. See also E. Feldman in *Tradition*, Vol. 21, no. 3, pp. 98 ff. for similar argument.

tionally, a long array of authorities are cited who denounce any attempt to deviate from established custom. Some responses have even impugned the sincerity of these feminists, pointing at the general movement which purportedly is a movement for greater sexual license.[81]

The demand which has received extensive treatment and yet which the Halakhah finds almost impossible to satisfy, is the inequality in the Jewish divorce process. Rabbenu Gershom had reduced this inequality somewhat by instituting that a woman cannot be divorced against her will;[82] but the law still requires the free consent of the husband, and as long as he witholds it his wife remains his wife halakhically with all its ramifications even though the couple are living apart and have been divorced by the civil courts. Numerous proposals have been suggested to remedy this situation, about which women have been clamoring more and more. Most of these proposals are based upon some pre-nuptial contractual obligation which would penalize the recalcitrant party when the giving of a *get* is ordered by the rabbinical court. However, poskim have found one flaw or another in such arrangements, and to-date no proposal has been accepted by the religious authorities.[83] Even in Israel, where the rabbinic courts are empowered to impose various pressures upon the party concerned, even to the extent of imprisonment, the *dayyanim* are reluctant to impose them.[84]

There is one radical solution which has a precedent in a Talmudic ruling; the annulment of the marriage by a rabbinic court declaring that the marriage ceremony was invalid *ab initio*. This was a case where a man compelled a woman to accept his proposal of marriage by threatening her. "He acted improperly, therefore the rabbis dealt with him improperly;"[85] i.e. by invalidating his marriage

---

81   Teshuvah of Yeshiva Univ. rabbis, unpublished. For the author's opinion, see below, pp. 253–254.

82   See above, p. 122.

83   See E. Berkowitz, *Tenai B'Nissuin U'Beget2* (Jer. 5727) and J.D. Bleich, *Contemporary Halakhic Problems* (N.Y. 1977), pp. 154–159. See also M. Chigier, *Husband and Wife in Israeli Law* (Jer. 5745), who argues that changed social attitudes should negate the halakhic presumptions of the Talmud which render pre-nuptial conditions void.

84   See Z. Wahrhaftig in *Shnaton ha-Mishpat ha-Ivri*, Vol. 3–4 (Jer. 5736–7).

85   *Bava Batra* 48b.

though not strictly according to the law. Already in the Middle Ages, the Rishonim were reluctant to exercise such authority; how much more so are Aḥaropnim reluctant to exercise such sweeping judicial powers.[86]

An additional consideration which inhibits the halakhist today from making any concessions to feminist demands are the concessions which the Conservative movement has already made in this respect; such as calling up women to the reading of the Torah and, more recently, the ordaining of women to the rabbinate. Orthodox Judaism, in its attempt to preserve the line of demarcation between it and Conservative Judaism, is responding to any demand for change in the same manner that its forebears two centuries ago responded to the movement for Reform; namely, with the slogan "anything new is forbidden by the Torah."[87] It proceeds on the assumption that any breach, no matter how slight, in accepted practice will only strengthen the Conservative movement and eventually undermine the authority of the Halakhah in other areas as well. As the halakhist sees it, his responsibility is not only to teach the Halakhah but to preserve its integrity and authority in Jewish life. And the only way to accomplish this is not by sanctioning a deviation from tradition arising from fresh attitudes, but rather by reaffirming our faith in and commitment to tradition's inviolability.

86   M. Elon, *Ha-Mishpat Ha-Ivri*, *op. cit.*, pp. 689 ff.
87   See above, p. 185.

13

Challenge and Response IV:
Zionism and the State of Israel

אמר עולא אין ישראל נפדה אלא בצדקה
שנאמר ציון במשפט יפדה ושביה בצדקה (ישעי' א, כז)

Ulla said, "Israel will be redeemed only through righteousness,
as is said, *Zion shall be redeemed with justice,
and her returnees with righteousness* (Isaiah 1:27)*

Opposition to Zionism

In our Introdiction (above, pages 5–7), we have pointed out the
distinction between Aggadah, the homiletical branch of Rabbinic
literature, and Halakhah, its legal code. The latter is mandatory,
binding upon its adherents; the former is hortatory at best, oftimes
legendary in character. When it came to the modern Zionist movement, however, the rabbinic opposition based its objections upon
two Talmudic statements which apparently are aggadic in nature
and not to be taken as mandatory. "Do not join the wicked," we are
exhorted in Ethics of the Fathers;[2] and since the leaders of the
Zionist movement, having abandoned traditional Judaism, are in
the category of "the wicked", we are forbidden to associate with
them. Even more to the point, assert the opponents of Zionism, is
the statement of R. Yose b. Ḥaninah that the Almighty made Israel
swear "that they should not go up as a wall (Rashi, all together, with
a strong hand) and that they should not rebel against the nations."[3]
This implies that the Jewish people should not undertake any

---

* *Shabbat* 139a.

1　The printed edition reads *Yerushalayim* instead of *Yisrael*; see the gloss *ad loc*.
　　Some translate *shave'hah* "her repentant ones," instead "returnees."
2　*Avot* 1:7.
3　*Ketubot* 111a.

concerted action for the reconquest of Eretz Yisrael from a foreign power. Rather, they are adjured to wait passively for the coming of the Messiah, who will lead all the Jews of the Diaspora back to Eretz Yisrael in some miraculous fashion.[4]

There were distinguished rabbis, such as Yehudah Alkalai and Zvi Hirsch Kalisher and Shmuel Mohliver, who refuted the arguments of the anti-Zionists, asserting that it is a mitzvah to resettle Eretz Yisrael and bring about the reestablishment of Jewish sovereignty in the anciet Homeland even before the coming of the Messiah.[5] Many halakhists contend that the issue of whether or not it is a mitzvah to settle the land is a matter of dispute between the two great masters, the Rambam (Maimonides) and the Ramban (Naḥmanides). The former does not include the mitzvah of *Yishuv Eretz Yisrael* in his *Sefer ha-Mitzvot*; whereas the latter, in his commentary to the verse *You shall take possession of the Land*[6] (Num. 33:53), states, "My opinion is (apparently disputing the Rambam) that this is a positive commandment...That our Sages emphasizing the importance of dwelling in Eretz Yisrael and saying that it is forbidden to depart from it[7]... it is here that we are commanded to do so, for this verse is a positive commandment." The *Tosafot*[8] ruled that the mitzvah does not apply nowadays (i.e. in their time, in the Middle Ages) because of the dangers involved in traveling to the Holy Land. Another justification offered there for declaring the mitzvah presently inapplicable is the fact that there are so many mitzvot which we would be required to observe in Eretz Yisrael (e.g. the Shemittah year and the tithing of agricultural products) but which we are incapable of observing (so it is better to remain outside the Land).

---

4   For this author's personal view, see *Religious Foundations etc., op. cit.*, pp. 161–162.

5   For a few details, see *ibid.*, pp. 164–165.

6   Thus JPS translation of *ve-horashtem*. Classical commentators, such as Targum and Rashi, translate "you shall drive out".

7   Cf. *Ketubot* 110b–111b.

8   *Ibid. s.v. hu omer.*

Settlement in Eretz Yisrael and the Halakhah

There is no doubt that for Jews who had lived for centuries in *ḥutz la-aretz* (outside the Land), settlement in Eretz Yisrael would create almost insurmountable halakhic problems, particularly if they were to engage in agriculture. One of these problems, the Biblical prohibition of working in the fields during the Sabbatical year (*Shemittah*; Lev. 25:1–5), became the subject of fierce controversy among the rabbis at the very beginning of modern Jewish settlement on the land. Paradoxically enough, in 1888 the foremost poskim in Eretz Yisrael, Shmuel Salant and Yehoshua Leib Diskin,[9] ruled that there must be strict adherence to the laws of Shemittah; whereas the foremost posek in Europe, Yitzhak Elhanan Spector of Kovno,[10] was inclined to be lenient in view of the immense hardships experienced by the new settlers. The halakhic basis for such leniency was the fact that practically all Rishonim ruled that the restrictions of the Shemittah year nowadays (i.e. after the destruction of the Bet ha-Mikdash) are only *mid'rabbanan*, of Rabbinic force, and not of Torah law. This ruling in itself is based upon the Talmudic exposition of the verse *You shall sanctify the fiftieth year* (the Jubilee year) *and proclaim freedom in the land for all its inhabitants* (Lev. 25:10): "As soon as the tribes of Reuven and Gad and half of Menasheh were exiled, the laws of the Jubilee year became null and void since *all its inhabitants* are not in the land."[11] And once the Jubilee became null and void. it follows that the Shemittah year also becomes null and void.[12]

Rabbi Abraham Isaac ha-Cohen Kook

Little more than two decades later, in 1910, the controversy over Shemittah raged even more fiercely. By this time, the chief Orthodox ideologue and champion of modern Zionism, Avraham Yitzḥak ha-Cohen Kook (1865–1935), was in Eretz Yisrael, and he immediately took up the cudgels for the religious settlers. He ruled

9 See above, p. 204.
10 See above, p. 180.
11 *Arakhin* 32b.
12 Cf.*Gittin* 36a and commentators *ad loc.*

that the land may be tilled during the year of Shemittah if sold beforehand to a non-Jew for that year;[13] but emphasized that the *heter* (permission) was only an emergency measure "since it is impossible for the Yishuv in general to exist without it." He therefore urged that the few who wanted to observe the shemittah restrictions should be encouraged and supported. Despite the personal villification he suffered from those who disagreed with his ruling, he maintained his opinion and wrote a volume entitled *Shabbat ha-Aretz* analysing the entire problem and vindicating his pesak halakhah.

Rabbi Kook grappled with all the other problems facing the settlers on the land. Various species of grain and legume had to be identified for the law of *Kil'ayim*, the mixture of diverse seeds (Deut. 22:9), as well as the grafting of one type of citrus on a tree of another type (e.g. grapefruit with orange). We have already mentioned[14] the problem of milking a dairy herd on Shabbat Rabbi Kook could find no heter for this (it was before the introduction of automatic milking machines), and suggested that a non-Jew be hired for this task. (Religious kibbutzim were loathe to accept this ruling as a matter of principle; they argued that a Torah-abiding community in Eretz Yisrael should not be compelled by the Halakhah to resort to non-Jewish labor). These and numerous other

---

13   Somewhat similar to *mekhirat hametz*, the selling to a non-Jew of one's leavened food before Pesah in order to avoid the Torah's proscription, *Seven days no leaven shall be found in your houses* (Exod. 12:19). Objections to Rabbi Kook's ruling are based both on halakhic and ideological grounds. The Halakhah forbids selling land in Eretz Yisrael to non-Jews (*Avodah Zarah* 20a): "It is written *You shall not show them mercy* (Deut. 7:2, implying that you shall not give them a resting place in the land" (from the similarity between *t'hanem* "show them mercy" and *hanayah* "camping-ground"). Tosafot *ibid*. maintains that this prohibition applies to all non-Jews, whereas Rambam (*Hilkhot Akum* 10:13) limits this ruling to the "seven nations" which occupied Eretz Yisrael at the time of Joshua. Ideologically it is paradoxical that land should be sold to non-Jews at a time when every effort is made to redeem the land from them. Nevertheless, it is now accepted practice for the Israeli Chief Rabbinate to arrange a bill of sale of all Jewish land to an Arab for the year of Shemittah. The agricultural settlements of Agudat Yisrael do not accept this *heter*, and avoid doing work on the land that is prohibited by the Torah. Even the Kibbutz Hadati settlements of the Mizrachi movement, who accept the heter, refrain from work that is dispensable.

14   Above, p. 212.

questions are dealt with in the two collections of Rabbi Kook's Responsa, *Mishpat Kohen* and *Da'at Kohen*. We see in them the great posek, whose familiarity with the halakhic sources is phenomenal and whose approach is a combination of the traditional and the pragmatic. But Rabbi Kook towers above all his contemporaries—*from his shoulders up he was taller than all the people* (I Sam. 9:2) — for his independent espousal of Zionism and for his many-faceted talents and pursuits. He was both halakhist and aggadist, poet and kabbalist, indefatigable correspondent,[15] visionary and man of action, saintly but not solitary. He laid the foundation for the Israeli Chief Rabbinate and was its first Ashkenazi head. He chided his rabbinic colleagues for their narrow views, and recommended secular studies as ancillary to Torah studies. He founded a Yeshiva — *Merkaz Ha-Rav* in Jerusalem — which he hoped would provide his type of leadership for world Jewry. Though his influence is still strong a half-century after his demise, it is confined to a comparatively small group of followers, and regrettably has not succeeded in penetrating the strongholds of the traditional Yeshiva world.

Rabbi Kook, stimulated by both the Zionist settlement and the Balfour declaration, foresaw the establishment of an independent sovereign Jewish State in Eretz Yisrael.[16] One of his most significant halakhic rulings is the equating of the authority of such a State with the authority granted by the Torah to the king of Israel.[17] He states, "At a time when there is no king, all royal prerogatives are transferred to the nation in general, since the rights of a kingdom include that which concerns the general situation of the nation."[18] Thus Rabbi Kook affirms the halakhic legitimacy of legislation passed by the parliament of an independent Jewish State, above and beyond the legitimacy granted to any sovereign state by the halakhic principle of *Dina d'Malkhuta Dinah*, "The law of the kingdom is law."[19]

---

15 Collected in several volumes entitled *Iggerot Ra'iyah*.
16 Cf. Zvi Yaron, *Mishnato shel harav Kook* (Jer. 5734), p. 319, n. 63.
17 Cf. *Sanhedrin* 20b.
18 *Mishpat Kohen*, pp. 337–338.
19 Cf. Sh. Shilo, *Dina d'Malkhuta Dina* (Jer. 5735), pp. 101 ff.

The Ḥazon Ish

In the years immediately preceding the establishment of the State of Israel, the foremost posek among the non-Zionist rabbis was Avraham Yeshayahu Karelitz (1878–1953), better known as the Ḥazon Ish, the title of his halakhic writings. Though he had no official position in the rabbinate, nor was he head of a Yeshiva, he enjoyed wide recognition as a posek because of his keen analysis of the Halakhah, as is evidenced by his commentary to the Shulhan Arukh, and his saintly character. Though his followers gave him a reputation as a *maḥmir*, one who invariably decides in a very stringent manner, his decisions were never arbitrarily so, but were rather based upon his unwillingness to compromise.[20] Where he found reason to be lenient he was so. Thus, he permitted the use of milking machines on Shabbat, with certain qualifications. He also took into account the changing attitudes in Jewish society. In commenting upon the Talmudic ruling that heretics are to be indirectly done away with,[21] he writes, "It appears that this law obtains only when religious commitment is widespread... Today, however, such strict measures against heretics would only increase heresy, since in their eyes it looks like violent extermination."[22] The Ḥazon Ish was a *maḥmir* when it came to *shei'urim*, the quantities and dimensions mentioned in the Halakhah. For example, the required quantity (*ka-zayit*, the size of an olive) for the mitzvah matzah at the Pesaḥ Seder for the Ḥazon Ish is approximately fifty cubic centimeters (two-thirds of a machine-baked matzah); whereas other poskim require only twenty-five and a half cubic centimenters. The esteem in which he was held even by the non-religious was demonstrated when the late Prime Minister David ben Gurion visited him to discuss the question of drafting religious girls in the Israeli Defense Forces.

---

20   His followers are also wont to add restriction (*ḥumra*) upon restriction. Thus in the case of the matzah eaten at the Seder, they insist that the entire quantity be swallowed at once.
21   *Avodah Zarah* 26b.
22   *Ḥazon Ish, Yoreh De'ah* 16:2.

The State of Israel and the Halakhah[23]

The Torah laid down the foundations for a Jewish State. It prescribed a dual governmental authority, that of the Judges and that of the King.[24] When the Hasmoneans established a kingdom in Israel during the days of the Second Temple, this dual system came into operation, with the authority of the judges concentrated in the Sanhedrin, also referred to as the *Bet ha-Din ha-Gadol*, the Supreme Court.[25] Though the Jewish kingdom ceased to exist with the destruction of the Second Temple — except for a very brief period under Bar Kochba — the Sages of the Talmud continued to discuss the extent of authority granted by the Torah to the king, providing in many essential matters of government collaboration with the Sanhedrin.[26] Post-Talmudic halakhists — with the exception of the Rambam — did not deal with *Hilkhot Medinah*, the Laws of the State, in any systematic fashion. Thus when Medinat Yisrael was established, there was not much in the vast halakhic literature that could be applied directly to a state functioning in the 20th Century. Two basic branches of government laid down by the Torah were missing: A kingdom that theoretically at least was bound by the Halakhah, and a Sanhedrin that could initiate Halakhah by adapting laws of the Torah to this novel situation.

Rabbi Yitzhak Isaac ha-Levi Herzog

An attempt to fill at least one of these lacunae by reestablishing the Sanhedrin was made by the first Israeli Minister of Religions, the late Rabbi Yehudah Leib ha-Cohen Fishman-Maimon; but his proposal was rejected outright by the Israeli rabbis. Many preliminary steps had yet to be taken before the revival of that central institution in Jewish life — characterized by Maimonides as "the root of the Torah-she-b'al-Peh"[27] — could become a reality. First

---

23 For a somewhat different treatment of this problem, see *Religious Foundations etc., op. cit.*, 197 ff.
24 Cf. Deut. 16:18–20, 17:8–20. For a detailed treatment of this subject, see *ibid.* chap. 1.
25 See above, p. 59ff.
26 Cf. Mishnah *Sanhedrin* 2:3.
27 *Hilkhot Mamrim* 1:1.

of all, the Halakhah as defined in the existing Codes of Jewish Law had to be adapted to all the requirements of 20th Century society; and secondly, rabbis had to be both persuaded to accept such adaptation and trained to execute such law. A great halakhist who set himself to initiate the taking of such steps was Yitzhak Isaac b. Yoel ha-Levi Herzog (1888–1959), successor to Rabbi Kook as Ashkenazi Chief Rabbi in Israel.

Even before his appointment in 1937 to such office, Rabbi Herzog was known for his distinguished erudition in Jewish Law, buttressed by his academic training in the Sorbonne. He published in English his *Main Institutions of Jewish Law*, two volumes dealing with the laws of property and contracts. Upon arrival in Israel, little more than a decade before the establishment of the State, he established the *Makhon Harry Fishel Lidrishat Ha-Talmud U'Mishpat ha-Torah* for the twin purpose of bringing Jewish civil law up-to-date and the training of *dayyanim*, judges for the *batei-din rabbaniyyim*, the religious courts recognized by the British mandatory power for the Jewish inhabitants. In collaboration with his Sephardi colleague, Ben Zion Meir Hai Uzziel (1880–1953), he instituted takkanot for regulating the batei-din. He also established the *Institute for Otzar ha-Poskim*, the Thesaurus of Rabbinic Decisions,[28] to serve as handy reference for the dayyanim. After the State came into being and the Knesset began legislating for its Israeli citizens, Rabbi Herzog proposed takkanot that would align halakhic law with the secular law that provided for equality of the sexes in matters of inheritance. However, the other members of the Chief Rabbinate refused to accept his recommendations. "The rabbis," he wrote, "were not inclined to institute any takkanah whatsoever."[29]

The exigiencies of the post-war period deflected Rabbi Herzog from his preoccupation with the Halakhah as he concentrated his efforts towards the rescue and ingathering of Jewish children who survived the evil design of the Nazis. However, over the years he rendered many important halakhic decisions, particularly in marriage and domestic law, which have now been published posthumously in three volumes under the title *Hekhal Yitzhak*. We see in them both his keen perception and his human sympathies.

28 See above, p. 194.
29 *Talpiyot*, Yeshiva Univ. N.Y. 5725.

Rabbi Ben Zion Hai Uzziel

One rabbi who shared Rabbi Herzog's efforts and hopes for the restoration of Jewish Law as incorporated in the Halakhah to its primal authority was his Sephardi colleague mentioned above. Rabbi Uzziel was the author of several volumes of Responsa, *Mishp'-tei Uzziel*, characterized by their up-to-date approach . Thus he writes in his Introduction to the volume on Even ha-Ezer, "One is obliged to investigate all the problems that the present conditions of life place before us. We dare not push them aside through fear that perhaps there being no precedent halakhah we will be branded as halakhic innovators." In this connection, he does not hesitate to express his opinion — sharply contested by most rabbis — that women have the right to vote, with the following argument: "Assuming that halakhically women are not subsumed in the terms *kahal* or *eidah* (community of Israel), are they not creatures created in the image (of God) with understanding!" He further argues that women may even be elected to office, a ruling which seems to be contrary to an express ruling of the Rambam.[30]

In his Introduction to the volume on Yoreh De'ah, Rabbi Uzziel writes, "With God's grace and wonders the day has arrived to which we have aspired (i.e. the establishment of Medinat Yisrael). Regrettably, full authority has not been granted to judge all according to the judgments of the Torah; and that supreme institution which is both judge and legislator has not yet been established. However, we have been given the full right to judge (i.e. in the Rabbinic courts) according to the laws of the Torah without any interference from any foreign ruler." His Responsa reveal a combination of both Ashkenazi and Sephardi approaches to questions of Jewish Law. Like the former, he analyses in depth the original sources, Talmud and Rishonim; like the latter he cites a whole string of his Sephardi predecessors before stating unequivocally his own opinion. It is only through the persevering efforts of Rabbis Herzog and Uzziel that the jurisdiction of the Rabbinic courts in all aspects of Family Law is firmly anchored in the laws of the Knesset.

We have from time to time made reference to the differences between Ashkenazi and Sephardi poskim. The latter, generally speaking, deal almost exclusively with practical problems and are

---

30 *Hilkhot Melakhim* 1:5.

less inclined in their Responsa to include pilpulistic diversions. This can be seen in the published works of several Sephardi ḥakhamim of the first half of this century, of which two are worthy of special mention. Yaakov Moshe Toledano (1880–1960), who was appointed Chief Rabbi of Tel Aviv in 1942 after serving in Tangiers and Egypt, is the author of Responsa *Yam ha-Gadol*. Among the practical problems he deals with is the halakhic status of voices heard over recordings (gramaphone), the telephone and radio; are they as valid as hearing the speakers directly.[31] Ovadia Hadaya, erstwhile member of the Sephardi Bet-Din in Jerusalem, is the author of Responsa *Yaskil Avdi*. Remarkably, he includes questions concerning Kabbalistic practices. A question dealt with exclusively by the Sephardim is the one concerning the use of public transportation on Shabbat. It seems that a Sephardi rabbi had permitted such use on the grounds that the labor is performed by non-Jews and not specifically for Jews,[32] and this heter was accepted in Baghdad and by the Sephardi community in New York City. However, the rabbis mentioned above have condemned this practice; and one of the reasons mentioned is that such practice would look peculiar in the eyes of the Ashkenazim. It is to be regretted that the works of these latter-day Sephardim are practically unknown, let alone studied, in Ashkenazi circles. It should be noted in this connection that at a recent conferece of dayyanim the chief Sephardi Rabbi of Jerusalem, Shalom Mashash, and the Sephardi head of the Rabbinic courts in Petah Tikvah, Moshe Malka, called upon the rabbis to follow the example of the rabbis in Morocco, who did not hesitate to adopt takkanot when the social situation warranted it.

Mishpat Ivri : Jewish Civil Law

When the newly-founded Knesset over three decades ago laid the foundation for the legal system for the State of Israel, it based it upon a hybrid melange of the Ottoman law in force when Palestine was under Turkish rule, and British Common law introduced by the mandatory power. It took years of gentle persuasion for the Israeli legislators to overcome their prejudice against Jewish tradition and

31   See above, p. 211.
32   Cf. Mishnah *Shabbat* 16:6.

begin to appreciate the value, both on legal and moral grounds, of traditional Jewish law. Credit for this development must be attributed, in addition to Rabbis Herzog and Uzziel, to two non-rabbinic — though rabbinically trained —personalities, Dr. Zerah Wahrhaftig, for many years chairman of the law committee of the Knesset, and the late justice of the Israeli Supreme Court, Dr. Moshe Silberg.[33] Thus in 1980 the Knesset enacted the Foundations of Law Act which abolished the link of Israeli law with the English legal system and declared: "If the court in considering a legal question requiring determination finds no answer to it in any enactment, in decided law or by way of analogy, *it shall determine the question in the light of the principles of liberty, justice, equity and peace in the Jewish heritage.*" This is a far cry from adopting the laws of the Shulhan Arukh, at least in so far as they are applicable to present day practice; but it does represent an advance towards the increasing introduction of traditional law, in contradistinction to "principles", in the Israeli courts.

Much is being done presently to hasten this advance. Israeli law schools are including in their curricula more and more courses in Jewish Law. In addition to Bar-Ilan University, both the Hebrew University in Jerusalem and the Tel Aviv University have special faculties and departments for research in Mishpat Ivri, each of them publishing annuals with the results of their research.[34] The recently published monumental survey of Mishpat Ivri by Justice Menahem Elon will do much to make Talmudic law more understandable, and thus more acceptable, to Israeli jurists. However, it should be emphasized that Mishpat Ivri and Halakhah are two separate entities. Halakhah is a religious concept and comprises not only civil law — "between one man and his neighbor" — but ritual law as well — "between one man and his Maker." Not all rabbis or poskim are ready to accept as halakhically binding the laws of the Knesset, though the recently elected Ashkenazi Chief Rabbi, Avraham Shapira, suggested that the rabbinate recognize these laws as having received the assent of the community, a requirement of the

---

33 M. Silberg, *Ba'in ke-Ehad*, Jer. 5742, pp. 180 ff. See also Y. Bazak (ed.) *Ha-Mishpat Ha-Ivri U'Medinat Yisrael*, Jer. 5729.

34 For Hebrew Univ. *Sh'naton Ha-Mishpat Ha-Ivri* (10 volumes to date); for Tel Aviv Univ. *Dinei Yisrael* (ed. Z. Falk and A. Kirschenbaum; 10 volumes to date).

Halakhah for the adoption of takkanot. At times, there are clashes between the State courts, including the Supreme Court, and the Rabbinic courts; though it should be noted that the latter are bound by Knesset law in certain areas; for example, in the rights of women and minors in inheritance and alimentary obligations.[35] Further-more, there are basic differences in the two disciplines, between students of the Halakhah in the Yeshivot, the potential dayyanim, and the students of Jewish Law in the universities. The religious commitment of the former makes them somewhat less sensitive to social considerations than the latter, who are more amenable to extraneous factors. Research into Mishpat Ivri includes the study of comparative law and historical development which may reveal insights to which halakhic scholars are indifferent.[36]

Dat U'Medinah : Religion and State

Though much has been written about the problem of the interrela-tionship between the Jewish religion and the Jewish State, the matter is extremely complex and far from settled. On both sides of the fence, the religious and the non-religious, there remains funda-mental disagreement. The latter constantly proclaim that Medinat Yisrael is a *Medinat Hok*, a state governed by secular statute, and not a *Medinat Halakhah*; yet the Knesset cannot avoid dealing with laws that are essentially religious in nature. This problem is clearly accentuated in legislation surrounding the basic law of the State, the *Hok ha-Sh'vut*, the Law of Return, which guarantees the right of every Jew to immigration and citizenship in the State of Israel. This law has raised the subtle question of "Who is a Jew;" perplexing the Supreme Court and dividing both the Knesset and the people.[37] The religious camp continues to be divided as to the religious signifi-

---

35   Z. Falk, *Dinei Nissuin*, Jer. 5743, pp. 38 ff.
36   See S. Shilo, *Tradition*, Vol. 20, No. 2, pp. 91–100, and M.S. Feldblum, *Emergence of the Halakhic Legal System*, in Jewish Law and Current Legal Problems, (*op. cit.*).
37   The anomaly of the situation is borne out by the fact that Moslem members of the Knesset also vote on the question of Who is a Jew. For a discussion of the problem of Jewish identity in our times, see M. Lewittes, *Light of Redemption* (Jer. 5731), pp. 25–45; also *Jewish Identity, Modern Responsa and Opinion* (Jer. 5730).

cance of the State and the concomitant halakhic problems, such as reciting Hallel on Yom ha-Atzmaut. Another ramification of this question of *Dat U'Medinah* is the position of the ostensibly non-halakhic Conservative and Reform branches of Judaism; are their religious leaders to be recognized as valid functionaries in marriages and conversions, or not.[38]

To many less significant questions the Talmud oftimes answers, *Teiku*, "Let the matter stand" (unresolved for the time being). Commentators have seen in this word a subtle hint to the Messiah, who will come to resolve all our problems.[39] Certainly to resolve the thorny problem of the State of Israel and the Halakhah we may have to wait for the fulfillment of the prophecy of Isaiah (1:26), *I will restore your judges as of yore and your counsellors as at the beginning.* Is it too sanguine to hope that this may come to pass "speedily and in our day, Amen."

---

38 There has been a great deal of obfuscation in this debate. On the one hand, it is not true as has been widely touted that the Halakhah would read Reform and Conservative Jews outside *k'lal Yisrael*, the House of Israel or the community of the Jewish people. On the other hand, Conservative leaders claim that they act within the framework of the Halakhah and yet are ready to adopt certain procedures which to the Orthodox are contrary to Halakhah.

39 Cf. *Eduyot* 8:7, "R. Shimon says, "The Messiah will come to bring agreement in disputed matters."

Epilogue

עת לעשות לה' הפרו תורתך. רבי נתן אומר הפרו תורתך עת לעשות לה'

*It is time for the Lord to act; they have transgressed
Your Torah* (Psalms 119:126). Rabbi Natan says,
"They have transgressed Your Torah because it is
a time to act for the Lord."*[1]

Modern Orthodoxy

My purpose in composing this admittedly sketchy review of the
history of traditional Jewish law has been twofold. Firstly, the
obvious one of supplying the student or the interested layman (and
hopefully the scholar as well as a succinct refresher course) a
concept of the Halakhah and its development as reflected in the
major halakhic writings. Secondly, I have attempted to demonstrate thereby the thesis that Halakhah, even in its post-Talmudic
history, has been sensitive and yielding — though assuredly in a
limited way — to the changing circumstances in which the Jewish
people have found themselves through the ages. This is the view
ascribed to the modern or neo-Orthodox Jew, who contends that it
is consonant with authentic traditional Judaism and within the
parameters of the Halakhah, and not — as the ultra-Orthodox
would have it — an attempt to justify one's unlawful concessions to
the demands of modern society.

---

* Mishnah, end of *Berakhot*

1   R. Natan interprets the verse to indicate that the Sages may transgress a
     particular ruling of the Torah for the higher purpose of strengthening loyalty to
     Torah in general; cf. *Menahot* 99b.

The modern Orthodox Jew, whose fealty to the Halakhah is an absolute commitment, would like to see the halakhic authorities of today approach Jewish law cognizant of its development in the past and interpreting it in the light of contemporary thinking and living. Thus they would not close their minds to secular knowledge or philosophic inquiry, though aware that these may influence their halakhic decisions. Indeed, we believe that meta-halakhic considerations, particularly the rationale of the mitzvot, would render halakhic practice more meaningful. This openness of modern Orthodox Jews leads them not to shun association in certain areas with non-Orthodox individuals and groups. By cooperating with Reform and Conservative Jews in communal endeavor, or even in polemic discourse, we indeed recognize them as Jews while not necessarily sanctioning their views about Judaism. By the same token, we sanction cooperation with non-religious Jews in the building and strengthening of the State of Israel. Modern Orthodoxy would also like to see contemporary authorities draw upon the results of modern scholarship, making them better able to fathom the opinions of the early authorities. Finally, and perhaps most significantly, we would like them not to be fearful of suggesting amendments to the existing Code of Jewish Law and adopting *takkanot* so that Halakhah would respond positively to the legitimate demands of modern Jewry.[2]

It is our conviction that the Torah was given to us for all times. Masters of the Halakhah in previous generations have demonstrated the processes by means of which we can apply its directives to any given situation, no matter how novel and unprecedented. These processes are continuing to operate today, as we have shown in the chapter on modern technology, though perhaps not with the rapidity that our hurried lives crave. However, satisfactory solutions in our Nuclear Space Age will be given only if certain truths are acknowledged and accepted by more and more contemporary rabbinic scholars. The answers to our problems will not be found in our shutting ourselves out of modern society, if that were at all possible for more than a small minority. Halakhic scholars will not produce any valid and tenable solutions if they are forbidden any and all contact with the surging tempo of modern life or familiarity with advancements in secular knowledge.

2   See R.B. Bulka (ed.), *Dimensions of Orthodox Judaism* (N.Y. 1983).

247

Acceptance of the fact that there has been change in ritual and custom in the past, and that therefore there can be legitimate change in the present, need not signify a break with halakhic tradition. Indeed, the rule of precedent opinion need not confine contemporary authorities so rigidly as to preclude the maintaining of a contrary opinion in the light of our understanding of the purposes of the law as it applies to present day circumstances. Instruction given to the *posek* of Talmudic times can well serve as a guide to the *posek* of today. "When one of my decisions," said Rava to Rav Pappa and Rav Huna the son of Rav Yehoshua, "comes before you and you question it, do not reject it summarily before you discuss it with me. If I have grounds for maintaining my opinion, I will state them; if not, I will reverse my judgment. After I pass away, do not destroy my opinion, though you need not accept it...for a judge must decide only on the basis of his own insights."[3] The essential requirement for making an halakhic decision, and this is true in all generations, is a thorough knowledge of the law as found in the major sources, and a proven loyalty to halakhic tradition and practice.

In the light of the foregoing, Modern Orthodoxy recognizes the new situation in Jewish life brought about by the establishment of the State of Israel, and the necessity to make certain revisions in our religious practice to conform to the new situation. It cannot agree, for example, with the fundamentalist position that has been expressed by leading rabbis that we may not change, even by addition of one word,[4] the wording of the Tisha B'Av prayer which speaks of a Jerusalem "whose dwellings are destroyed and is barren of inhabitants" at a time when the Holy City is thronging and expanding. Nor do we hesitate to celebrate Yom ha-Atzmaut with the recitation of Hallel preceded by a benediction, since we regard the establishment of an independent Jewish sovereignty in the Land of our Fathers even more significant than an event of "redemption from a distress."[5] Furthermore, we see no reason in insisting that such documents as the *Ketubah* and the *Get*, which were originally

---

3   *Bava Batra* 130b. See also *Pithei Teshuvah* to *Yoreh De'ah*, sec. 242, n. 2, for the right of later authorities to disagree with earlier ones.

4   I.e., by adding, as it has been suggested, the word *hayatah*, changing the phrase from present to past tense; cf. Isaiah 62:4. *Thou shalt no more be termed Forsaken, neither shall thy land any more be termed Desolate.*

5   Cf. *Pesahim* 117a, statement of *Hakhamim*.

written in Aramaic because it was the language of the people,[6] may not be written today in Hebrew.[7]

The fundamentalist refusal to acknowledge the religious significance of the establishment of Medinat Yisrael is — to my mind — based upon their narrow conception of the age-old hope for *bi'at ha-Mashiah*. To the fundamentalist, the coming of the Messiah is conceived as a sudden instantaneous and radical transformation of the world from *olam ha-zeh*, the unredeemed world of Galut or Exile, to the glorious days envisaged by the prophets when *all the children will be learned of the Lord* (Isaiah 54:13); and until that day arrives, as long as there are Jews who do not follow all the provisions of the Halakhah, we are still in Exile and nothing of halakhic significance has changed. Rational-minded Jews, on the other hand, are more inclined to follow Maimonides' thinking in this matter. He speaks of a "tentative" Messiah who has to achieve certain goals, something that can only be done in stages and in the course of time.[8]

There is a widespread reluctance in halakhic circles to discuss the possibilities of change in the Halakhah, and even a tendency to condemn the person who dares raise the question. In fact, the slogan adopted by Orthodoxy is "The Halakhah never changes." The alarming growth of the Reform and Conservative movements, which have weakened considerably the hegemony of the Halakhah, has led many to assert that the slightest amendment to the existing Code would open the floodgates and release a torrent of reckless demands which would change the whole character of Jewish life and sweep away many of the hallowed traditions that are an inseparable part of Jewish practice and thinking. Is this fear justified, and must it be assumed that legitimate change would perforce lead to unwarranted and illegitimate change? Should we not distinguish between those who would topple the whole structure and those who simply want to remove some of the out-moded customs that have accumulated in the course of time and are no longer compatible with our present standards of propriety and religious significance.

6   Cf. *Bava Metzia* 104a.
7   See the discussion in *Noam*, Vol. IX.
8   *Hilkhot Melakhim* 11:3–4. Cf. the Rabbinic comment to the verse *I the Lord will hasten it in its time* (Isaiah 60:22), "If Israel is worthy, then I will hasten it; if not worthy, then in its due time" (*Sanhedrin* 98a).

Could it not be argued that if qualified masters of the Halakhah were to carry on their traditional role of being the judges of halakhic questions according to their own insights and taking cognizance of the situation at hand, then the wind would be taken out of the sails of Conservative and Reconstructionist Judaism? One is reminded of the discussion recorded in the Mishnah:[9] Rabbis were asked in Rome, "If God has no desire for idolatry, why does He not abolish it?" They answered, "If people would worship only that which the world has no need of, then He would abolish it; but people worship the sun and the moon and the stars. Should God's world be destroyed because of these fools?" By the same token we should ask ourselves, Should we abandon the normal processes of the Halakhah because of the fools who have rejected it entirely?

The tension that exists in Jewish Law between the timeless and timeliness, between the abiding and the changing, is well-known.[10] Someone has phrased the dialectic in pragmatic terms. "Religion, if it is to succeed in remaining a central influence in the lives of its adherents, must lay stress upon its roots in the past, its traditions, its heritage, its permanence and stability. At the same time, it must guard against the loss of relevance, for if it loses its relevance it will lose its influence."

The Sages of the Talmud have expressed this seeming paradox in a more classical way. In a homily on the verse (Eccl. 12:11) *The word of the wise are as goads, and as nails planted,*[11] they comment, "If like a nail, shall we assume that just as a nail decreases (the wall into which it is hammered) but does not increase, so also the words of the Torah decrease but do not increase? No, for it says *planted,*[12] just as a plant grows and increases, so the words of the Torah." Here is an affirmation of the principle that the Torah possesses both the fixity of a nail and the evolutionary growth of a plant. And it is common knowledge that for a plant to grow and develop an occasional trimming is required. More pertinent to our discussion is the

---

9   *Avodah Zarah* 4:7.

10   See, e.g. Z. Falk, *Erkei Mishpat be-Yahadut* (Jer. 5740), chap. 4.

11   *Ḥagigah* 3b.

12   The usual translation for *netu'im* here is "well-fastened" or "fixed". JPS notes, "Hebrew uncertain". Cf. *Kohelet Rabbati* 12:11.

comment of the Midrash,[13] "It does not say 'like *fixed* nails,' but 'like *planted*' nails.' Why? Because He made them like nails, and a nail has a head so that it can easily be drawn out."

In the perspective of the past hundred and fifty years following the inception of the Reform movement, we can see that the stand taken by the Ḥatam Sofer that "anything new is forbidden by the Torah" and reiterated uncompromisingly by the Orthodox leadership today has not proved itself. It did not stem the tide of Reform, nor did it prevent the breakaway of Conservative Judaism from the established Orthodoxy. As for those who remained loyal to the rigid conception of the halakhic tradition, their rejection of any and all demands of modernity has in the main led to their increasing intolerance of controversial opinion. The fact of the matter is, though we may theoretically deny all change, resistance ot adaptation to modernity is in the long run futile. Thus, for example, a conference of Hungarian rabbis in 1866 declared a ban against rabbis preaching in Hungarian. Nevertheless, even in Pressburg, the city of the Ḥatam Sofer and at a time when his son was rabbi of the *kehillah*, the community engaged a preacher who preached in the "alien tongue".[14] A more significant deviation from the traditional Halakhah because of a change in values and attitudes is the teaching of Torah today to women, albeit accepted with much reluctance on the part of the ultra-Orthodox.[15]

Which brings me to my personal view of the feminist demand that a quorum of women gathered for prayer constitute a *minyan*, allowing them to recite those portions of public prayer restricted by

---

13   *Bamidbar Rabbah* 14:13.

14   L. Greenwald, *Hara'u Mesadrei ha-Bavli* etc., p. 20, n. 26.

15   See above, p. 228–229.

16   See J. Blidstein in *Sh'naton Ha-Mishpat ha-Ivri*, Vol. IX– X (Jer. 5742–43), p. 167, n. 190. A precedent to this ruling may be seen in *Mo'ed Kattan* 27b, which states, "At first they would purify the utensils of women who died in their menstrual impurity. Since this caused embarrassment to living menstruating women, they instituted that the utensils of all women be purified after they die." It is interesting to note the partial concession of Yosef Ḥayyim of Baghdad, who wrote, "During a woman's menstrual period, it is forbidden for her to stop praying or reciting benedictions. On the contrary, she has to pray and recite benedictions as is her custom. However, she should not go to synagogue while a menstruant, but should wait until her menstrual period has ceased. Nevertheless, during the months of Elul and Tishri, which are known as "awesome days" (*yamim nora'im*), she may go to the synagogue even while a menstruant" (*Ḥukot ha-Nashim*, chap. 39).

the Halakhah to a minimum of ten adult males. Conceding to this demand would not be the first concession to women desiring to fulfil equally with men certain mitzvot of the Torah. No less an authority than Rabbenu Tam ruled that women may recite the benediction over such mitzvot and say, "and has commanded us etc." even though the Halakhah asserts that they are not commanded. A sensitivity to women's desire to pray at all times was manifested by Yisrael Isserlein, author of *T'rumat ha-Deshen*, when he ruled that women may enter the synagogue to pray even during their menstrual period on the grounds that to deny them that privilege would cause them "distress and shame."[16]

My learned colleagues muster an impressive array of both medieval and modern poskim who maintain the Talmudic position that women do not constitute a minyan.[17] It seems to me that they miss the point. The question confronting the posek today is this: Is our contemporary evaluation of the nature of women and their role in religious life compelling enough, and is this specific demand reasonable enough, to allow us to make a further concession to women's importuning even though it runs contrary to the categorical restriction imposed by the Rabbis? Reliable precedent can be found in the opinion of Rabbis Yose and Shimon that women may "lay hands upon a sacrifice, not because the laying of hands is required for women, but in order to grant them gratification."[18] The ruling requiring a minyan for certain recitations in public prayer is based upon the verse *That I may be sanctified in the midst of the children of Israel* (Lev. 22:31).[19] Are women by nature incapable of sanctifying God,[20] and are they by nature excluded from the community of Israel?

17 See Aryeh Frimer in *Ohr ha-Mizrah*, Vol. XXXIV, no. 1–2 (N.Y. Sept. 1985) for references and analysis of the various opinions..

18 *Ḥagigah* 16b.

19 *Megillah* 23b.

20 A classic example is that of "Hannah and her Seven Sons" of the Hasmonean period; see Maccabees 2:7.

21 See above, p. 60.

Yom Tov Sheni shel Galuyot : Second Day Yom Tov in the Diaspora

I would like to illustrate with a concrete example how the modern approach to Jewish Law would introduce change in a traditional practice which has persisted without change from Talmudic times to the present. I refer to the obbservance by Jews living outside Eretz Yisrael of a second Festival Day (*Yom Tov Sheni*), in addition to the one prescribed by the Torah. It is well known that this practice originated at a time when the Sanhedrin in Eretz Yisrael would fix the calendar each month by declaring a certain day to be the first of a new month (*Rosh Ḥodesh*).[21] The Jews living more than twelve days distant by horse-rider from the seat of the Sanhedrin would not know whether the 30th or the 31st day of the passing month was declared to be Rosh Ḥodesh, and thus they would be in doubt which day was the 15th of the new month, particularly in the months of Nisan and Tishri when the festivals of Pesaḥ and Sukkot are celebrated. Consequently, they were obliged to observe two days of the Festival instead of the one prescribed by the Torah.[22]

In what category is this obligation? Is it *gezerah* or *takkanah* which cannot be revoked, as some Rabbinic authorities insist; or is it a *minhag* which does not possess an absolutely irrevocable character?[23] Let us review the Talmudic text upon which this observance is based. After a discussion about the sanctity of the Second Day, the Gemara asks, "Why do we observe two days nowadays when we already know the fixing of the month?" and replies, "Because they (most probably the Nasi and his Bet Din) sent from there (i.e. from Eretz Yisrael) 'Be careful to continue the *minhag* of your fathers (to observe two days); sometimes the (non-Jewish) kingdom issues a decree (Rashi, "against the study of the Torah") and you may be upset (in your calculations).' "[24]

---

22 The rider would not travel on the Sabbath or Rosh Hashanah or Yom Kippur, thus there were communities twelve days distant from Jerusalem who would know the exact day for the beginning of Pesaḥ but not for Sukkot; see *Rosh Hashanah* 21a.

23 Rambam asserts several times "It is only a minhag;" see *Hilkhot Yom Tov* 1:21, 6:14, *Hilkhot Talmud Torah* 6:14(11). *Ran* to *Sukkah* 44, however, calls it a "fixed takanah." See also *Tosafot ibid.*, where it is called "minhag". For a contrary opinion see J.D. Bleich, *Contemporary Halakhic Problems* (N.Y. 1977)., pp. 56–60.

24 *Betzah* 4b.

This is not the place to enter into a detailed analysis of the above text, which has been commented upon extensively by both Rishonim and Aḥaronim. Suffice it to say that the Second Day Yom Tov has been observed scrupulously in the Diaspora for centuries without question. However, the situation today is so radically different from what it was even less than a century ago, that the time has come for our religious authorities to examine the matter anew. From the discussion in the Talmud which preceded the directive sent to the Diaspora from Eretz Yisrael it is apparent that prior to then changes took place in the observance of the Second Day, depending upon the means of communication between Eretz Yisrael and the Diaspora (essentially to the Jews in Babylonia). When it was possible to signal the Diaspora by the relaying of flares,[25] the Diaspora celebrated only one day. When the flares had to be discontinued because of interference by the Cutheans, they celebrated two days. When once again the flares could be operated they returned to one day,. When messengers were sent to report the fixing of the new month, wherever they arrived before the 15th of the month only one day was celebrated. These facts, as Rashi explains, "indicate that this observance was not instituted for all times." In other words, it was not a takkanah which according to the Halakhah cannot be cancelled until an equally authoritative Bet Din cancels it; it is — as Meiri says[26] — "in our times nothing more than a minhag of the fathers." If we insist that it was a gezerah lest future generations be upset in their calculations due to the decree against Torah study, now that Eretz Yisrael has become the center of the Torah world with the security provided by the State of Israel that fear cannot be entertained any longer. Furthermore, it is no longer a matter of calculations; the calendar has already been fixed and determined for all time to come.[27]

If we argue that this minhag cannot be abandoned lest — and this is a hope rather than a fear — the Sanhedrin be reconstituted and once again it will fix the calendar at the beginning of each month; at such time the means of communication with the Diaspora at its disposal will be such that its proclamation of Rosh Ḥodesh will be transmitted in a matter of seconds to all corners of the globe. If the

25   Mishnah *Rosh Hashanah* 2:2.
26   *Bet ha-Beḥirah ad loc.*
27   Cf. Rambam, *Hilkhot Kiddush ha-Ḥodesh* 1:5, quoted above, pp. 60–61.

Second Day was a gezerah, it certainly was not intended for a time when instantaneous world-wide communication is a daily feature of life.

Why do we present these arguments? Again, because our situation today is so different. Travel between the Diaspora and Eretz Yisrael has now become so frequent and relatively easy, that the distinction between the two communities is fast disappearing. The frequency of visits to Israel on the part of those who observe Second Day has led to an anomalous situation which is contrary to the basic law of minhag, that one should not act differently from the minhag ha-makom. Though I have demonstrated elsewhere[28] that the Halakhah does not require a person from *Ḥutz la-Aretz* who happens to be in Eretz Yisrael on a Festival to observe the Second Day, many rabbis — and for different reasons — rule that they should observe the additional day. As a result, we have yet another unhalakhic phenomenon of *agudot agudot*,[29] people in the same community — indeed, praying in the same synagogue — observing the Holiday differently. The same disharmony exists in Ḥutz la-Aretz with so many Israelis visiting there and observing one day while their co-religionists observe two days. We must also be mindful of the increased integration in our times of Jews in the economic life of the general community, imposing an added difficulty to their maintaining their religious traditions. This added burden is also imposed upon the many observant Jewish students attending university.

The Sages made the following pertinent comment: Who is responsible that I observe two days of Yom Tov in Syria; because I did not observe one day in Eretz Yisrael properly. I thought I would receive a reward for observing two days, but I receive a reward only for one day. To this we apply the verse, *Moreover I gave them laws that were no good* (Ezek. 20:25)[30] We have long ago — considering the length of our years in Galut — expiated the sin of not observing Yom Tov properly in Eretz Yisrael. If we wish — as we undoubtedly

28 *The Light of Redemption* (Jer. 5731), pp. 26 ff.
29 See above, p. 71.
30 *Yalkut Shimoni ad loc.*

should — to establish the centrality of Eretz Yisrael in Jewish life today, one way would be for the Diaspora to celebrate the Festivals as they do in Eretz Yisrael, and become once again *One people in the Land* (II Sam. 7:23).[31]

Conclusion

Let it be clearly understood. We are in no way advocating that an individual person or group decide that this or that practice is not in harmony with the needs and attitudes of the day, and that therefore he or they may feel free to abandon it. What we are pleading for is the creation of a Chief rabbinical Council — the term Sanhedrin is too far-reaching at present — whose members are sensitive and responsive to contemporary values[32] and are ready to exercise their prerogative to institute *takkanot* and render halakhic decisions in the spirit of an evolutionary development of the Halakhah. True, we do have a Chief Rabbinate today in Israel, and modern Orthodox Jews, in contradistinction to the ultra-Orthodox, do recognize its authority. However, as presently composed it is limited both in the number and the type of its membership. More than the present insistence that there be an equal number of Ashkenazim and Sephardim, we would like to see an equal number of university and non-university trained rabbis. Instead of its membership being limited to Israelis whose appointment is linked to Knesset law and thus open to political influences, we would like to see candidates for membership selected from halakhic scholars all over the world; a procedure which would undoubtedly lead to greater universal recognition of its authority. And only such a body, and not the secular Knesset, would be competent to decide *Who is A Jew* for the entire Jewish people.

31 See *Sukkah* 43b–44a, where the mitzvah of Lulav was cancelled in Eretz Yisrael because it was not observed in the Diaspora. Rashi *ad loc.*, "That Israel should not be divided into *agudot agudot*, and it would seem as if (we have) two Torahs."

32 In the spirit of the Tanna R. Yose, who said, "Do not give the Sadducees occasion to ridicule us" (for insisting on absurd procedures; *Parah* 3:3). Quite a few customs sanctioned by the Talmud were dropped by the Rishonim because of their absurdity in the eyes of our non-Jewish neighbors; see Yitzhak Zev Kaḥane, *Mehkarim B'Sifrut ha-Teshuvot* (Mossad Harav Kook, Jer. 1973), pp. 307 ff.

Someone has said that "we must look to the living community of faithful adherents for the development of Jewish law." Undoubtedly, the majority of such adherents today look to the heads of the traditional Yeshivot, who are fundamentalist in both theory and practice, as their halakhic authorities. However, the fact that at the moment the ultra-Orthodox are dominant does not necessarily imply that they are the more authentic. Nor does it mean that the Modern Orthodox should refrain from articulating their point of view. If the ideas expressed by them seem far-fetched and impractical, we must remember that many things have come to pass which at first seemed impossible of realization; and this only because there were idealists who were convinced of the truth of their cause and strove for its realization against all odds. We would rather follow the advice of Rabbi Tarfon, who said, "It is not your responsibility to finish the task; yet you are not free to desist from it. "[33] Instead of *waiting*, as the fundamentalists do, for the realization of the Divine promise that *I will restore your judges as of old, and your counselors of yore* (Isaiah 1:26), we prefer to *prepare* for it. It is our humble hope that this volume may signal others to join in the preparation.

33   *Avot* 2:16.

Bibliography

Albeck, H., *Mavo l'Talmudim* (Tel Aviv 1969)

Albright, W.F., *From the Stone Age to Christianity*

Assaf, S., *Tekufat ha-Geonim* (Jer. 1955); *Mekorot l'Toldot ha-Ḥinukh*

Bar-Asher, S. (ed.), *Toldot ha-Yehudim B'Artzot ha-Islam* (Jer. 5741)

Baron, S.W., *Social and Religious History* (Phila. 1952); *The Jewish Community* (Phila. 5702)

Bazak, Y. (ed), *Ha-Mishpat ha-Ivri U'Medinat Yisrael* (Jer. 5729)

Berkowitz, E., *Halakhah, Koḥah ve-Tafkidah* (Jer. 1981); *T'nai B'Nissuin U'Beget* (Jer. 5727)

Berger, Y.D. in *Seridim* (Vol.4, Jer. 5743)

Birmingham, S., *Our Crowd* (N.Y. 1977)

Bleich, J.D. in *Jewish Bioethics* (N.Y. 1979); in *Tradition* (Vol. 21, No.2); *Contemporary Halakhic Problems* (N.Y. 1977)

Blidstein, J., *Sh'naton ha-Mishpat ha-Ivri* (annual), Vol. 9-10

Breuer, M., *Keter Aram Tzovah* (Jer. 1976)

Bright, J. in *The Bible and Ancient Near East* (N.Y. 1965)

Buber, M., *The Prophetic Faith*

Bulka, R.B., *Dimensions of Orthodox Judaism* (N.Y. 1983)

Cassuto, U., *Commentary to Exodus*; *Torat ha-Te'udot*

Chajes, Zvi H., *Kol Sifrei Maharitz* (Jer. 5318)

Chavel, H.D., *Kol Kitvei ha-Ramban* (Jer 5723); *Mishnato shel R. Akiva Eger* (Jer.-N.Y. 5732)

Chigier, M., *Husband and Wife in Israeli Law* (Jer. 5745)

Dinari, Y.A., *Ḥakhmei Ashkenaz B'Shilhei Y'mei ha-Binayyim* (Jer. 1984)

Drazin, N., *History of Jewish Education* (Baltimore 1940)

Drori, M., in *Jewish Law and Current Legal Problems* (Jer. 1985)

Dupont-Sommer, A., *The Dead Sea Scrolls* (N.Y.1955)

Ellinson, E.G., *Ha-Ishah ve-ha-Mitzvot* (Jer. 5742); *Procreation in the Light of the Halakhah* (W.Z.O. Jer.)

Elon, M., *Ha-Mishpat ha-Ivri* (Jer. 5733)

Epstein, B., *Torah Temimah*

Epstein, I., in *The Jewish Library* (ed. Leo Jung, N.Y. 1943)

Epstein, Y.N., *Mavo'ot l'Sifrut ha-Tannaim* (Jer. 5717); *Mavo'ot l'Sifrut ha-Amoraim* (Jer. 1962); *Meḥkharim B'Sifrut ha-Talmud* (Jer. 5744); *Peirush ha-Gaonim* (Jer. 5742)

Falk, Z., *Dinei Nissuin* (Jer. 5743)

Feldblum, S., *Dikdukei Soferim, Gittin* (N.Y. 5726); in *Jewish Law and Current Legal Problem* (Jer. 1985)

Feldman, D.M., *Birth Control in Jewish Law* (N.Y. 1968)

Feldman, E., in *Tradition* (journal) Vol. 21, No. 3

Finkelstein, L., *The Pharisees*

Frankel, Z., *Mavo l' Yerushalmi*

Friedlander, M. (trans.), *Guide of the Perplexed* (J.P.S.)

Freiman A.H., *Seder Kiddushin ve-Nissuin* (Jer. 5725)

Frenkel, D.A., in *Jewish Law and Current Legal Problems* (Jer. 1985)

Frimer, A., in *Or ha-Mizrah* (Vol. 36, No. 1-2, N.Y. 1985)

Fuchs, A., *Yeshivot Hungaria be-Gedulatan U'b'Hurbanan* (Jer. 5739)

George, Henry, *Progess and Poverty* (N.Y. 1879)

Gerhardsson, B., *Memory and Manuscript, Oral Tradition etc.* (Uppsala 1961)

Ginzberg, L., *On Jewish Law and Lore* (Phila. 1955)

Gotthold, Z., in *Sefer ha-Yovel l'Histadrut ha-Rabbananim* (Jer. 5745)

Graetz, H., *History of the Jews* (J.P.S. English ed.)

Greenbaum, A., *Peirush ha-Torah l'R. Shmuel b. Hofni* (Jer. 5739)

Greenberg, B., *On Women and Judaism* (Phila. 5742)

Greenwald, L., *Ha-Ra'u Mesadrei ha-Bavli et ha-Yerushalmi* (N.Y. 1954)

Grossman, A., *Hakhmei Ashkenaz ha-Rishonim* (Jer. 5741) *Ha-Hashmal B'Halakhah (Makhon Mada'ei Technologia*, Jer. 5738)

Halevy, Isaac, *Dorot ha-Rishonim*

Helmreich, W.B., *The World of the Yeshiva* (N.Y. 1982)

Herford, R.T., *The Pharisees*

Hershman, A.M., *The Book of Judges* (trans. New Haven 1949)

Hoenig, S.B., *The Great Sanhedrin* (Phila. 1952)

Hurvitz, E. (ed.), *Mossad ha-Yesod*

Husik, I., *A History of Medieval Jewish Philosophy* (Phila. 1947)

Jakobovits, I., *Jewish Medical Ethics* (N.Y. 1959)

James, William, *Varieties of Religious Experience*

Jung, Leo, *The Jewish Library* (N.Y. 1934)

Kahane, Y.Z., *Mehkarim B'Sifrut ha-Teshuvot* (Jer. 1973)

Kapah, Y., *Halikhot Teiman* (Jer. 5728)

Kasher, M., *Ha-Rambam ve-ha-Mekhilta etc* (N.Y. 5703); *Torah Shelemah*; *Haggadah Shelemah*; in *Leo Jung Jubilee Volume* (N.Y. 1962)

Katz, D., *Tnu'at ha-Mussar* (Tel Aviv 5714)

Katz, Y., *Halakhah ve-Kabbalah* (Jer. 5744); *Goy shel Shabbat* (Jer. 5744)

Kaufman, Y., *The Religion of Israel* (Chicago 1960)

Klein, Isaac, *A Guide to Jewish Religious Practice* (N.Y. 1979)

Kleinberger, A.P., *Ha-Maḥashavah ha-Pedigagiyut shel ha-Maharal* (Jer. 5722)

Kohut, Alexander, *Arukh ha-Shalem* (Jer. 5699 Shilo ed. 5730)

Kook, A.I., *Orot ha-Kodesh* (1925); *Olat Re'iyah* (N.Y. 1966); *Iggerot Re'iyah*

Lamm, N., *R. Ḥayyim of Volozhin* (N.Y. 1966)

Lieberman, S., *Tosefta Ki-P'shuta* (N.Y. 5715 - 5733); *Talmudah shel Kesarin* in *Tarbitz* (Jer. 5691)

Leibovitch, N., *Iyyunim Ḥadashim B'Sefer Vayikra* (Jer. 5743); *Studies in Devarim* (Jer. 5743)

Leiman, S.Z., *The Canonization of Hebrew Scripture* (Hamden, Conn. 1976)

Leon, H.J., *The Jews of Ancient Rome* (Phila. 1960)

Levi, E., *Yesodot ha-Halakhah* (Tel Aviv 5720)

Levin, B.M., *Otzar ha-Geonim* (Jer. 5691)

Levita, E., *Masoret ha-Masoret*

Lewittes, M., *Religious Foundations of the Jewish State* (N.Y. 1977); *Light of Redemption; Tzemihat Ge'ulateinu* (Jer. 5744)

Lifshitz, B., *The Judicial Status of the Responsa Literature* in *Shnaton HaMishpat ha-Ivri*, Vol. 9–10

Litvin, B., *The Sanctity of the Sages* (N.Y. 1962)

Loewy, Yehudah (Maharal), *Tiferet Yisrael*

Maimon, Y.L., *Sarei ha-Me'ah* (Jer. 5710)

Malter, H., *Saadia Gaon* (Phila. 5702)

Mantel, H., *Studies in the History of the Sanhedrin* (Cambridge, Mass. 1961)

Margaliyot, M., *Bein Bavel l'Eretz Yisrael* (Jer. 1938); *Encyclopedia l'Ḥakhmei ha-Talmud* (Tel Aviv); *Encyclopedia li-Gedolei Yisrael* (Tel Aviv)

Margaliyot, R., *Sefer Sha'arei Zohar*

Margolis and Marx, *A History of the Jewish People* (Phila. 1938)

Margolis, M.L., *The Story of Bible Translations* (Phila. 1917); *The Hebrew Scriptures in the Making* (Phila. 1922)

Mirsky, S.K., *Bein Shekiah l'Zeriḥah* (N.Y. 1951)

Montefiore, C.G., *A Rabbinic Anthology* (Phila. 1960)

Moore, G.F., *History of Religions* (N.Y. 1958)

Neubauer, Y.Y., *Ha-Rambam al Divrei Soferim*

Neuman, A.A., *The Jews in Spain* (Phila. 5705)

Noam (journal)

Rabinowicz, H.M., *The World of Hasidism* (Hartford 1970)

Rabinowitz, R.N., *Dikdukei Soferim*

Rafael, Y., *Sefer ha-Ḥasidut* (Tel Aviv 5715)

Reider, J., *Deuteronomy* (Phila. 5697)

Revel, H., *Ha-Masoret b'Sifrei ha-Rambam* (N.Y. 5702)

Rosenblatt, S., *The Book of Beliefs and Opinions* (trans. New Haven 1948)

Rothkopf, A., *Bernard Revel* (Phila. 1972)

Rubenstein, A., *Bein Ḥasidut l'Shabta'ut* in Bar-Ilan Annual 5727

Schechter, S., *Seminary Addresses* (Cincinnati 1915); *Studies in Judaism* (Phila. 1908)

Scholem, G., *Major Trends in Jewish Mysticism* (N.Y. 1941)

Segal, M.H., *Masoret U'Bikoret* (Jer. 5715)

Shilo, S., *Dina d'Malkhuta Dina* (Jer. 5735); in *Tradition* (Vol. 20, No. 2)

Siev, A., *Rema* (N.Y. 1972)

Silberg, M., *Ba'in ke-Eḥad* (Jer. 5742)

Soloveitchik, J.B., *Confrontation* in *Tradition* (N.Y. 1963); *The Lonely Man of Faith* in *Tradition* (N.Y. 1965)

Spero, S., *Morality, Halakhah and the Jewish Tradition* (N.Y. 1983)

Spiegel, S., *The Last Trial* (Phila. 1967)

Steinberg, A., *Hilkhot Rof'im U'Refuah* (Jer. 5738)

Tcherikover, V., *Hellenistic Civilization and the Jews* (Phila. 1959)

Tikuchinsky, A., *Takkanot ha-Geonim* (Tel Aviv-N.Y. 5720)

Twersky, A., *Rabad of Posquieres* (Phila. 5740), *Intro. to Code of Maimonides* (New Haven 1981)

Urbach, E.E., *Ba'alei ha-Tosafot* (Jer. 5715)

Wahrhaftig, Z., in *Shnaton ha-Mishpat ha-Ivri*, Vol. 3–4 (Jer. 5736)

Weiss, I.H., *Dor Dor ve-Dorshav* (Berlin 5684)

Weiss, A., *Hithavut ha-Talmud* (N.Y. 5703)

Wertheim, A., *Halakhot ve-Halikhot B'Ḥasidut* (Jer. 5720)

Wolfson, H.A., *Philo* (Cambridge, Mass 1947)

Yaari, A., *Sh'luḥei Eretz Yisrael* (Jer. 5711)

Yaron, Z., *Mishnato shel Harav Kook* (Jer. 5734)

Yavetz, Z., *Toldot Yisrael* (Tel Aviv 5692)

Yehudah, Z.A., in *Tradition*, Vol. 8, No. 2

Yellin and Abrahams, *Maimonides* (Phila. 1944)

Yosef Hayyim, *Ḥukot ha-Nashim*

Yosef b. Naim, *Malkhei Rabbanan* (Jer. 5691)

Zaks, M. *Peirushei R. Eliyahu mi-London* (Jer. 5716)
Zeitlin, S., *The Rise and Fall of the Jewish State* (Phila. 1962)
Zevin, S.Y., *Ishim ve-Shitot* (Tel Aviv 5712)
Zimmels, H.J., *Ashkenazim and Sephardim* (London 1976)
Zohar, Z., in *Studies in Contemporary Jewry* (Indiana Univ. 1986)

Index of Biblical References

Index of Rabbinic References

268

MIDRASH

RISHONIM

General Index

Aaron the High Priest, 51
Abba Arikha (*Rav*), the Amora, 5,
84, 85
Abbahu of Caesarea, the Amora, 83
Abbaye, the Amora, 113, 114
Abel son of Adam, 6
Abortion, 214ff., 221, 227, 230
Abraham the Patriarch, 13, 22, 26,
27, 104, 106; selection of, 17
Abraham ibn Daud, 129
Abraham b. David of Posquieres
(*Ravd*), 136, 143, 152
Abuhazeira, Yaakov, 200
Abulafia, Hayyim, 204
Abulafia, Hayyim Nissim, 205
Academies, see Yeshivot
Adam of Creation, 6, 13; and Eve,
95
Adultery, 18, 217
Aggadah, Haggadot, 5ff., 55, 85, 233
Agudat ha-Rabbanim, 223
Aha of Shivha, the Gaon, 117
Aharon b. Asher, 47
Aharon ha-Cohen of Lunel, 136
Aharon ha-Levi of Barcelona, 135
Aharonim (later authorities), 91, 193,
220, 232, 254
A'H'U' (Altona, Hamburg and
Wandsbek), 160, 164
Akavia b. Mahallalel, 71
Akiva b. Yosef, the Tanna, 46, 47,
57, 65, 74, 75, 102, 109, 165, 168, 178
Albeck, H., 82, 86, 195
Albright, W.F., 23
Alexander the Emperor, 152
Alexandria, 129, 201
Alfasi, Yitzhak b. Yaakov ha-Cohen,
(*Rif*), 88, 130f., 137, 142f., 151
Algazi, Yom Tov b. Yisrael
Yaakov, 203

Algiers, 200, 201
Al Hayyakh, Uzziel, 201
Aliyah, to Eretz Yisrael, 92, 204;
women to the Torah, 167, 232
Alkabetz, Shlomo, 151
Alkalai, Yehudah 234
Alliance Israelite Universelle, 201
Almighty, see God
Alshikh, Moshe, 151
Altar in the Temple, 6
Altona, 160, 164
America (U.S.), 184, 189, 221
Am ha-Aretz, 80, 168
Ammon, 18
Amora, Amoraim, 83f., 96, 111, 143
Amsterdam, 160, 164
Amulets, 164, 171, 173
Ankawa, Avraham b.
Mordekhai, 200
Antigonos of Sokho, 69
AntiSemites, antiSemitism, 183
Antoninus, 77
Anusim, see Marranos
Apocrypha, 47
Arabic, culture and language, 115,
129, 139, 196
Aramaic, 78, 87, 115
Arba'ah Minnim, 170
Arbitration, see *Pesharah*
Ari ha-Kadosh, see Luria, Yitzhak
Aristotelian doctrine, 133
Aron Kodesh, 185
Artifical Insemination, 217f., 223,
226
Arukh, 123f.
Arukh ha-Shalem (Completum), 85,
114
Asceticism, 30, 139
Asher b. Yehiel, (*Rosh*), 89, 91, 93,
96

273

Index of Halakhic Works

(the word Sefer has been omitted from the title)